The
EVERYTHING®
TAROT BOOK
Second Edition

Dear Reader,

If you're like most people, you've played card games many times without realizing there was anything mystical or magical about the pieces of paper you held in your hands. But that ordinary poker deck has an ancient link to a most amazing oracle—the Tarot, which wise men and women have consulted for centuries to discover the secrets of the universe. Now you, too, can unveil the mysteries of the Tarot and use it as a road map to your destiny.

People often ask me, "How can a deck of cards reveal the future?" My reply is simple: by revealing yourself to you. Like dreams, Tarot cards contain meaningful symbols that trigger your intuition. They expand your vision and let you see what lies beyond the limits of everyday reality. They speak to the creative part of your mind, the part that serves as the architect of your life, to help you make informed choices and design your future the way you want it to be.

Initially, you'll probably be intrigued by the images on the cards. Why is that man hanging upside down? Why are those Sphinx-like creatures pulling a chariot? But the Tarot isn't just a collection of pretty pictures. Each card is a treasure chest full of knowledge encoded centuries ago to protect it (and the people who used it) from being destroyed by misguided zealots. Once you learn the secret language of the cards from this book, you'll be able to access the hidden wisdom of the Tarot and the magic behind it.

Explore. Engage your curiosity. Use your imagination. Keep an open mind and an open heart. Your future really is in the cards!

With best wishes,

Skye Alexander

The EVERYTHING® Series

Editorial

Publishing Director	Gary M. Krebs
Director of Product Development	Paula Munier
Associate Managing Editor	Laura M. Daly
Associate Copy Chief	Brett Palana-Shanahan
Acquisitions Editor	Lisa Laing
Development Editor	Rachel Engelson
Associate Production Editor	Casey Ebert

Production

Director of Manufacturing	Susan Beale
Associate Director of Production	Michelle Roy Kelly
Cover Design	Paul Beatrice
	Matt LeBlanc
	Erick DaCosta
Design and Layout	Colleen Cunningham
	Jennifer Oliveira
	Brewster Brownville
Series Cover Artist	Barry Littmann

Visit the entire Everything® Series at *www.everything.com*

THE
EVERYTHING®
TAROT BOOK

SECOND EDITION

Reveal your past,
inform your present,
and predict your future

Skye Alexander

Adams Media
Avon, Massachusetts

An Everything® Series Book.
Everything® and everything.com® are registered trademarks of F+W Publications, Inc.

Published by Adams Media, an F+W Publications Company
57 Littlefield Street, Avon, MA 02322 U.S.A.
www.adamsmedia.com

ISBN 10: 1-59337-656-1

ISBN 13: 978-1-59337-656-7
Printed in the United States of America.

J   I   H   G   F   E   D   C   B   A

Library of Congress Cataloging-in-Publication Data
Alexander, Skye.
The everything tarot book / Skye Alexander. -- 2nd ed.
p. cm.
Includes index.
ISBN 1-59337-656-1
1. Tarot. I. Abadie, M. J. (Marie-Jeanne). Everything tarot book. II. Title.
BF1879.T2A27 2006
133.3'2424--dc22
2006014737

This publication is designed to provide accurate and authoritative information with regard to the subject matter covered. It is sold with the understanding that the publisher is not engaged in rendering legal, accounting, or other professional advice. If legal advice or other expert assistance is required, the services of a competent professional person should be sought.

—From a *Declaration of Principles* jointly adopted by a Committee of the American Bar Association and a Committee of Publishers and Associations

Many of the designations used by manufacturers and sellers to distinguish their products are claimed as trademarks. Where those designations appear in this book and Adams Media was aware of a trademark claim, the designations have been printed with initial capital letters.

This book is available at quantity discounts for bulk purchases.
For information, please call 1-800-872-5627.

Illustrations from the Rider-Waite Tarot Deck® reproduced by permission of U.S. Games Systems, Inc., Stamford, CT 06902 USA. Copyright ©1971 by U.S. Games Systems, Inc. Further reproduction prohibited. The Rider-Waite Tarot Deck® is a registered trademark of U.S. Games Systems, Inc.

Contents

10

11

12

13

To Ron, my port in the storm

Top Ten Ways the Tarot Can Help You

1. It can allow you to gain insight into yourself.

2. Tarot can help you gain insight into other people.

3. With Tarot you can get answers to questions and concerns.

4. It can train your ability to see into the future.

5. It can enable you to see the present more clearly.

6. Through Tarot you can better understand the effects of the past.

7. You can use it as a tool to work through personal problems and challenges.

8. Tarot can help you strengthen desirable qualities and traits.

9. It can allow you to develop and sharpen your intuition.

10. Perhaps most importantly, Tarot can enhance your connection with your Higher Self.

Introduction

▶ No one knows exactly when or where the Tarot originated. The earliest known book of Tarot cards still in existence dates back to the early 1840s; seventeen of those antique cards still remain. The first entire deck still in existence was painted by the Italian artist Bonifacio Bembo for the Duke of Milan.

Many theories abound about the Tarot's beginnings. One is that the great library of Alexandria in Egypt, whose female librarian Hypatia was world-renowned for her wisdom and learning, housed scrolls containing all the knowledge of the ancient world. Among these scrolls was the legendary Book of Thoth, derived from the mystery schools of ancient Egypt. The allegorical illustrations on Tarot cards are said to contain these secret teachings, which in the Major Arcana represent a course in personal and spiritual development. The Minor Arcana, which was added to the Tarot at a later date, may have derived from an Italian card game known as tarrochi. Our present-day poker decks closely resemble the Minor Arcana of the Tarot.

Tarot images are inextricably linked to ancient beliefs, mythologies, and religious systems such as the Hebrew Kabbalah. The cards' numerological associations have been tied to the Greek mathematician Pythagoras, who taught that letters and numbers contain divine essence and extraordinary powers unrealized by the uninitiated.

Gypsies may have carried the cards to Europe. (The term gypsy is considered to be a corrupt form of the word Egyptian.) The Church, however, believed the Tarot was "the devil's picture book," and the cards were quickly condemned as heretical. To possess them was dangerous. Thus, during the Middle Ages, the Tarot went underground, along with astrology and many other forms of occult knowledge. (Occult simply means hidden.) Yet despite persecution, the ancient knowledge contained in the Tarot continued to be passed down in secret, until interest in the cards surfaced again during the Renaissance.

Though we may never know their true history, we can still use Tarot cards to advise and guide us, to show us what lies ahead in the future, and to help us gain access to our inner knowing and the Divine. The amazing insights contained in the Tarot and the deck's inherent flexibility make it just as relevant to contemporary Westerners as it was to the ancients.

In the view of alchemists and mystics, the symbols preserved and presented in the Tarot spring from the *anima mundi,* or soul of the world, a vast repository of knowledge, like a cosmic library, filled with all the memories and wisdom of the entire human race, past, present, and future. Sometimes called the Akashic Records, this source of knowledge could be accessed by anyone willing to make the effort to develop his psychic link to the source.

Within this collective pool are all the basic figures found in myths, legends, religions, and fairy tales. Taken together, these figures encapsulate a magical storehouse of profound esoteric knowledge. For example, The Empress in the Tarot symbolizes the feminine archetype, the great mother goddess of the world's most ancient religion, what Goethe called "the eternal feminine."

Each figure in the Tarot calls forth from the individual's unconscious a deep resonance. When a user consciously contacts these images in the Tarot, their hidden counterparts in the collective unconscious are allowed to surface and become integrated into the person's life.

A properly conducted Tarot reading is a story. As in myths, the images on the cards meld into a meaningful pattern that can clarify the issues confronting the person for whom the reading is being done. In a sense, the reading can act like a dream or a flash of inspiration to impart understanding.

Tarot cards are wonderful tools to use for meditation, as well as for divination. They stimulate the intuition, which is the key to the gateway of the unconscious. They illuminate the hidden factors in a person's life, factors that the person may not be aware of that are secretly shaping her existence. Thus, the Tarot is not only a tool for answering everyday questions or telling fortunes; it is also a beacon that shines light into the darkest recesses of your inner self and illuminates the vast realms that lie beyond the limits of the conscious mind.

Books

rot

ypical Tarot deck consists of seventy-
ht cards. Of these, the first twenty-
are identified as the Major Arcana.
fifty-six remaining cards are called
Minor Arcana, presumably because
contain information that is of a less
rtant or mystical nature. Because
arot can be viewed and understood
body of wisdom and guidance, it
metimes thought of as a book—
more accurately, as two books—of
knowledge.

The Major Arcana

These arcana (which means mysteries or secrets) represent the mysteries or secrets of the universe that reflect universal law. As such, they are the most complex cards in the deck and require more diligence to understand. Each of the Major Arcana cards, which are also often called trump cards, is illustrated with specific symbols or scenarios, which are basically the same in all decks, even though they may differ thematically according to the philosophy of the designer. Each of the Major Arcana cards has a title, such as The Magician, The Empress, The Lovers, The Moon, The Tower, and so forth. They are numbered from zero—The Fool—to twenty-one—The World. (In Chapter 12, the individual cards are discussed and interpreted in detail.)

As seems to be the case in most schools of thought, particularly those that have been around for a while, there is disagreement about many aspects of the Major Arcana. Some scholars and authors focus primarily on the numerical order of the cards (zero to twenty-one) contending that they form a system through which the development of an individual's life can be traced. Some interpreters have interjected psychological meanings into the Major Arcana, while others have viewed them as a representative of spiritual development and growth.

Sally Gearhart, in *A Feminist Tarot*, asserts that the various systems of organizing the Major Arcana came into being as a result of the oral tradition. People developed stories to help them remember the specific attributes of each card. In her opinion, it is easier to remember what the individual cards mean if we relate them to each other in groups.

The Major Arcana cards also describe a path to enlightenment—The Fool's Journey. Beginning with The Fool, which represents innocence and the initial step of the journey, and ending with The World, which signifies wisdom and completion, the twenty-two cards can be viewed as stages in the seeker's personal development. According to some schools of thought, they outline a course in initiation into the mysteries of life and the nature of the universe. (Chapter 8 examines this process and its significance in greater depth and detail.)

Fate and Universal Forces at Work

The cards in the Major Arcana represent forces beyond yourself and the limits of mundane, earthly, human existence. Depending on your personal worldview, you could think of these forces as fate, god, goddess, cosmic, karma, or your own Higher Self. Whichever way you choose to see the energies or entities behind the cards, they indicate that something larger, outside yourself is operating and influencing you and the issue about which you are seeking advice.

[There are] forces operating within that are capable of producing phenomenal results. That is, the power of your own suggestion starts the machinery into operation or causes the subconscious mind to begin its creative work [that] leads to belief, and once this belief becomes a deep conviction, things begin to happen.

—**Claude M. Bristol, *The Magic of Believing***

When many trumps turn up in a reading, it's a signal that the situation is not entirely in your own hands or that you are not alone in the matter that concerns you. Spiritual or higher forces outside your control may be at work, perhaps guiding the outcome. Because these cards can be linked with archetypes, they may portray dimensions of greater significance that are influencing your situation.

A reading that contains more cards from the Major Arcana than from the Minor Arcana suggests that you may not have a great deal of choice in how your question or issue turns out. You might not be able to control what happens. In some cases, a predominance of trump cards shows that previous actions or decisions have set things in motion, and now you are being propelled toward the inevitable result.

The Major Arcana cards possess many different layers. As you work with them, these layers reveal themselves. It's a bit like digging into an archeological site. For example, on a strictly practical level, The Empress may be a direct reference to your mother or your desire to become a mother. On the mundane or worldly level, The Magician may refer to your desire to live a more creative life, to be more creative in your work. On the level of spiritual development, The Devil may indicate that it is time for you to throw off the obstacles that are preventing your living more fully and deeply, that you should tend to your soul needs rather than your material concerns.

Each individual unfolds according to his or her own inner blueprint. There's no hurrying the process, which ultimately takes place on its own time schedule. The cycles in life show you the patterns you are following and suggest new directions. (These are most clearly shown in the astrological chart, which is an excellent adjunct to the Tarot.) The Major Arcana can be a guide that helps us to explore universal concepts as they apply to our lives at any given moment.

The Minor Arcana

Most scholars agree that the Minor Arcana were added to the Major Arcana sometime in the fourteenth or fifteenth century. It is believed that this portion of the Tarot was originally used for fortune-telling, and that in earlier times, it was considered safe for nonadepts to have access to this part of the Tarot. The Minor Arcana consists of four suits of fourteen cards each: Wands, Pentacles, Swords, and Cups. Each suit contains four Court Cards (King, Queen, Knight, and Page) and ten number cards from Ace through Ten, also called pip cards.

Everyday Guidance

The Minor Arcana cards can be extremely accurate in answering questions about the here and now, as they refer to specific areas of everyday life and human experience. They do not describe spiritual growth per se, but each of the areas to which these cards refer can certainly be incorporated into a pattern of spiritual development. You don't need to search for some deep mystical meaning to attach to them, however.

To understand the Minor Arcana, it's important to realize that they serve as an adjunct to the Major Arcana—a sort of commentary within the context of the reading. This is not to imply that they have no real significance on their own, but rather that they are an integral part of the context of the entire reading. Their main function is to relate the readee (the person for whom the reading is being done) to the elements of the everyday world, which exist for all of us no matter how spiritual we are or how seriously we pursue a spiritual path.

Generally speaking, the cards of the Minor Arcana represent lesser, or mundane, lessons. They show the everyday concerns, situations, challenges, and achievements you experience in your personal life. As such, they also present advice and describe conditions and possibilities related to the subject of a reading.

The Minor Arcana may seem less important, but they provide immediate information. Through the study of the Minor Arcana, you can observe the ongoing process of how you grow and develop.

When many (or all) of the cards in a reading come from the Minor Arcana, it's safe to say your future is in your own hands. Your decisions and actions will produce your future. You have the ability to control your destiny.

Real Life Situations and Solutions

As you begin to study the Minor Arcana, especially if you read different books on the subject, you will find a mixture of interpretations, some of which conflict with each other. Some experienced Tarot readers have developed their own unique views about the cards and their meanings. Your intuition plays a key role in interpreting the Minor Arcana, as will your own experiences with the cards. Take what you like from the "expert" information you read and leave the rest.

In time, you will begin to develop your own renderings of the cards, discovering by trial and error what works and what doesn't. Bear in mind that what works for one reader may not work for another, and that your own insights and experiences with the cards are just as valid as anyone else's.

As you explore the suits and the numbers and begin to test interpretations in actual readings, you will become aware of an overall system operating. It's kind of like learning to play the piano. You first have to learn the notes (symbols), then practice the scales to get familiar with fingering (readings), and then you begin to understand how the composer created a piece of music. In time, you may even write your own music.

Life Situations Represented by the Four Suits

In medieval times the four suits (usually called Wands, Pentacles, Swords, and Cups) represented the four main classes of people—the nobility, the clergy, the merchant class, and the working class. In today's society, there are correspondences—an elite, or old money, class is the nobility; today's version of the clergy has expanded to include the professions and academia; the merchant class includes businesses and people employed by corporate institutions; and those in blue collar or service positions are the working class.

It is clear that civilization cannot evolve further until the occult is taken for granted on the same level as atomic energy.

—**Colin Wilson,** *The Occult*

These suits help us pinpoint the areas of life that need our attention, because each of the suits represents a distinct realm of activity, experience, and personal growth. When many cards of the same suit appear in a reading, it's a clear indication that the person consulting the Tarot is concerned about a particular area of life—or should be. A reading about a relationship will usually turn up several cards in the suit of Cups, whereas Pentacles are likely to predominate in a reading about finances. (See Chapter 5 for more information on the symbolism of the suits.)

Court Cards

In most decks, each suit contains fourteen cards, including four Court Cards. Usually these cards are called the King, Queen, Knight, and Page, although some designers use labels such as Knave, Prince, Princess, Lord, and Lady. The images on the Court Cards are usually quite similar to those on ordinary playing cards—straightforward illustrations of a King, a Queen, a Knight, and a Page. Though there may be some variation in costume or colors, depending upon the philosophical orientation of the deck's creator, sometimes the only way to differentiate the suits is to note the symbol of the suit—Cup, Sword, Wand, or Pentacle—which is usually held by the person on the card.

In some cases, a King could represent a woman with the qualities of that particular King card. For example, the King of Pentacles could signify a strong, successful businesswoman.

The Court Cards often represent actual people in the life of the individual for whom a reading is being done, or they may personify the readee. They can also be used as Significators. (Significators are discussed in further detail in Chapter 10).

King

A king is a powerful ruler who exercises absolute authority over the territory he rules. He is, so to speak, at the top of the heap. Thus, the King of any suit represents a completion point: There's no higher position to attain. A cycle that began with the Ace has been completed, and it's now time to either consolidate your position or begin a new cycle. The level of the King is where you release and let go, complete old tasks, and prepare for a new and more fulfilling way of life. An example of this could be a man who is a highly placed corporate executive, who's reached the pinnacle of success in his field and made a lot of money, and who now decides that it's time to give back to the world. Former U.S. President Jimmy Carter is a good example of the person signified by the King in the Tarot.

Queen

The Queen is a mature woman who is also a ruler in her own right; she's not just the King's consort. As such, she represents a woman who embodies and expresses the feminine qualities of rulership, or leadership, most importantly the qualities of creativity and cooperation. She has developed skills and wisdom that come only through years of experience. With the Queen, you achieve a level of maturity and self-confidence. You know when to compromise and when to take a firm stand. You are not intimidated by any situation. Yet you remain able to grow and evolve, and you can be flexible through understanding.

The Queen may portray a mature, capable woman, an authority figure who is nurturing and understanding, or a mother image, sometimes the querent's real mother. In certain instances, a Queen card can refer to a man who has the qualities of the Queen—in other words, a man who is deeply attuned to his own feminine nature, such as an artist or a musician.

Knight

A Knight is someone who has been singled out and honored by the ruler for having performed valuable services. A Knight takes on responsibility to the Crown he serves. At the level of the Knight, you are fully aware of your path, and your aims are clear. You want to get on with it in the most direct way possible, not waste time on irrelevancies. You feel an intense sense of dedication—to a project, an idea, a person. You've taken risks and gotten yourself together for the task at hand, and you are focusing your energies totally toward accomplishing your goal, to make the risk worthwhile. This is a time of vertical thinking, for the point of our devotion is where the divine enters. The Knight, who is often considered a messenger or an agent of movement, can refer to a woman as well as to a man. The message the Knight carries or the movement he suggests corresponds to the suit to which the card belongs. The Knight of Wands, for instance, might indicate a message about a creative project or a trip taken for fun and adventure.

Page

The Page is a personal attendant of the royal family, often an errand boy (or girl). It's his or her job to serve in order to advance. The Page represents preparing yourself to succeed at something. It involves being willing to assume a subordinate role—as younger people often do—and to learn about commitment. The Page is about challenging yourself, developing your inner resources, and taking something to a greater stage of accomplishment. You may experience some hesitancy, or feel that you are not fully prepared for the task, but you still hope the situation will turn out as you anticipate.

ALERT!

The Page cards can represent either sex, but they usually refer to a young person or a child who is involved in the experiences related to the suit to which the Page belongs. Pages can indicate messengers, students/apprentices, youths, or immature adults.

In addition to representing actual people in your life—family members, spouses or lovers, friends, coworkers, neighbors, etc—the Court Cards can symbolize influences in your environment. They can also refer to situations, conditions, or characteristics of the querent. Because our society today is more egalitarian than it was at the time the Tarot originated, it is possible to see a woman through a male card and vice versa. Here, feedback from the readee can help you to identify the person to whom a Court Card is referring.

The Numbered Cards

Each suit also includes an Ace, which is considered to be the One card, followed by cards numbered Two through Ten. Also known as pip cards, these combine the qualities of the suit with those of the number.

Interpretations of the Minor Arcana are likely to vary, according to the worldview and intentions of the deck's designer. Some writers of books on the Tarot pay little attention to the Minor Arcana; others approach them mainly from the perspective of numerology. In many decks, the pip cards do not display any scenarios to suggest the card's meaning but merely show the corresponding number of the suit symbol. For example, the Three of Cups may simply depict three cups, without any storytelling imagery.

FACT

Pythagoras, a famous Greek philosopher, metaphysician, and mathematician, pursued the mystical significance of numbers as a science in the sixth century B.C.E. He studied numbers for their mathematical qualities and taught that each number contained specific mystical significance. In Pythagoras's philosophy, numbers were an expression of the fundamental laws of the universe.

Although five hundred years' worth of Tarot students and masters have produced some agreement on the meanings of the Minor Arcana cards, there is also a good deal of disagreement, and sometimes the pictures on the cards tell a different story than would be indicated by the combination of number and suit. The Eight of Cups in the Waite deck, for example, shows a man walking away from eight cups, which suggests leaving a relationship or emotional situation behind. However, the number Eight connotes sincerity, abundance, and achievement, so drawing this card would suggest success in matters of the heart. Therefore, you may prefer to base interpretations of the pip cards on the number rather than on any particular illustration—unless, of course, your intuition hooks into the picture and it reveals something.

The Minor Arcana and Playing Cards

By now you've undoubtedly noticed the similarities between an ordinary deck of playing cards and the Minor Arcana. The Court Cards, with the exception of the Page, are virtually the same as the King, Queen, and Jack in a poker deck. The Ace and numbered cards, too, echo a deck of playing cards, although in the Tarot the Ace represents a beginning and is never a high card.

The four suits divide the Minor Arcana, just as they do a poker deck. Some people believe that Wands equate to Clubs, Swords to Spades, Cups to Hearts, and Pentacles to Diamonds. It's even possible to do readings with regular playing cards, though of course the cosmic, spiritual factors indicated by the Major Arcana cards will be missing.

Many researchers believe that our present-day playing cards evolved from the Minor Arcana cards. It's also likely that in earlier times, the Minor Arcana were used as a type of game and were added to the Major Arcana to form the two books that exist today. Perhaps the only Major Arcana card to make its way into our modern playing cards is The Fool, whom we see depicted as the Joker.

Chapter 2

Exploring the Tarot

The Tarot is a powerful tool, but it must be used properly and with respect, not only for the knowledge it contains but for its ability to connect with the deepest recesses of the human psyche. Although the Tarot can be successfully used to answer mundane or practical questions, its highest value is as a guide to developing your intuition, which in turn leads to spiritual development.

A Tool for Divination

Imagine this scenario: You need information about the future ramifications of a decision regarding a major life change. It could involve your career, your marriage, a relocation, a pregnancy, or someone close to you. Instead of worrying and wondering—or swinging back and forth between two alternatives—you simply take out your Tarot cards (or you consult a professional reader).

Preferably, you have a special private place where you can be quiet and alone. Before using your cards, you take a few moments to relax completely according to your preferred method, slowly allowing your conscious mind to sink to the deep level of your inner nonconscious mind. While holding your cards, or shuffling them, you formulate a succinct question about the situation for which you are seeking counsel. Calmly, you feel this question becoming a part of your entire being. Then you lay out your cards in a predetermined spread and voilà—the answer to your question is right there before you!

Believe it or not, you already have the innate ability to get the answers you want. The Tarot, or any other physical tool, simply enables you to focus your intuition, the part of you that already knows the right answer. The Tarot cards are simply a convenient way to get at the inner truth of the situation.

Sound impossible? It isn't. Right now, today, you have this power. The problem is that you don't know you have it, and you don't know how to use it. But in fact your nonconscious mind is already programmed to give you the answers you seek and need—once you know the correct keys to press to access the vast resources of information already in your mental software. That's where and why the Tarot can help.

The answers will amaze you. The Tarot has the ability to reach right around surface problems and get to the root of the situation. So often we displace what is really bothering us onto a simpler issue. For example, a woman may come to a reading saying she wants advice about whether or not to go into business for herself. However, when the cards are laid out, the references are all to the state of her marriage. This could be puzzling if you aren't fully aware of the uncanny ability of the cards to get at the heart of the matter, regardless of the actual question.

When asked about her marriage, the woman bursts into tears and says that the only reason she is thinking of quitting her job and going into business for herself is as an escape route from a difficult marriage. She figures setting up her own business will require every minute of her time and every ounce of her energy, effectively removing her from participation in her marriage. After the reading, she understands that if she is ready to make progress in her life, she must face and resolve her marriage issue. Her nonconscious mind knew all along what the root of the problem was, and its promptings had directed her to come for a reading, which cut through her avoidance of the real problem.

Tapping Your Intuition

The word psychic evokes conflicting and sometimes negative emotions. Fear of the unknown and of those who supposedly can manipulate hidden forces has led many people to believe all things connected with the sixth sense—including divination tools such as the Tarot—are dangerous. This is simply nonsense. Intuition is a basic component we all possess from the start, an innate sense like sight, hearing, taste, smell, and touch. Children, in fact, often exhibit astonishing feats of intuition, perhaps because no one has told them yet it is wrong or weird to be able to access direct knowing.

Everyone is psychic, to one degree or another. Naturally, as in all of the arts—and divination is an art—talent is a factor, and some people are naturally more talented than others. The beauty of the Tarot, however, is that the more you work with it, the more adept you become. Therefore, the first requirement in using Tarot is to take it—and yourself—seriously, and to keep an open mind. Fear will block results, so will a frivolous attitude.

Humans are only at the beginning stages of discovering our almost unlimited capabilities. Scientists say that we use, at best, only 10 percent of the brain's capacity—and that's when we are being especially productive. Most of us jog along in our daily lives using only about 5 percent, or even less. Can you imagine what would happen if we all used substantially more of our innate intuitive ability? What problems we could solve, what progress we could make!

One of France's most eminent brain specialists, Dr. Frederic Tilney, puts it bluntly: "We will, by conscious command, evolve cerebral centers which will permit us to use powers that we now are not even capable of imagining." Not only New Age practitioners like Tarot card readers are aware of this, but scientists, educators, theologians, and psychologists as well know that the potential for the human race is, in the words of paleoanthropologist and environmentalist Dr. Richard Leakey, "almost infinite."

FACT

In 1909, Arthur Edward Waite commissioned artist and dramatist Pamela Colman Smith to illustrate a Tarot deck. It was published as *The Pictorial Key to the Tarot* and became famous in its own time.

Releasing your mental potential is a little like being the conductor of a great orchestra, except that you are also all of the instruments. The conscious mind is the conductor, whose job is to get all the parts going in concert, in harmony. Most people have heard of the right-brain and left-brain. The so-called left-brain rules your analytical, rational thinking while the right-brain presides over nonverbal, imaginative thinking. The challenge is to learn to blend all your parts into one harmonious whole, to allow each one to interact with and enhance the others. In this endeavor, the Tarot is an excellent method of integration.

By focusing the conscious mind on the question and on the spread of cards, the intuitive self is engaged. Designed to draw on your own innate clairvoyance, the Tarot acts as a catalyst to produce information you need. It provides clues to self-awareness, especially things you may have hidden from yourself. Because the Tarot is specific and detailed, it allows the left-brain and the right-brain to interact smoothly, the way a navigator directs a pilot. Once we understand that two sides of the brain are better than one, we are in a position to tap into the reserves of the mind for any purpose we wish.

As you begin your study of the cards, let them speak directly to your inner self. Tune in to what you feel about each card. The interpretations given in this book are useful, but they are not carved in stone. You are free to be creative in how you use the cards. The cards in a spread act as a template, or a field, through which information flows. You must, of course, first learn the standard meanings of each individual card before you can see a whole, a gestalt, within a spread. The more you practice, the better you will get at sensing which meaning is appropriate.

Early Tarot Decks

No one knows exactly where or when the Tarot originated. Evidence suggests that seventy-eight-card Tarot decks much like the ones we're familiar with today, such as the beautiful fifteenth-century Visconti-Sforza deck, may have been used in Italy and France during the Renaissance for telling fortunes. During this period, the nobility in Milan used the Tarot for gaming and gambling.

It's believed that the first Tarot decks contained only the Major Arcana; the Minor Arcana were added later. Early packs portrayed people solely on the Major Arcana and Court cards. The numbered or pip cards showed only the suit's symbol—Cups, Swords, Wands, or Pentacles—in the corresponding quantity (One through Ten). Some, such as the Visconti-Sforza deck, didn't even include labels on the Major Arcana cards—perhaps because novices were discouraged from doing readings and adepts would recognize the symbolism without needing labels.

Storytelling Decks

Storytelling images were added to the basic symbolism of the Minor Arcana cards in the first part of the twentieth century. Many of the most popular decks today, including the Waite deck and the Thoth Tarot, developed during this period. Instead of merely showing the appropriate number of symbols (Cups, Swords, Wands, or Pentacles) on the numbered cards, these decks portrayed activities or scenarios that described, through the language of pictures, the cards' meanings. People were depicted in relationship to the number of objects representing the suit.

These images made it easier to understand the meanings of the individual cards. For example, the vivid illustration on the Three of Swords—three swords stuck through a large red heart—certainly does convey a strong sense of heartache and suffering. However, some experts say the pip cards were illustrated as a memory aid rather than as an attempt to interpret the cards in a specific way.

If the doors of perception were cleansed, everything would appear to man as it is, infinite. For man has closed himself up, till he see all things thro' narrow chinks in his cavern.
—**William Blake,** *The Marriage of Heaven and Hell*

One problem with specific illustrations, though, is that they may cause confusion. In some cases, an illustration may seem contradictory both to the meaning of the suit involved and to the number being represented. The graphic portrayals may also limit individual interpretation and free association. Not everyone interprets the cards in exactly the same way, of course, and the meanings can vary depending on the question asked. It's usually best to trust your own intuitive responses and to use the images on the cards as guides or prompts rather than as rigid definitions.

The Rider-Waite Deck

Since its introduction in 1909, the Rider-Waite deck (which is also sometimes called the Waite deck) has been one of the most influential and popular Tarot decks. The deck was illustrated by Pamela Colman Smith, a theatrical designer, artist, writer, and member of the occult Order of the Golden Dawn. The deck expresses Smith's knowledge of magick (spelled with a k to distinguish it from stage illusion and magic tricks) and mysticism. Guided by Arthur Edward Waite, she produced a series of seventy-eight allegorical paintings that included storytelling images on the Minor Arcana as well as the Major Arcana cards. Unfortunately, the innovative deck, which broke away from the standard Tarot designs that had been used for centuries, bears the names of Waite and sometimes that of its publisher, William Rider and Son, instead of Smith's.

More than six million Waite Tarot decks are now in print. Smith's original images have spawned numerous variations over the years, including the popular Universal Waite deck, brightly recolored by Mary Hanson-Roberts. Today you can buy miniature versions, oversized versions, and even glow-in-the-dark versions of the Waite deck. This classic deck is widely used to illustrate books about the Tarot, including this one, and as a teaching tool for beginning diviners.

The Crowley Thoth Deck

Another innovative and influential Tarot deck emerged during the early part of the twentieth century, birthed by a collaboration between the notorious British occultist Aleister Crowley and Lady Frieda Harris. Known as the Crowley Thoth deck, it features dramatic artwork, vivid colors, and striking imagery. The deck contains many Kabbalistic, magickal, and astrological symbols, as described in *The Book of Thoth*, which Crowley authored—hence the name of the deck. Like the Waite deck, the Thoth deck has been reproduced in different variations and translated into numerous languages.

The Encyclopedias of Tarot

For more than a quarter century, Stuart Kaplan, head of U.S. Games Systems, Inc., has been compiling encyclopedias of Tarot. A long-time enthusiast and collector, Kaplan has cataloged more than 1,500 different decks, dating back to the fifteenth century. The beautiful four-volume set contains more than 25,000 card illustrations, along with extensive information about the development of the oracle since the Renaissance. Hundreds of as yet unpublished decks as well as rare and unique cards, including many from Kaplan's own collection, are featured in these encyclopedias. Exhaustive bibliographies, methods for dating antique cards, examinations of styles and techniques, artists' biographies, and other information make these volumes essential reference texts for collectors, dealers, and fans of the Tarot.

Variations in Terminology and Numbering

If you examine several different Tarot decks, you'll probably notice that they don't all use the same terminology. For instance, Wands may be called Rods or Staves in some decks. Cups are sometimes named Chalices, and Pentacles might appear as Coins or Discs.

Figures in the Major Arcana often go by various names, too. The Hierophant, High Priest, Pope, and Jupiter are all names for trump five. In his Thoth Tarot, Crowley switched the names and the order of some Major Arcana cards. Instead of Strength, he gave us a card called Lust. The familiar Temperance card became Art in Crowley's deck, and Judgment was replaced with Aeon. The designers of some new decks take great liberties, renaming many of the cards and ordering them to suit their own purposes.

Some decks rearrange the numerical order of the cards. Strength and Justice (trumps eight and eleven), for example, are sometimes reversed.

These unique approaches show the inherent flexibility that exists within the structure of the Tarot, which like any esoteric system of knowledge is enriched by diversity.

Recent Developments

The twenty-first century confronts us with unprecedented opportunities and conundrums, many of which have no easy answers. During times of transformation, when we must face challenges, make decisions, or change our familiar ways of doing things, oracles can serve as road maps on the journey into unknown territory. Sometimes they are our only guides. The Tarot and other divination aids shine light into the darkness to help us see where we are going.

It's no surprise, then, that oracles and other tools for transformation have gained popularity in recent years. Tarot sales have increased markedly since the turn of the millennium, and new products are continually being introduced into the marketplace.

As enthusiasm for the Tarot continues to expand, imaginative artists are interpreting the oracle in original and distinctive ways. Some alter the usual twenty-two-card Major Arcana and fifty-six-card Minor Arcana decks by adding a few extra cards or providing a blank so users can customize their decks. Others blend two or more divination systems. One World Tarot, for instance, combines Tarot with astrology. Tarot of the Sephiroth blends Kabbalah and the Tarot. The Celtic Dragon Tarot, Animal-Wise Tarot, the Unicorn Tarot, Australian Animal Tarot deck, and Tarot of the Cat People incorporate animals or mystical beasts into their imagery.

In addition to the many innovations and new approaches, some older decks and designs are now being revisited. The Minchiate Tarot, by Brian Williams, is one example. This updated version of the ninety-seven-card Renaissance oracle includes cards for the twelve astrological signs and four elements, along with the usual seventy-eight cards of the Major and Minor Arcana.

The Shape of Things

Although virtually all Tarot cards are rectangular in shape—except for the Motherpeace deck, which is round—their dimensions vary markedly. Most are larger than regular playing cards. Some, including the Medieval Cat Tarot and the Cary-Yale Visconti Tarocchi deck, are long and narrow; others, such as the Goddess Tarot and the Lover's Path Tarot, are nearly square. The Waite deck and other popular packs come in giant versions as well as miniature models small enough to hang on a key chain. Select a deck that appeals to your eye and your hands; the choice is purely personal.

Cultural and Spiritual Themes

Trends in both political ideology and spiritual development in culture can be tracked through the Tarot. In the 1970s, the Motherpeace Tarot, which celebrates 30,000 years of women's culture, expressed the emergence of the feminist movement. Decks with Native American and shamanic themes appeared in the 1980s and early 90s. In the late 1990s, a revival of interest in Celtic spirituality launched a series of decks with Celtic motifs, including Sacred Circle Tarot, the Arthurian Tarot, Glastonbury Tarot, and Celtic Dragon Tarot. Wicca's expansion at the turn of the new millennium brought about a plethora of goddess-oriented decks along with decks that honor the "old religion." Some decks, including the Universal Tarot and the Wheel of Change Tarot, incorporate a variety of traditions into their multicultural imagery, echoing the cultural diversity and spiritual melding that's taking place throughout our shrinking world.

Some recent Tarot decks focus on a particular area of life, such as the Lover's Path Tarot, whose images and interpretations are devoted to understanding relationships. Others incorporate symbolism, concepts, and designs from other countries, including Japan, China, Egypt, and Russia.

Modern decks also attract young users. Their designs often echo youth culture. Hero/adventure decks, goth decks, and wizard and fantasy decks, for instance, tend to be popular with teen and young adult audiences. Some decks, including Quick & Easy Tarot and the Instant Tarot Reader, are intended for beginners. Others, such as the Gummy Bear Tarot, take a playful approach to a serious subject.

The Tarot in an Age of Computers

Desktop publishing and elegant graphics software have made it easier for artists to design, publish, and distribute their own original Tarot decks. Some even come on CDs instead of card stock. Many original decks that have not been printed can be viewed online, and you can even get free, instant Tarot readings online.

Chapter 3

Choosing a Tarot Deck

Whether you choose a standard deck, such as the Waite deck, which is the most popular deck in the world, a more modern deck, or one reproduced from a Renaissance pack, the decision is strictly up to you. The illustrations in this book are based on the Waite deck, but that's not an endorsement of this classic. So many wonderful and diverse decks exist these days, with new ones being introduced regularly, that the hardest part might be making up your mind!

Finding the Right Deck

Much will depend on whether or not you are primarily a visual person. The symbolism of the Major Arcana is pretty much the same in all decks, even if it is depicted through different themes (e.g., Celtic, Native American, Japanese, etc.). For some people, the pictures on the Minor Arcana serve as memory aids to the cards' meanings. Other readers prefer to dispense with storytelling scenarios on the Minor Arcana and are more comfortable with a simpler deck. In some decks it's difficult to tell immediately if a pip card is upright or reversed; in others it's obvious. Look at a number of decks and if one strikes your eye, try it out. Many stores keep sample packs available for you to examine and test before you buy. If you are less adventurous, just start with the Waite deck, as most books about the Tarot are based on those illustrations.

If after using a deck for a while you do not feel entirely comfortable with it and its symbols, get another deck. Feeling an affinity for the deck you are using is essential. You need a deck that will resonate with your own inner symbology, and that is compatible with your own belief system. Therefore, if the symbols make you anxious or uncertain, you have chosen the wrong deck. If you like the imagery—possibly crystals, animals, angels, herbs and flowers, or some abstract configuration—and if it seems to suit your personal point of view and you feel good using it, then you have found a good deck.

You can choose a deck intuitively. A pendulum can help you make the decision successfully, or you can hold a deck in your hands, close your eyes, and see what vibrations come through to you about the deck. Different decks give off different vibrations, and different people receive different vibrations from the same deck. It's a personal decision!

When choosing a deck, bear in mind that in some decks the Minor Arcana cards are not to be taken at face value (when illustrated). As discussed in the previous chapter, there is no historical precedent for illustrating the pip cards; they are not derived from any ancient mystical tradition so far as historians can ascertain. Whether or not you choose a deck with storytelling images on these cards, interpret them first according to their suit and numerical divinatory meanings.

Using More Than One Deck

Many people like to have two or more decks, sometimes for different purposes. You might decide to keep one deck for your own spiritual development and use another deck for readings. These can be identical or of two different designs. If you read for other people, you'll probably want to have one deck for yourself and another for others to use.

ALERT!

If a deck in your possession does not seem right to you, lay it aside for a time. You can go back to it later on. During the interim, you may have changed, your intuition may have reached a different level, and the deck may work. If it still doesn't feel right, give it away or discard it.

Become thoroughly familiar with one deck first, using it until you understand the symbolism and can remember the meanings of the cards. Mastery of a single deck will make mastery of secondary or additional decks much simpler.

If after meditating on the Major Arcana of one deck you then meditate on the Major Arcana of a second deck, you will begin to intuitively understand the differences between the two decks. Follow the same process given above for choosing a single deck when selecting additional decks.

The deck you begin with might not be the one you continue using forever. Many Tarot enthusiasts collect decks and may be proud of their libraries, but most have a favorite that they turn to whenever they want advice.

Handling Your Deck

How should you handle your Tarot deck? With utmost care and respect. Treat it as you would any precious possession of great value. Never leave it lying about unattended. Always return it to its special place immediately after you have finished using it for practice, meditation, or a reading.

It is important to clear the vibrations from your deck each time you use it, especially if another person handles the cards. However, if you use a totally separate deck only for your own spiritual practice it is not necessary to clear out your own vibrations. In fact, you want the deck to be impregnated with your personal energy. But, if you do readings with that same deck even if only for yourself, you should clear it after each reading so that no residue remains that might affect the next reading.

Blessing and Purifying the Cards

It is a good idea to bless your deck each time before you use it. When you get a new deck, you may want to have a short blessing ceremony before you use it for the first time. This need not be complicated. If you already use blessing rituals as part of your usual activities, that will be sufficient. If you do not already have blessing rituals, simply place the cards in front of you, hold your hands palms down over them, and say, silently or out loud, "I call upon the divine powers to bless and protect these cards, for my intention is to use them for good only. I declare that only good shall come from their use and that all negativity shall be turned away from them."

There are many methods of clearing, or purification. The following methods are based on the four elements: Fire, Earth, Air, and Water.

Fire Purification

Fire is excellent for clearing and cleansing. Fire has been used for ceremonial procedures since the beginning of time, and many deities are linked with the divine fire. Fire is associated with Spirit, with the primal spark of life, and is, of course, necessary to our existence. Fire represents pure energy: It comes from a material source (such as wood or coal), but fire itself is immaterial. Thus it has the capacity to mediate between the visible and the invisible worlds. It transcends form into formlessness.

To clear with fire, you can place your deck of cards in bright sunlight for an hour or more. Or you can light a candle and set it in a candleholder on the table (or the floor—wherever you usually work with your cards). Lay your cards near the candle and allow it to burn beside them (being careful, of course, to watch over the process) while you silently invoke the Spirit of Fire, asking it to remove the old vibrations. You may choose to purchase a long-burning pillar candle and dedicate it to the purpose of clearing your deck. Do not use the candle for any other purpose. If possible, put it in a glass receptacle that will enclose it entirely. When you finish clearing your cards, thank the Fire Spirit for its help.

Earth Purification

Of all the four elements, none is as revered as the earth, for it is our home and our source of all sustenance. Many people feel a deep, sometimes mystical, connection with the earth. Just a pot of soil with a plant in it reminds us that we are fundamentally connected to our Mother Earth, from which all life springs. Stable, serene, and enduring, earth grounds us in the physical realm, the body, and in the present. In fact, we call the soil under our feet ground.

FACT

Ancient Kabbalists assigned a numeric value to each letter of the Hebrew alphabet. In the Kabbalistic tradition, salt is a sacred word because its numerical value is the same as god's name of power, Yahweh, multiplied by three.

To clear with earth, use salt—preferably coarse sea salt (available in health food stores). Salt, the essence of earth, was once one of the most valuable commodities available to humans. Indeed, we cannot live without it. Salt is also a crystal, which makes it useful for realigning energies.

For a salt-clearing, put your unwrapped deck into a small bowl and lay a sheet of clean white paper over it to avoid getting salt on the cards themselves. Make sure the cards are completely covered. Then, while silently invoking the Spirit of earth, pour a layer of salt over the cards—on top of the paper—and leave it for at least twenty minutes. Afterward, pick up the paper with the salt on it and dissolve the salt in water. Pour the salt water down the sink drain (not the toilet) and run clear water after it. Give thanks to the earth Spirit.

Another earth-clearing method uses natural quartz crystals. Place a large crystal on top of your unwrapped deck for an hour, preferably in a sunny location. It is best to reserve a crystal for this purpose alone. If you use a crystal, you must also periodically cleanse the crystal by the salt method (or with a special citrine crystal). To do this, simply make a solution of one-half teaspoon salt to one cup water and let your crystal soak in the solution for twenty-four hours. Depending on the frequency with which you use your cards, and need to clear them, cleanse your crystal more or less often.

Air Purification

Of all the elements, air is perhaps the most intimate to you, as you experience it constantly with the in-and-out flow of your breath. You cannot survive for more than a few minutes without it, and through your breathing, you are in constant communication with the element of air. You share this element with all other humans—indeed with most other living entities on earth, plants as well as animals. Air as a cleansing method is invisible, but very powerful.

To clear with air, you can follow the Native American tradition of using smoke, called smudging. With this technique (which is incidentally the quickest of the clearing practices mentioned here), the ascending smoke serves as a channel connecting you to the Great Spirit. Smudging consists simply of lighting a bunch of herbs and wafting the smoke over or in what is to be cleared.

Although different herbs are used for different purposes, sage is the most common (and most readily available—you can get it in the supermarket). To smudge your deck, simply put a few sage leaves (or a heaping tablespoon of the ground herb) into a fireproof dish or vessel (such as a large shell) and set fire to it. When the smoke begins to form, hold the deck in the wafting smoke while you invoke the Spirit of Air. Do this for a few minutes until the smoke begins to dissipate.

Whole leaves burn better than ground sage. You can even purchase smudge bundles of dried leaves with the stems still on them from stores specializing in natural foods and herbs, from some New Age shops, or from organic producers of herbs (who often sell by mail). If you are a gardener or a cook, you may already grow your own herbs. If so, simply gather a bundle and tie the stalks and leaves tightly together with string, then hang them upside down in a cool, dry place to dry.

ALERT!

When using fire in the home, be cautious. If you light a bundle of sage, hold a fireproof bowl under it to catch any sparks. Never leave burning herbs unattended, and when finished make sure that all smoldering remains have been extinguished completely. Stir smoking herbs with a fork until the smoke dies out, then leave the bowl in a sink until cold.

The beauty of the smudging technique is that not only do you clear your deck, you clear yourself and your room as well. You can also use this technique to clear your space after a client leaves, if you do readings for others.

Water Purification

The idea of water evokes thoughts of cleanliness and freshness. Water has been used in spiritual ceremonies in all cultures since the beginning of time. Water can make you feel renewed; a long, cold drink of spring water on a hot day refreshes; a bath or shower can change your outlook. Using water to cleanse your Tarot deck is an excellent way of clearing any negative emotions that may have been provoked by your reading.

The power of the Spirit of Water relates to intuition, to renewal, and rebirth. It is central to the Christian tradition of baptism. Clearly you cannot soak your deck of cards in water, but you can create a water atmosphere with a mister. Simply fill the mister with pure water (distilled or from a spring), invoke the Spirit of Water, ask it to cleanse and renew your cards, and then spray-mist the air above and around you.

Misting produces negative ions that literally change the energy in a room. When misting, use the finest spray you can, sending light puffs of mist into the air above your cards. Be careful not to get them wet. If you read for others, misting is also a good way to clear the energy field in your environment between clients.

Another method is to take a sprig from a plant—a pine sprig is especially good—dip it into a bowl of pure water and sprinkle the water around the area where you work with your cards. Putting cut flowers in a vase of water and setting it nearby where you work will serve the same purpose.

If you like, you can make charged water by leaving a bottle of water in sunlight or moonlight, or by putting water in differently colored bottles that relate to the seven chakras, then misting the air with this "charged" water.

Shuffling the Deck

Most Tarot decks are larger than a deck of ordinary playing cards. A new deck will be stiff and usually slick because the cards are treated with a protective lacquer-type coating. You will need to break in a new deck just as you must break in a new pair of shoes. Ruffle the cards at the edges a few times to give them flexibility. In time, as you handle the cards, they will become softer and easier to use.

FACT

When doing readings for other people, you can let them decide how they will handle the cards. Some people are shy, reluctant, or unsure. You can tell these people to simply hold the entire deck in both hands while they formulate clearly in their minds what they want the reading to achieve for them. Then you do the shuffling.

How you shuffle the cards is up to you. Shuffling, cutting, and handling the cards puts your individual vibrations onto them, so they can absorb your energy and respond to your concerns. Perhaps you've seen psychics read a person's life from a piece of jewelry or other personal object; the principle is similar. Most Tarot readers have a special method or ritual that allows them to connect with the cards, whether they are reading for themselves or for others. In time, you'll probably develop your own. Whether you cut, tap, or blow on the cards, the object is to establish a link between yourself and the oracle.

Oversized decks are difficult to shuffle overhand, as you might an ordinary playing deck (the way a professional card dealer shuffles). You may prefer to hold the pack in one hand and with the other slide out small sections and reposition them, doing this several times until you feel the cards are well mixed. Some people spread the cards out and stir them around with both hands. A third possibility is to cut the cards into several stacks, restack them, cut into more stacks, restack, and so on until you feel right about the amount of mixing you have done.

Whether you allow anyone else to shuffle or touch your deck is a matter for you to decide. Some card readers ask the person being read for to handle the cards (whether they simply hold them, shuffle them, cut them, or mix them in another manner), to put their personal vibrations on the cards. But other readers adamantly refuse to allow anyone else to shuffle (or handle) their decks. If you decide to allow others to handle your deck, use one of the methods given previously for purifying the deck in between users.

Before you handle your deck, be sure to wash your hands thoroughly in warm water, preferably with a sweet-smelling, pure soap. Soap made from glycerine or vegetable oils is the best because it contains no animal products. Dry your hands on a soft towel and lightly apply some neutral greaseless lotion to them. Treat your hands with care and respect, for they are the physical conduit through which your vibrations flow into the cards.

Storing Your Cards

Most readers also have methods and rituals for storing their Tarot decks. Many wrap their decks in silk, for silk is believed to possess special protective qualities that prevent the cards from becoming tainted by ambient energetic vibrations. You can use a silk scarf that has special meaning to you. Some people like to find a silk remnant from an older tradition, perhaps from an antique tapestry or a piece of cherished clothing such as a grandmother's wedding gown. You can simply fold your deck into the piece of cloth or make a pouch, either like an envelope or one with a drawstring.

Some Tarot enthusiasts insist that the cards should be kept in a pine box (as well as wrapped in silk) to keep bad vibrations from contaminating them. Care for your cards as you would any treasure or valued tool, but there's no need to get caught up in any rigid superstition about them.

Some companies make beautiful velvet, satin, and tapestry pouches—with zippers or drawstrings—specially designed to hold Tarot cards. You could also store your deck in an attractive wooden box. Whatever you choose to store your cards in, keep your cards in a special, private place—you'll always know where they are when you want them and you can be sure they won't fall into the wrong hands.

Chapter 4

Learning to Interpret the Tarot

The first step in learning to interpret the Tarot is to familiarize yourself with your own deck of cards. The images on the cards resonate differently with different people and your interpretation will depend upon your individual temperament as well as on your purpose for using the Tarot. Your own first impressions of the cards may differ from the interpretations you read here, or in any other book. This does not mean you are wrong; this book is only a guide. The rule of thumb is to do what makes sense to you.

Teaching Yourself Tarot

As you study your cards, bear in mind that they have been derived from multiple cultures, and that behind them stands a mystery. Each person's reaction to the cards is as unique as a fingerprint. However, at first it is best to learn the standard interpretations. You can take off from there once you have studied and practiced with the cards.

Begin by studying each of the cards and their meanings, noting which especially appeal to you for whatever reason. Use your own deck alongside the illustrations shown here (taken from the Waite deck) until you begin to get a feel for the cards.

Then practice. Learning to read the Tarot is like learning to play a musical instrument. It takes time, and the more effort you invest, the more proficient you will become. To aid you in your practice, some Tarot packs are designed especially for beginners. These decks provide keywords or written information along with images, symbols, and numbers to help novices learn the meanings of the individual cards. The Beginner's Tarot by Samantha Lynn, for example, is illustrated with simple line drawings that show the suit symbols, numbers, and a few words of explanation—such as joy and pleasure. The Quick & Easy Tarot deck includes brief divinatory and reversed interpretations printed on each card, along with images from the Universal Waite deck.

Decks such as these make it easy for beginners to start doing readings right away and help them learn as they go, without having to stop and look up the meanings of the individual cards in a book. Instructional aids like these, however, may interfere with the intuitive process and lead new users to rely on the words rather than the symbols on the cards.

One Step at a Time

When you first begin the serious study of the Tarot, you may wish to spend the first hour of every day working with the cards. You can also learn the symbols and their meanings bit by bit as you practice laying out cards and interpreting them.

If you do not have the leisure to spend the first hour of the day with your cards, at least set aside some specific time, preferably daily, or as often as you can manage. Much will depend on your aims. If you want merely to do fortune-telling or predictions into the future, you can concentrate on the interpretations offered in this book and the sections related to the spreads and readings. However, if you limit yourself to divination alone, you'll miss out on many of the benefits the Tarot can give you. Many people find the Tarot helps them to access psychological states and enhances their spiritual development.

> The highest purpose of the Tarot is as a system of self-initiation or enlightenment. It is a map into the realms of spiritual bliss. It is a record of man's relationship with the cosmos. In short, it is a textbook of occult teachings.
>
> **—Gerald and Betty Schueler, *The Enochian Tarot***

Step One

If you decide to make a serious study of the Tarot to access its wisdom, begin by concentrating on each of the Major Arcana cards in turn. Begin with trump zero, The Fool. Read the description and the interpretation, compare the symbolism on the card to its counterpart in your deck (if you are not using the Waite deck).

Step Two

After you have familiarized yourself with the Major Arcana—the heart of the Tarot—turn to the Minor Arcana. Study the meanings of the four suits, for each suit corresponds to an area of life and represents a mode of interacting with the world. (The suits are discussed in more depth in Chapter 5; the correlations between the suits and astrological elements are examined in Chapter 6. You'll find interpretations of the individual cards of the Minor Arcana, arranged by suit, in Chapters 13 through 16.)

Step Three

Next, move on to the Court cards: the Kings, Queens, Knights, and Pages. These cards often are used to represent people, although they have other meanings and purposes, too (as you'll see when we get to Chapter 5). Become familiar with the images on these cards and the distinctions between them.

Step Four

Last, examine the numbered cards of the Minor Arcana. (Chapter 5 describes these cards and their link with the study of numerology.) When you have become familiar with all seventy-eight cards, you can begin to practice readings.

At first the task of remembering all seventy-eight cards may seem a bit overwhelming. But little by little, you'll find yourself growing more comfortable with the images, and you'll start to grasp the inherent system at work within the two books of the Tarot. Your intuitive responses will begin to make sense. You'll start to see connections between the cards that turn up in your daily sessions and what's going on in your life. Before long, you will find yourself gaining an appreciation of the breadth and depth of this time-honored source of wisdom that has fascinated some of the world's greatest minds for centuries.

Using Your Intuition

Remember, when you use the Tarot you are tapping your intuition, and intuition is not logical or rational. If you tend to be predominantly left-brained (as most of us are), this might at first seem a bit strange. You may experience odd sensations, such as a mild pulsing in the forehead, a tingling, lightness, or an impression of being pulled inward. Do not let this frighten you. Your intuition cannot hurt you; it's a natural part of you, just like your other senses.

Your intuition, or sixth sense, is a valuable and often underutilized resource. In your unconscious, you have a huge data bank of experiences upon which to draw, most of which you are not even aware. As a result, you really know much more than you think you know. Your intuition has the unique ability to access knowledge and to correctly interpret the cards for you. In short, your unconscious is an innovator with great creative ability. Pay attention to it, trust it, let it guide you in your study of the Tarot—and in life.

ALERT!

If at any time you feel uncomfortable while using the cards, stop and try again later. Pay attention to negative feelings. Make notes about any cards or symbols that produce anxiety or discomfort. Negative information is only that—information. Psychic information is like a weather forecast: if we know the weather is going to be stormy, we can take sensible precautions.

Communicating with Your Selves

Psychology and spiritual traditions have a great deal to say about the various selves that comprise us. Whether you subscribe to a psychological concept of an unconscious, subconscious, and superconscious, or believe in angelic guardians and a Higher Power who guides you, the Tarot can help you connect with these various levels of being.

Symbolism is the language of the Tarot. Its symbols speak to a very deep, ancient part of you that is often ignored or discounted. By using the Tarot on a regular basis, you strengthen the connection between your ordinary, rational, mundane way of thinking and the other levels of existence—whether you view them as being inside or outside yourself. It's a bit like paying attention to your dreams. After a while, you'll start to understand things you didn't understand before.

When meditating on the cards or doing readings for yourself, you may get sudden, unexpected ideas or impressions that may—or may not—be directly related to a particular card or spread before you. These insights arise because working with the Tarot opens a portal between the selves (or between the different levels of reality) so that uninhibited communication can take place. Often these instantaneous revelations that slip in the back door of your mind are as meaningful as the reading itself. Sometimes, while you shuffle the cards, a single card will fall from the deck. Usually this card answers or sheds light on the question you're contemplating at the time. Is this just coincidence, or something akin to what C. G. Jung called synchronicity?

FACT

C. G. Jung was a Swiss psychologist who, in addition to studying with Sigmund Freud in Vienna, made his own valuable contributions to twentieth century psychology, including his theories about the unconscious. He coined the term synchronicity to describe the occurrence of meaningful coincidences, or events, that may appear to be simple coincidences but in fact are deeply related.

Like all oracles, and all intuitive tools, the Tarot lets you access wisdom in myriad ways. As you work with your deck, pay attention to all your experiences, your thoughts, feelings, impressions, and sensations. Like a good interpreter, the Tarot will enable you to communicate with parts of yourself that may have been shut off from you until now because you lacked an interface that would bring you together.

Keeping a Tarot Journal

As you study the Tarot, it's a good idea to keep a journal. Use a bound notebook or three-ring binder with loose-leaf pages. At the top of each page write the name of a card. Each time you examine the card, date your entry. If you are doing readings, sketch the spread you've used and label each card. (Spreads are explained and demonstrated in Chapter 10.) Add comments about your state of mind, situations in your life, or anything else that you feel may be relevant.

Once you have a journal devoted to your study of Tarot, make a covenant with your Tarot journal. Think for a few minutes about why you are doing this and why you are willing to make a commitment to writing your experiences—and copying your layouts, indicating what cards appear in which positions—regularly in your journal. Then put this into words. Study what you have written for a few minutes and see if you are satisfied with your purpose. You may want to make changes. Your statement of purpose might go something like this:

> I'm keeping my Tarot Journal for the purpose of getting in touch with my Higher Self, my intuition, and with the aim of generating heightened consciousness. My goal is to become more aware of messages from my sacred mind and to act on this information for my spiritual growth and development. I believe that keeping this journal will aid this process by providing me with a framework in which I can record and reflect upon my experiences and wherein I can chart my progress.

You are making this agreement with yourself, and it is up to you to keep to the terms you make. Trust your inner self to keep up its part of the bargain.

Where to Start

Begin by examining the cards of the Major Arcana, the more important and complex cards in the deck, as they are considered to contain secret or spiritual knowledge. Carefully note each of the main figures on the cards—what they are doing, whether they are sitting or standing, their postures, the positions of their hands and limbs (what today is called body language), what they are looking at, etc. Pay attention to any other beings—human, animal, or spiritual—that appear with them. Some decks, including the Gilded Tarot and the Sacred Circle Tarot, incorporate animals, birds, insects, and reptiles into the cards' imagery to convey specific information. Notice also the background and the foreground, for each detail is an intentional and meaningful symbol. Even something that may seem minor, such as a flower or familiar household object, is a factor in the overall interpretation of the card. Then study the Minor Arcana in the same way.

Don't analyze your initial, immediate responses to the cards—just write down what comes to you spontaneously. If a question arises in your mind, write it down but don't try to answer it right away. Return to it later.

Make notes of your impressions—of the card as a whole and of individual symbols. Accustom yourself to noticing details and try to relate to the details on a personal level, asking yourself, "What does this mean to me?" For example, in the Waite deck, The Fool carries a rose. The rose has a generally accepted universal meaning, but your own interpretation might be different. Maybe roses hold a strictly personal meaning for you, based on your own life experience. Maybe you don't particularly care for roses. Maybe when you see a rose you think of the thorns instead of the fragrance. You can go with the standard interpretation, or substitute your own. As is true of dream symbols, your individual impressions are usually more significant than the commonly accepted ones.

Let your Tarot journal be a gift you give yourself, one that makes a wonderful learning tool. Rereading what you have written is a way to show yourself how much progress you have made. Reviewing it regularly is like having a teacher at your elbow.

Over time your impressions will change and expand. You may find that if you go back to a card after you've worked with the Tarot for a while you'll have a different slant on it. This means that the illustration has penetrated deeper into your unconscious. Remember that the cards are multilayered in meaning. What you derive from your initial free examination of the pictures as well as the insights you glean over time will be important factors in how you understand and use the Tarot.

The natural inclination, for a beginner, is to interpret each card individually in a reading, and then to try to put together a whole picture from the individual pieces. But once you have impressed the meanings on your unconscious, you will find that a glance at an entire layout of cards will give you a picture of the totality. However, this only comes after much study and practice. By keeping a detailed record, to which you can return just as you might reread a diary, you will create the building blocks that enable you to get a comprehensive take on the reading before going into its details. Once you complete an intensive study of the Tarot, you'll be amazed at how significant your first impressions were to your entire process of learning to interpret.

Chapter 5

Tarot Symbolism

Every detail on each card—especially those in the Major Arcana—is a meaningful symbol. Symbols resonate on different levels of the psyche. One of the best ways to connect with these symbols is to contemplate and meditate upon those that are meaningful to you. The symbols produced by your unconscious mind are truly yours. Thus, there are as many interpretations of the symbols of the Tarot cards as there are readers. How a card speaks to you and how you feel about the symbols it presents is what's important.

Different Strokes

Individual Tarot decks express the themes that are important to their creators. Some use obviously Christian symbology, others are frankly Pagan. Some decks express feminist sensibilities, while others depict Native American, Asian, or African motifs. Some, such as the Wheel of Change Tarot and the Universal Tarot, mix imagery from a variety of cultures and spiritual traditions. It is important that you are both aware of the symbols on your personal deck of cards and feel comfortable with them or them to reach into your unconscious depths. Make friends with your cards and let them speak to you in terminology that is relevant to you.

As mentioned earlier, there are literally thousands of different Tarot decks in existence, and each is as unique as its creator. Some decks, such as the Artist's Inner Vision Tarot, by NoMonet Full Court Press, combine the creativity of several artists and thus offer the user a smorgasbord of ideas, images, and themes to ponder. Some packs are quite elaborate; others, such as the Minimalist Tarot, present very simple imagery. Some Tarot artists are influenced by designs from centuries past; others take full advantage of modern computer imagery and digital technology.

Suit Symbols

Regardless of what spin a particular artist chooses to put on her deck, certain basic concepts will generally prevail. The four suits, for example, are fundamental to the Tarot's structure and composition. These suits correspond to the four elements, which are the building blocks of life, the vital and primal forces of the universe. These elements—Earth, Air, Fire, and Water—exist everywhere in our world, not only in a physical sense, but also as vibrations or energies. We find them depicted not only in the Tarot but also in the four primary tools magicians use, the four directions, the four seasons, the Four Gospels in Christianity, and the Four Noble Truths in Buddhism.

Although the suit symbols are most evident on the Minor Arcana cards, they also appear in the Major Arcana. The Magician or Magus, for instance, is usually pictured with the symbols of all four suits before him, indicating his mastery of all the elements. The four suits may turn up on The World card, too, where they suggest a balance of these fundamental forces.

Wands

The suit of Wands corresponds to the element of Fire. Fire is active, outer-directed, linked with Spirit, will, self-expression, and inspiration. It suggests growth, expansion, and personal power. Because Fire represents archetypal masculine or yang energy, the symbolism used to depict this suit in the Tarot is distinctly phallic. Some decks use other images for the suit of Wands—rods, staves, clubs, branches sprouting leaves, lances, arrows, torches, or divining rods. Tarot of the Old Path shows them as brooms.

Often the people on the Wands cards (in storytelling decks) are shown as warriors, heroes, leaders, or magicians, dynamic and creative people who charge forth into life with confidence and enthusiasm. They may ride proud steeds, wave flags, or wear garlands. Whatever they are doing, they seem to be enjoying themselves. Even when they face challenges, as the Five and Ten cards frequently show, these courageous and hardy individuals seem fully capable of handling the difficulties placed before them and succeeding at whatever they undertake.

FACT

You can find a Tarot deck to suit almost anyone's interests. The Baseball Tarot depicts Wands as—you guessed it—baseball bats. The Cooperstown Tarot depicts Cups as baseball gloves.

When Wands appear in a spread or reading, it's usually an indication that some sort of action or growth is afoot. You might be embarking on an adventure of some kind or may be required to muster your courage in a challenging endeavor. Perhaps you could benefit from using your intuition instead of logic to solve a problem. Maybe you need to have fun, take some risks, assert yourself, or be creative.

Swords

The suit of Swords relates to the element of Air. Like Fire, Air is a masculine/yang force, so its symbol, too, is obviously phallic. Although usually depicted as a mighty battle sword, the suit's symbol may be represented by ordinary knives, athames (ritual daggers used by magicians), scythes, axes, guns, or spears. Some swords are sturdy and functional, others are ornate, reminiscent of King Arthur's Excalibur. In The Wheel of Change deck, Swords are presented as shards of broken glass. However, the "weapon" represented by this suit is the intellect. As such, Swords symbolize rational thinking, logic, analysis, communication, and the power of the mind. The Child's Play Tarot uses pencils to denote the intellectual quality of this suit.

Storytelling decks frequently show the characters on the Swords cards as warriors, scholars, sages, teachers, or seekers, serious and dispassionate individuals who pursue answers to life's great questions. Often the images reveal suffering or strife, perhaps indicating the struggle involved in transforming experience into knowledge, or to illustrate the way in which Rudolf Steiner, on whose work the Waldorf Schools are founded, describes wisdom, which is as "crystallized pain." The Nine and Ten of Swords, in particular, frequently depict painful scenes of worry, anxiety, and stress, which may be the result of too much thinking or relying too heavily on the intellect.

When Swords turn up in a reading, it often means that mental or verbal activity is a priority. Perhaps you are overworking your mind. Or you might need to use your head and examine an issue clearly and rationally. The King of Swords, for instance, can advise you not to let your heart rule your head. Swords also represent communication, study, or cutting through murky situations with logic and discrimination.

Cups

The suit of Cups is associated with the element of Water. Water's energy is receptive, inner-directed, reflective, connected with the emotions, creativity, and intuition. Because Water is a feminine or yin element, its symbols suggest the womb. In the Tarot, Cups are usually shown as chalices or goblets, but any type of vessel can depict the nature of the suit. Some decks picture them as bowls, cauldrons, vases, urns, flowers, pitchers, coffee mugs, steins, baskets, or bottles. Regardless of the imagery, the principle is the same—Cups represent the ability to receive and hold.

For the most part, the scenes that appear on these cards suggest comfort, security, and contentment. Because the suit of Cups represents the emotions, the people on the cards are usually shown in relationships of some kind—romantic, familial, friendship. The Two of Cups symbolizes partnership, and frequently a man and woman appear together in a loving manner on the card. Three women friends often grace the Three of Cups, while the Ten of Cups depicts a happy home and family life.

Because Cups represent water and its ability to be reflective and recep-tive, Cups can also describe a person who is intuitive, compassionate, sensitive, creative, or nurturing. All of these characteristics are tradi-tionally feminine and relate to the inner reflections of a person and her emotional awareness.

A reading that contains many Cups usually emphasizes emotions and/or relationships. Depending on the cards involved, you may be enjoying positive interactions with people you care about or are seeking greater ful-fillment in matters of the heart. Perhaps you are suffering a loss or disap-pointment, or are on your way to recovery and emotional renewal.

Pentacles

Pentacles or pentagrams (five-pointed stars) correspond to the earth element. Like Water, Earth is a feminine/yin force that energetically relates to our planet as the source of sustenance, security, and stability. The suit of Pentacles represents practical matters, money and resources, the body, and the material world. Tarot decks often portray the suit as coins or discs, some-times as shields, stones, rings, shells, crystals, wheels, stars, clocks, or loaves of bread. Regardless of the actual image used, the suit symbolizes physical resources, values, practical concerns, material goods, property, and forms of monetary exchange—things that sustain us on the earthly plane.

Storytelling decks often depict people on the Pentacles cards engaged in some form of work or commerce, or enjoying the fruits of their labors and the things money can buy. The Three of Pentacles in the Waite deck, for instance, shows a craftsman working at a forge. The Ten of Pentacles

THE EVERYTHING TAROT BOOK

presents a picture of domestic security, abundance, and comfort. The Five of Pentacles, on the other hand, portrays a sad image of poverty and need.

When Pentacles appear in a spread, it's a sign that financial or work-related matters are prominent in the mind of the person for whom the reading is being done. In some cases, these cards can also signify physical or health issues, or other situations involving the body or one's physical capabilities. The Queen of Pentacles, for example, can indicate a sensual woman who is at home in her body, who loves good food, creature comforts, and the finer things in life. Depending on the cards, this suit may suggest a need to focus on practical concerns. Or you could be too security-conscious and are putting emphasis on material things at the expense of spiritual, emotional, or intellectual considerations.

Numerology and the Tarot

The numbers on the pip cards of the Minor Arcana are of primary significance. Regardless of whether the deck you use includes storytelling images on these cards, pay attention to the number and the suit, for this combination provides the essential information in a reading.

Symbolically speaking, numbers are not merely arithmetic used to denote quantities. Each number also has a unique power and secret significance, applicable both to the spiritual and the material worlds. Numerology, the spiritual art of numbers, is thousands of years old. Cultures with an esoteric tradition have long honored and understood the sacred symbology of numbers. Numbers are indeed symbols and each possesses its own special characteristics. In fact, numbers could be considered our most common and familiar symbols.

When interpreting the number cards of the Minor Arcana, the suit will tell you the area of life to which the number card refers—the nature of the influences and forces at work and on which the specific number is commenting. By combining the meanings of the suit and the number featured on a card, you can determine how the card applies to the particular situation for which the reading is being given.

Ace (One)

One signifies new beginnings. It implies something coming into being, the starting point of a whole new cycle. It represents self-development, creativity, action, progress, a new chance, a rebirth.

FACT

Barbara Moore, author of *The Gilded Tarot Companion*, calls Aces gifts from the universe. They symbolize a chance to start anew and realize possibilities and potential.

The Ace shows that a seed has been planted, meaning that something has begun, though you may not yet know how it will develop. The Aces symbolize potential growth. When an Ace appears in your reading, you are at a starting point, being offered a new opportunity. It's up to you to follow through—it won't automatically happen. The Ace indicates you have the choice to initiate something, that the time is ripe for new possibilities and growth.

The energy of One is solitary and self-contained. Drawing an Ace may indicate being alone or withdrawing into isolation to nurture a new idea, project, or experience before going public with it. Aces also can show focus, concentrated energy, and clarity of purpose.

Two

The essence of Two is duality. This number depicts some kind of union or partnership, with another person, a spiritual entity, or two parts of yourself. Two also represents the balance of polarities such as yin and yang, male and female, private and public, separate and together.

Two furthers the direction initiated with the Ace. It represents stabilizing and affirming the new opportunity. Sometimes Two shows a need to achieve balance with whatever new factor is being added to the situation that began with the Ace. Whether favorable or unfavorable, this addition will be of importance to you. Depending on the reading, the Two suggests either increased chances for a desirable outcome or greater obstacles involved in achieving that outcome.

Two's vibration can indicate sensitivity to others, perhaps to the point where you consider their needs over your own. "Two-ness" can also mean a state of immersing yourself in another person or in an idea or project.

Three

We see the essence of Three expressed in the trinity of Mind, Body, and Spirit. It is the number of self-expression and communication, of expansion, openness, optimism, and clarity.

With the Three, you begin to open up and see the big picture, understanding the details of how One and Two combine in your own process of growth and evolution. This is the point at which the project, idea, or relationship you initiated earlier now begins to take form. Three says "Go," but if unfavorable factors are involved, caution is advised.

The number three represents movement, action, growth, and development, but in some cases expansion can happen too fast. You may scatter your energies or spread yourself too thin. There is a tendency to leap before you look, or to buy now and pay later. However, properly handled, Three's vibration is cheerful, optimistic, and pleasant, representing a period of happiness and benefits, so long as you pay attention to what you are doing.

Four

The number Four equates with foundation. There are four elements, four directions, and four seasons, so Four suggests totality, stability, and security. When Fours appear in a reading, it can indicate a time for self-discipline through work and service, productivity, organization, and pragmatism to establish a sound foundation.

Clarity is important now, so that you can work effectively to make your situation turn out positively. If you are in a place you want to be—a home, job, relationship—you might have to work to maintain stability; if you aren't where you want to be, drawing Fours suggests it's time to plan and work to make appropriate changes.

At this time, life can seem to be all work and no play, but sometimes that's necessary for you to accomplish your objectives. If your goals and purpose are clear, you won't mind doing the work, for you see the end result as beneficial. When Fours turn up in a reading, the message is to take slow, steady, determined steps and move patiently to bring your dreams to fruition.

Five

Five is the number of freedom, instability, and change. Its vibration is active, physical, impulsive, impatient, resourceful, curious, and playful. Drawing Fives in a reading suggests excitement, adventure, movement, and challenges afoot. It might even indicate a rollercoaster ride!

ALERT!

Although Fives are an indication to go for it, consider the risks involved, too. When Fives appear in a reading, you are willing to take risks because you love the excitement involved in the situation. The cards around the Five will indicate whether there is real danger or if things will work out to your advantage.

Sometimes, Five can be too much to handle, especially if you tend to be a quiet, sensitive person. The excitement and changes in your life may seem to be happening too fast, so that you feel you are caught in a whirlwind—or a hurricane. Thus Fives are often connected with stress and instability. You might need to slow down a bit and get some perspective before moving ahead. If an important decision is involved, "take five" before you make any commitment.

Six

Six is the number of service and social responsibility, caring, compassion, and community involvement. It signifies peace and quiet after the storm of Five. This is a time to keep it simple and attend to everyday needs, to rest, and to get into harmony with yourself and your surroundings. Any misunderstandings that occurred during an earlier period of upheaval can now be resolved harmoniously.

When Sixes appear in a reading, it's time to stop and catch your breath, realizing that you have created a comfortable pattern and can reap the rewards of your previous planning (Four) and risk-taking (Five). You feel centered and at ease with yourself and your circumstances. Unfavorable cards in the reading may indicate difficult circumstances yet to be faced, but Six cards rarely show anything negative themselves.

Six's vibration is cooperative; it can represent working with others or providing service of some kind. Just remember to take care of your own needs, too. In some cases, Sixes in a reading can show a tendency toward reclusiveness—just vegging out at home to enjoy a time of ease, especially after a period of intense activity or stress.

Seven

The number Seven symbolizes the inner life, solitude, and soul-searching. Seven is a mystical number depicting wisdom and spirituality; there are seven heavens, seven days of the week (the seventh being holy), seven colors in the visible spectrum, seven notes in a musical scale, and seven major chakras.

When Sevens appear in a reading, it indicates a time of turning inward to discover the meaning of life, what has been happening to you, and why. You may be searching, on a psychological or spiritual level, for answers. Perhaps you feel an intense need to be alone. Seven often refers to birth and rebirth, religious inclinations and spiritual resources. Some people retreat from the busyness of everyday life at this time, take vows of some kind, or begin to practice ritual as part of their inner development. Emblematic of the path of solitude, analysis, and contemplation, Seven marks a time when you are exploring your own individuality in your own way.

This is not a time to begin projects related to the material or financial world. Your energy is focused on the inner rather than the outer realm. Now is a good time to create a sanctuary for contemplation, a private place where you can examine your past experiences and evaluate the present. You might wish to study or research metaphysical subjects, start paying attention to dreams and ESP experiences—whatever will help you to find your own true path in life. In some cases, Sevens in the reading may indicate that you are spending too much time alone and need to socialize.

Eight

Eight represents abundance, material prosperity, and worldly power or influence. It is the number of leadership and authority. On the spiritual level, Eight symbolizes cosmic consciousness; infinity's symbol is a figure Eight turned on its side. This powerful number indicates you possess the organizational and managerial skills that contribute to material success—or that you need to develop them. If you have been devoting much of your time and energy to spiritual progress, the appearance of Eights in a reading indicates it's time to get your financial or worldly affairs in order.

As the infinity glyph symbolizes wholeness, the number Eight points to the development of multiple aspects of your life—physical, mental, and spiritual.

Eight's vibration is linked with honor, respect, equality, awards, public recognition, power, and abundance in all areas of life. When you draw Eights, the potential for achieving these benefits is likely, but sincerity and dedication are needed.

The Eight cards also caution you to consider the welfare of others as well as yourself. If there are unfavorable factors in the reading, you may need to be careful with money or possessions. Eights reversed can indicate that you have many issues around abundance—or the lack of it—yet to resolve.

Nine

The number Nine equates with humanitarianism. It represents universal compassion, tolerance for the many differences among different peoples, and the attainment of wisdom through experience. Drawing Nines suggests you have reached a level where you are comfortable dedicating your life to others' welfare, or to some worthy cause. The challenge is to avoid getting so caught up in the big picture—the greatest good for the greatest number—that you neglect what is closest to you.

Nine symbolizes integration and, in a reading, shows that you have established your life priorities—you know what you want and how you intend to get it. You feel a flow of vitality between all the different parts of yourself. You understand the interaction between you and the world as a continuing process of living, being, moving. The Nine vibration allows you to see beyond the boundaries of the self into the totality of the universal. You are able to give freely of yourself because you feel complete within yourself.

The last single-digit number, Nine represents the end of a cycle. It's time to tie up loose ends. In most cases, the Nine cards depict fulfillment, completion, wholeness, and the sense of satisfaction that comes from having reached a peak after a long, arduous climb.

Ten

Ten represents both an ending and a beginning, the point of transition from the completed cycle to the new cycle, which has not yet manifested. When Tens show up in a reading, whatever you have been working on or involved with is over. You've got whatever you are going to get out of it, and now it is time to bring in the new cycle that's been waiting in the wings.

Whether the cycle that's ending has been good or bad, you know it's over now, which is especially gratifying if you have been experiencing rocky times. If you have become complacent during a good period, drawing Tens tells you the time has come to challenge yourself and reach for a higher level. As a compound number, Ten, though a form of One, has more impact and therefore adds an extra dimension in a reading. Like ascending to a higher level of a spiral staircase, you can look down at precisely where you began and chart your progress. Now you have a choice to either stagnate in familiar and comfortable territory or to take a chance and start something new and different.

As happens in any period of transition, you may experience discomfort about making the decision to stay put or move on. Both options are available; both require thought and consideration. You might feel you are sitting on the fence, with one foot on either side, not sure whether to jump all the way over. Transitions are like that, and sometimes it takes quite a while to get both feet on the same side of the fence. However, you know that "he who hesitates is lost," and though you have the luxury of postponing both decision and action for a little while, when Tens show up in a reading it's a signal that a decision must be made.

Color Symbolism

Many Tarot decks display vivid and beautiful color palettes. But the colors shown on the cards are not purely decorative; they embody specific symbolic, spiritual, psychological, and physiological properties as well. For centuries, artists have used colors in their compositions, not only for their aesthetic properties, but also for their ability to convey moods and messages to those who view them.

In magical practice, colors correspond to the four elements. Red is associated with Fire, blue with Water, green with earth, and yellow with Air. Because each suit is linked with an element, many Tarot artists use the colors connected with the corresponding suits to trigger subconscious responses and insights. Therefore, some decks emphasize red on the cards in the suit of Wands, blue on the Cups cards, green on the Pentacles cards, and yellow on the Swords cards.

FACT

Early Christian paintings and stained glass windows often show Jesus and Mary dressed in blue robes, which suggest serenity and compassion. We connect orange with fire, the sun, and warmth, while green represents growth, health, and in some countries, money.

Studies show that people react psychologically and even physically to colors. For instance, red tends to make us feel stimulated, warmer, and can even raise pulse rate and body temperature slightly. Blue, conversely, calms and cools us. In some prisons, cell walls were painted pink and aggressive behavior among inmates declined. The table below lists qualities associated with different hues. As you familiarize yourself with your Tarot deck, notice how the artist has used colors to express certain qualities.

Color	Intention
Red	Passion, vitality, courage
Orange	Warmth, energy, activity, drive, confidence
Yellow	Creativity, optimism, enthusiasm
Green	Healing, growth, fertility, prosperity
Light blue	Purity, serenity, mental clarity, compassion
Royal blue	Loyalty, insight, inspiration, independence
Indigo	Intuition, focus, stability
Purple	Wisdom, spirituality, power
White	Purity, wholeness, protection
Black	Power, the unconscious, banishing, wisdom
Pink	Love, friendship, affection, joy, self-esteem
Brown	Grounding, permanence, practicality

Popular Symbols

In addition to the suit symbols, you'll find many familiar—and some not so familiar—images on the cards in your deck. Tarot artists intentionally choose symbols from various spiritual, cultural, magical, and psychological traditions to convey information directly to your subconscious. Like dream imagery, the symbols depicted on Tarot cards speak to people at a deep level and trigger insights in a way that's more immediate and succinct than words can.

Symbols and pictures offer other advantages over words, too. Because images are understood by our inner knowing, they are less likely to present you with dogma when you seek truth. They inspire you to think, but they don't tell you what to think. They bypass the analytical, orderly left-brain and strike up a lively conversation with the imaginative, flexible right-brain. Like myths, symbols transcend the boundaries of religion, nationality, and time, presenting universal themes and concepts that people everywhere can relate to.

The cards in the Major Arcana, in particular, are rich with meaningful imagery, although many decks include vivid symbolism on the Minor Arcana cards as well. Some of the symbols are universal in nature, found in many countries and time periods. Others are personal and may reflect the designer's intentions or beliefs, rather than holding broader meanings for all users. The Universal Tarot, by Maxwell Miller, incorporates a variety of symbolism from many different traditions to create a complex and comprehensive oracle.

Universal Symbolism

Symbols embody the essence of whatever they stand for; they aren't merely a convenient form of shorthand. That's why they have such power, why they appear in diverse and widely separated cultures, and why they have endured for millennia.

Symbol is myth's vehicle, the chariot by which legend and story, and myth's higher form, religion, is drawn through the heart and mind, and through time. Symbols express underlying patterns of thought and feeling stemming from the mythological roots that still affect people in a very real way.

Symbols that turn up again and again, in all parts of the world, possess universal appeal and resonate in what Swiss psychiatrist C. G. Jung called the collective unconscious. They mean essentially the same thing to everyone, regardless of age, race, religion, or nationality and get around the limitations of the rational, analytical, left-brain. Often we confront these symbols in dreams where they provide guidance and awaken us to parts of ourselves that we may have ignored in our waking lives. The Tarot works in a similar manner.

The following table shows a number of common, universally understood symbols that you may notice on the cards in your Tarot deck. They can be helpful keys as you examine the cards and learn their significances.

Symbol	Meaning
Circle	Wholeness, unity, protection, continuity
Square	Stability, equality, structure
Triangle	Trinity, three-dimensional existence, movement
Downward triangle	Divine feminine, earth or water elements
Upward triangle	Divine masculine, fire or air elements
Star	Hope, promise
Five-pointed star	Protection, the human body, physical incarnation
Six-pointed star	Union of male/female or earth/sky, integration, manifestation
Vertical line	Movement, heaven, sky, masculine energy
Horizontal line	Stability, earth, feminine energy
Cross	Union of male/female or earth/sky, integration, manifestation
Spiral	Life energy, renewal, movement toward the center
Sun	Clarity, vitality, optimism, contentment, masculine energy
Moon	Secrets, intuition, emotions, feminine energy
Dove	Peace, reconciliation, promise
Crane	Wisdom
Rose	Love
Mountain	Challenge, vision, achievement
Ocean/water	Emotions, the unknown depths of the psyche
Snake	Transformation, hidden knowledge, kundalini energy
Egg	Birth, fertility
Rainbow	Renewal, hope, happiness
Book	Knowledge
Lantern	Guidance, clarity, hope
Bridge	Connection, harmony, overcoming difficulty
Tree	Knowledge, growth, protection, strength
Butterfly	Transformation

When studying the symbolism in the Tarot, remember that your own responses and interpretations are what count most. Cars suggest movement and freedom to most people, but if you were in a serious auto accident when you were young, cars may represent pain or danger to you. Trust your own instincts and intuition. After all, your Tarot deck and your subconscious are attempting to communicate with you, and they will do it in imagery that you can understand.

Personal Symbols

Tarot decks can also contain their creators' personal symbols. These images may or may not mean the same thing to you as they do to their designers or to another person using the cards. Flexibility is part of what makes the Tarot so fascinating.

Perhaps the artist is attempting to get you to stretch your imagination by presenting you with new or atypical pictures. The noted and eclectic artist Salvador Dali repeats individual symbols such as a forked stick on some of the cards in his deck, as well as omitting or altering some familiar imagery entirely. The World card in his deck is anything but a pretty picture of joy, harmony, and abundance—possibly because the artist views our world as disturbing and never completely fathomable.

Daily silence experienced in humility and fervor as an indispensable exercise in spiritual nourishment gradually creates within us a permanent state of silence. The soul discovers in such a silence unsuspected possibilities. It realizes that life can be lived at different levels.

—Pierre Lacout in *God Is Silence*

Tarot decks that come packaged with their own books or instructional guides generally explain the significance of the symbols displayed on the cards. Even so, if your own feelings about the pictures on the cards don't coincide with the artist's, give your own responses precedence. And if your interpretations of certain symbols change over time, that's okay, too.

Chapter 6

Astrology and the Tarot

One of the most interesting things about the Tarot is the way in which it dovetails with astrology. In addition to the links between the suits and the four elements, which are cornerstones of astrology, many decks also include astrological factors in their illustrations to show celestial influences at work in the Tarot.

Astrological Indicators and Imagery

The Sun and The Moon in the Major Arcana are the most obvious examples of astrological imagery in Tarot. Many decks feature a crab, the symbol for the zodiac sign Cancer, which is ruled by the moon, on The Moon card. And Justice is often shown holding a scale or balance, the symbol for Libra.

Tarot artists frequently incorporate illustrations of the planets, constellations, zodiac wheels, astrological glyphs, and other symbolism into their compositions to convey insights and information. Ciro Marchetti's beautiful Gilded Tarot is one that liberally uses astrological imagery on the trump cards: The Empress holds the glyph for Venus, the planet of women, and is circled by the zodiac wheel; The Fool juggles the twelve sign glyphs.

The link between astrology and the Tarot was even more evident in some decks that appeared during the Renaissance. The Minchiate Tarot, for instance, featured ninety-seven cards instead of the usual seventy-eight. This interesting oracle included twelve cards for the twelve astrological signs plus one for each of the four elements in addition to the Major and Minor Arcana.

The Major Arcana

Of course, you can use the Tarot with absolutely no knowledge of astrology, but even a cursory understanding of the planets and the signs of the zodiac as they relate to the Major Arcana will enrich your understanding of the Tarot.

The Fool

The Fool is related to Uranus, the planet that destroys old ideologies, concepts, and structures. Uranus represents not only the advanced thinker, modern scientist, and esoteric occultist but also the bohemian, the beatnik, the hippie, revolutionaries, anarchists, rebels, and radical humanitarians—nonconformists of all stripes.

Uranus was discovered in 1781, just twenty-nine years after Benjamin Franklin made his famous kite experiment. Thus, the planet's discovery coincided with that of electricity and the subsequent development of electronics and telecommunications. Uranus produces sudden changes of all sorts, and, like a thunderstorm, often serves to clear the psychic air.

Esoteric astrologers believe that Uranus represents the unique task each person assumes in this particular incarnation, that the planet offers a clue to the soul's reason for making this earth-life journey. In a sense, the position of Uranus in a person's birth chart shows where the soul is most free of restrictions, for old karma has already been dissolved and you are able to be most truly yourself—unique and individual. For instance, someone born while Uranus was in Cancer might not be bound by familial expectations, ties, or traditions. Uranus reveals the places and ways in which we tend to behave in a free-spirited manner—where we act or think unconventionally, knock over tradition, be iconoclasts, do unusual things, or produce far-out ideas.

Uranus symbolizes Man's liberation from the bondage of the personality and signifies the power which may be achieved through the collected energies of truly individualized souls working toward a conscious connection with the Source of Life.

—**Alan Oken, *Complete Astrology***

Uranus is exalted in Scorpio, an indication of unusual daring and a willingness to stake life itself on adventures into the unknown—as The Fool is about to do. Uranus rules the sign of Aquarius, an air sign that emphasizes mental activity. Aquarius extols the idea of the individual as a cooperative member of the larger whole, and that all humanity is one coherent family, a concept that can be grasped only intuitively. Detachment is a primary quality of Aquarius, conferring the ability to deal with large issues that would be painful to others who lack emotional objectivity.

Aquarians tend to be original and forward-looking, even futuristic, and seek new experiences, even if danger is involved. Traditional ways of thinking and living bore Aquarians, who want to shape the future according to their own unique vision of how things should be. These people can be rebels and free spirits, willing to experiment with life, take chances, and deal spontaneously with whatever befalls them. The image of The Fool blithely embarking on a solo journey into uncharted territory typifies the Aquarian spirit.

The Magician

The Magician is related to the planet Mercury. It is interesting to note that Uranus, sometimes called the cosmic magician who rules magic and invention, is considered to be the higher octave of Mercury. Mercury is the planet of the intellect; it represents how the mind works, how you learn, and how you communicate. In astrology, Mercury is linked with cleverness, dexterity, quickness, and changeability, but it is also the mark of the trickster—all characteristics associated with The Magician.

In mythology, Mercury is the messenger of the gods, personified as fleet of foot and quick of mind. On the metaphysical level, Mercury mediates, or delivers messages, between the conscious mind, altered states of consciousness, and the unconscious mind. Dual in nature, Mercury represents the archetypes of both the eternal youth and the wise old man. Far more complex than astrologers generally credit it with being, on a spiritual level, Mercury is Thoth-Hermes, guide of souls.

Mercury is multifaceted, a god of many attributes. He governs all aspects of communication—writing, speaking, learning, commerce, and messages of all sorts. In psychological terms, Mercury's position in your birth chart describes your level of ability to communicate both what you think and what you feel. It illustrates the process by which you link your internal realm of both feeling and thought to the external world.

Mercury rules both Gemini and Virgo and is exalted in the sign of Aquarius, which is ruled by Uranus. Gemini is an air sign, and The Magician symbolizes the power of the mind to create ideas that eventually manifest in the physical world, shown by the earth sign Virgo. The Magician's ability to move easily between the two realms, heaven and earth, is one of this trump's most intriguing qualities.

The High Priestess

The High Priestess is linked with the Moon, which governs the emotions and intuition. The Moon is a metaphor for all that is instinctive. Cyclical and constantly changing, the Moon is called the soul of life, mediator between the planes of the spiritual (Sun) and material (Earth), reflecting back the light of the Sun it has received into itself. Thus, the Moon is also a metaphor for receptivity, the yin principle in Asian philosophy, and is emblematic of the container of life, that matrix that nourishes the process of manifestation. It is the protective surrounding that shields the growing, developing entity—be it a seed in the soil, the embryo in an egg, the fetus in the womb, or the creative act of making art.

Both physical and psychological crises can be indicated by the transits of the planets in relation to the natal chart. These constitute a transforming crisis, which is to say that one is presented with the opportunity—often the necessity—to make life-changing decisions with profound effects.

In astrology, the Moon's house, the fourth, reveals your experience of your mother, your early home, the past, and memory. The Moon rules the zodiac sign Cancer, a water sign symbolizing contact with the instinctive nature, the realm of the World Mother who brings forth abundant life even in the face of death. There is mystery here—the one of the relationship between life and death. Cancer also symbolizes emotional connectedness, or the invisible side of life epitomized by feelings—remember, the Moon has a hidden side that you never see. Your lunar self is the channel for the flow of the divine goddess energy, which is subtle and not always obvious.

Symbolically, the Moon serves to reveal the nonconscious side of human life, and in that diffuse light you can often see more accurately than in the glare of the noonday Sun. The Moon allows you to shine light into your inner spiritual world, to illuminate what springs naturally from inside yourself. In moonlight you perceive the reality of your inner spiritual self more fully. You are more aware of the shadings and nuances of feelings and inner perceptions, and you tune in more accurately to the spiritual vibrations of others.

The Moon is exalted in the zodiac sign Taurus, the bull, and The High Priestess is often depicted wearing the horns of the Moon—the same as the horns of the bull—on her headdress. As a lunar figure, she speaks to your deepest inner needs, your memories, feelings, moods, and internal rhythms.

The Empress

The Empress is related to Venus, the planet of women, love, beauty, desire, pleasure, and relationships. Venus symbolizes the deeply feminine part of all people, male as well as female, telling of their capacity to reach out to others in a loving way, not just sexually or erotically. She also represents the affections and symbolizes what people value in terms of social natures. Venus functions through relating—to other people, to your own desire, to nature, to the things you love, and to the outside world.

Venus rules both Taurus, an earth sign, and Libra, an air sign, and both signs are associated with affection, sociability, and love of beauty. The Taurean nature of Venus is more sensuous and materialistic, while the Libran side is more refined and artistic. Venus is exalted in Pisces where the transcendental vibrations of Neptune, the ruler of Pisces, make love the most transcendent of spiritual experiences. Here, romantic love is rendered more altruistic, singing in tune with the harmony of the spheres.

Taurus symbolizes connection to the earth plane with its reliance on the physical senses. The second sign of the zodiac, Taurus provides the matrix (a word related to mother) for the primary energies of life to come into being on the physical plane, through bearing children and growing plants. earthiest of the earth signs, Taurus is symbolic of the soil of Mother Earth herself. The receptive quality of Taurus is like that of the earth, which receives the seed, contains it, and enables it to grow.

Libra symbolizes the desire for balance in all things, and by extension, an urge toward relationships, from the personal to the abstract. The seventh sign of the zodiac, Libra is associated with beauty and harmony, the arts, partnerships in love and business, and aesthetics. The Empress embodies all these characteristics and energies, depicting the practical as well as the romantic aspects of the archetypal feminine force.

The Emperor

The Emperor is related to the sign Aries. As the first sign of the zodiac, Aries symbolizes leadership, initiative, action, energy, and new ideas. It is associated with beginnings of all kinds and the primary energy that gets things going. People born under this cardinal fire sign are self-starters, leaders—not followers. Willful and daring, with a strong desire to be first,

Aries people are always looking for the next adventure, challenge, project, or experience.

Aries is ruled by the planet Mars, the exemplar of all the traditional aspects that we esteem in the male of the species: sexual prowess, courage, energy, action, protectiveness, and valor. Though Mars is known as the god of war, he also represents daring and forthrightness. As a warrior, he is both aggressor and protector. Mars expresses the principle of action, in any and all spheres. In mythology, he was first trained as a dancer, then as a warrior. The war dance prepared the spirits of the warriors for physical danger and trial, joining them together as a group—what we today call male bonding.

FACT

An interesting aspect about Mars energy in women is not that the male-dominated military establishment permits women to serve, even to fly in combat, but that women want to do it, which proves that, given a chance, women can express Mars's sheer physical energy and daring as forcefully as men do.

Mars and The Emperor represent primal male energy, the archetypal masculine or yang force that is the counterpart and complement to Venus and The Empress.

The Hierophant

The Hierophant is related to the zodiac sign Taurus, which symbolizes connection to the material plane and, by extension, the accumulation of possessions. Gifted with patience, Taurus lets things happen in their own time. Like a good gardener, Taurus is content to wait until the right time comes along, knowing there's no point in pulling up the radishes to see if they are ready to eat. Taurus's patience may seem like slowness, but it is the slowness of certainty and self-confidence. Taurus rests secure in the knowledge that tomorrow is another day and that excess motion will not make the sun rise any earlier.

Rooted in the physical world, Taurus is quintessentially of the earth. Worldly concerns, material values, and things that are well established fall under the domain of this sign. Related to the second house of money and valuables, materialistic Taurus's natural instinct is to accumulate and preserve both things and institutions. Therefore, both Taurus and The Hierophant are associated with institutions that endure over time—religion, academia, jurisprudence—and The Hierophant represents that which is already established in the social order.

Taurus is ruled by the planet Venus, which also governs material pleasures, enjoyment, and the five physical senses. Though associated with love and pleasure, Venus, as Aphrodite, was a goddess of great power. The Hierophant represents this aspect of Taurus, our grounding in a society or community that allows us to venture forth as individuals and develop our talents, and the powerful institutions of state that both help and control their citizens. Thus, The Hierophant symbolizes the authority represented by social institutions and the security they provide.

The Lovers

The Lovers card is related to the sign Gemini, which symbolizes the dualistic character of humanity (male/female, yin/yang, left-brain/right-brain). The third sign of the zodiac, and an air sign, Gemini is associated with siblings, neighbors, and the immediate environment.

The most mutable of the mutable signs, Gemini's nature is to change. Its symbol, the Twins, clearly depicts its duality. The speed at which Gemini can change is sometimes daunting—as anyone who has ever been involved in a romantic situation with a Gemini can attest. But The Lovers card is not to be taken at surface value. It describes the reconciliation of opposites, or duality, either with another person or within yourself.

Gemini is ruled by the planet Mercury and, as Lois Rodden comments in her book *The Mercury Method of Chart Comparison*, it is Mercury who "opens the gates between two people," showing a "clear picture of both the attitude and the circumstances" between them. She states, "Mercury is the planet that carries the awareness, or level of communication, from one person to another."

The Chariot

The Chariot is related to the zodiac sign Cancer, which symbolizes the sheer tenacity of the life force. The Crab, Cancer's image, is known for its ability to hold on. If a crab has something in its grasp with one claw, the only way to get it loose is to cut off the claw. The Charioteer, likewise, holds firmly to his steeds. In the Waite deck, The Chariot depicts a man trying to control two animals that seem to be going in opposite directions. Cancer represents the process of the growth of the soul through the sustaining efforts of the life forces, which are by nature dual (masculine/feminine, yin/yang). Thus, Cancer's primary characteristic is tenacity.

> As we all know, science began with the stars, and mankind discovered in them the dominants of the unconscious, the "gods," as well as the curious psychological qualities of the Zodiac: a complete projected theory of human character.
>
> —C. G. Jung

Cancer is the first water sign, and like all water signs it represents relatedness, with other people and with the opposing forces within one's self. Associated with motherhood and family, Cancer is an extremely powerful sign whose energies initiate and sustain life. In the Cancer stage of development, we are required to play a larger role in our own development, to nurture ourselves, to learn to master our own opposite natures, and through that mastery to win victory over obstacles that stand in our way.

Cancer is ruled by the Moon, and it is this connection to the Great Mother that strengthens the inner life force this sign represents. Thus, The Chariot symbolizes the process of self-development through aligning yourself with the creative forces in the universe that sustain us here on earth. The card also shows the effort necessary to guide the two sides of yourself to move forward successfully in life.

Strength

The card Strength is related to the sign Leo, which, like the heart, symbolizes the center from which the life force emanates, from which all energy flows and returns. Strength shows the creative individual potential that can manifest into reality.

Leo is the sign of the personal ego, with strong needs for self-expression and admiration. A fire sign, Leo displays vital energy, action, and creative talent. A fixed sign, Leo represents the eternal flame that animates all of life.

Ruled by the Sun, Leo is the sign of the natural leader, who is not easily discouraged and who pursues goals with a great deal of persistence and devotion. The Lion, Leo's symbol, has long been an imperial symbol, appearing on the royal coats of arms of many noble houses of Europe. Astrologically speaking, the Sun represents individuality, or the essence of Spirit. In metaphysical terms, it is significant of each person's individual connection to the Light Source of the Divine. Psychologically, the Sun represents the archetypal father concept.

Strength, therefore, signifies the divine, creative force within you, which is your inner strength. It also describes the process of connecting with Source or Spirit and expressing that powerful, life-giving energy creatively in a disciplined, mature, courageous manner.

The Hermit

The Hermit is related to the zodiac sign Virgo, which symbolizes the quest for perfection. Virgo represents the ideal that resides in the divine essence and the knowledge that can only be harvested from the fields of experience.

The most mental of the earth signs, Virgo's hallmark is work; its canon is duty. Excellent critical faculties make people born under this sign perfectionists. Interested in learning all there is to know about the world, with an emphasis on practical skills and utilizing tools, Virgos aim to be useful to others.

FACT

Though Virgo has high aesthetic standards, art for art's sake doesn't interest people born under this practical sign, who always prefer things that serve a purpose. Their concern is what will be effective, not what will be fun. Thus, Virgo is called the sign of service.

Virgo is ruled by the planet Mercury, which also rules Gemini, and has been discussed previously in the section on The Lovers. In Gemini, Mercury expresses itself by gathering information; in Virgo the information is sorted and analyzed. The Hermit, too, depicts knowledge gained through experience as well as the process of carefully sorting and analyzing information so it can be used for the good of all. Notice that The Hermit is usually shown withdrawing from the world—for often the only way to gain wisdom is to retreat into solitude. However, he carries a lantern to light the way for others to follow the path.

The Wheel of Fortune

The Wheel of Fortune is related to the planet Jupiter, which marks the point in our solar system where we move from the realm of the strictly personal (represented by the Sun, Moon, Mercury, Venus, and Mars) toward the external world and society at large. This giant among the planets represents the principles of expansion and growth. Sometimes called the second sun and greater benefic, Jupiter generally symbolizes blessings and benefits such as prosperity, success, good luck, honor, and accomplishment. The Wheel of Fortune likewise is a card of good fortune and fulfillment.

Jupiter rules Sagittarius, the sign that signifies the interface between the individual and the institutions upon which the social order rests—schools and universities, churches, the legal system, philanthropic and social organizations, government, and the like. Jupiter's association with learning and religion represents the Higher Mind, and, consequently, the development of higher mental and spiritual attributes. He goes beyond the purely rational level of Mercury to seek an understanding of universal principles on which thought is based. Through acquiring and integrating higher knowledge (Jupiter), we can improve both our positions in the world and our connections with the Divine (The Wheel of Fortune).

In astrology, Jupiter symbolizes the ideological basis for systems of thought, be they philosophical or religious, orthodox or unorthodox. Thus, we look to Jupiter for spiritual as well as social development. Jupiter is exalted in Cancer, which rules the home where the principle of learning is first established. The family is the basic unit of society, therefore Jupiter represents how we grow beyond the personal sphere and how we integrate the personal with the nonpersonal, or outer world. The Wheel of Fortune also shows how our families, education, philosophies, and social positions influence our abilities to succeed in life.

Justice

The card Justice is related to the sign Libra, which has as its symbol a blindfolded woman holding a set of scales signifying impartial justice. Libra represents striving for balance in all things. By extension, relationships—personal and professional—fall into Libra's domain because we must balance our own needs and desires with those of other people if we are to live together peacefully on this planet.

Libra is the sign of peace and harmony. We can see its concern for harmony expressed in the arts, social graces, and aesthetics. But to insure peace and achieve balance, we need laws, contracts, agreements, and a system of justice—hence the connection between Libra and Justice in the Tarot.

Libra is ruled by Venus, the planet of love and partnerships. Divine love shows itself through human love, and through loving other people we discover the path to the Divine—the source of ultimate justice. Refer back to the sections on The Empress and The Hierophant for more about Venus.

The Hanged Man

The Hanged Man is related to the planet Neptune, a planet difficult to define for it symbolizes all that is unreal, ethereal, mystical, otherworldly, invisible, inspirational, imaginative, and creative. Neptune is also identified with escapism, drugs and alcohol, avoiding responsibilities, destructive self-indulgence, deception, fraud, delusions of all sorts, fascination with celebrities' lives, and involvement in religious cults.

Only two years after Neptune's first sighting, Madame Blavatsky, the founder of Theosophy (a religious movement based on ancient wisdom), journeyed to Tibet and India in search of spiritual enlightenment. Afterward, the late nineteenth century set off a wave of spiritualistic, psychic, mediumistic, and table-tapping experiences all over Britain and the United States. Is it only coincidence, one wonders, that Neptune is identified with the dreamer, the artist, the musician, the filmmaker, psychic power, mysticism, and spiritualism?

Astrologers view Neptune as the higher octave of Venus. Therefore Neptune's energy is expressed in music, poetry, and the arts in general. In its highest form, it represents the celestial musician who dances to the rhythm of the universe. This cosmic dancer is the progenitor of the seven Muses, those spinners of artistic inspiration. Such elevated inspiration may also fuel prophecy and visions, which reveal universal truth impenetrable by the power of reason alone. Through Neptune's vibration, we can contact the universal guides, or master souls, who govern our planet's evolution.

Ruler of the zodiac sign Pisces, which symbolizes that which is most ephemeral in human nature, the desire to unite with the cosmic consciousness, Neptune doesn't particularly care whether or not its vision is made manifest in the real world. Not surprisingly, Venus is exalted in the sign of Pisces, but while she deals with human love, Neptune is concerned with the transpersonal in the expression of universal love, which often means self-sacrifice.

FACT

The last generation of people born when Neptune was in Libra (1943–1957) brought forth the concept of the human rights movement and freedom for all peoples of the earth.

The Hanged Man also represents self-sacrifice or more accurately, ego sacrifice. This may mean letting go of your own desires to achieve a greater good or to align yourself with Divine Will. Either way, The Hanged Man often signifies a higher level of vision that requires you to see things in a different way, which is why the card depicts a man dangling upside down—by removing the blinders of the earthly or human realm.

Death

The Death card is related to the sign Scorpio, which represents the transforming powers of life and death. In dealing with the process of transformation, Scorpio embodies life's ultimate mysteries—sex and death, rebirth and regeneration. The eighth sign of the zodiac, Scorpio, the fixed water sign, is concerned with the processes of destruction and renewal.

In the news of children being born, ours or those of people around us, we may recognize powerful signposts of new beginnings taking place in our own lives. News of deaths often carries metaphors of significant closings or transformations in related areas of our experience.

—**Ray Grasse,** *The Waking Dream*

Scorpio is ruled by Pluto, the most recently discovered planet in our solar system. Found in 1930, it symbolizes the transformative processes of both the inner psyche and outer world—and the link between the two. Like Scorpio, the Death card shows the breakdown of a previous form and its transformation into something else. Vegetation rots and becomes mulch, from which arises new vegetation. The individual sperm and ovum both "die" to be transformed into the embryo.

Astrologers associate this most compelling—and most difficult—of the planets with the transformative process that goes on in the dark underworld of the psyche, sending up its aromas via dreams and, sometimes, compulsive behaviors. Here, we are in the realm of the ancient god Hades, as Pluto was called by the Greeks. Although the Death card can indicate physical destruction, it more often describes the death of old attitudes, behaviors, emotional patterns, or ego attachments. Interestingly, many researchers believe our fear of death and the fearful superstitions around the number thirteen are connected with this Tarot card.

Temperance

Temperance is related to Sagittarius, the sign of the truth seeker. It is concerned with all manifestations of the higher mind and universal values. The ninth sign of the zodiac, ruled by Jupiter (which we discussed in the section about The Wheel of Fortune), Sagittarius signifies the religious and intellectual institutions that bind society together and advance learning and morals. The Archer, Sagittarius's symbol, loves personal liberty and intellectual freedom and looks for the absolute truth underlying all causes, for the unifying principle at the center that binds all things into a single whole.

A mutable fire sign, Sagittarius is far-reaching conceptually and intellectually, eclectic in the quest for knowledge, wisdom, and experience. Ultimately, it seeks the inner teacher and guide and is related to the archangel Michael, who is the angel of fire. Sagittarius is the sign of philosophy, religion, and law as well as of long-distance travel, for all these endeavors help us to expand our knowledge. Like its image, the Archer, Sagittarius shoots his arrows as high as they will go, out of sight, in search of the ends of being and ideal grace.

The Temperance card describes not only the quest for knowledge and experience but also the qualities of self-discipline, faith, and vision, which temper desire and direct it in a purposeful way. Thus, Temperance represents personal will aligned with Divine Will.

The Devil

The Devil is related to the planet Saturn, known to astrologers as the lord of karma, and as the great teacher. Saturn is the planet of discipline and structure, time and ambition. Its placement in your birth chart represents where you are tested by the universe, where you face tasks and trials in the form of obstacles, which are the lessons you must learn. Saturn is also associated with stability, permanence, responsibility, dependability, endurance, and a capacity for self-sacrifice.

[Like in *Beauty and the Beast*,] Saturn's role as the Beast is a necessary aspect of his meaning, for as the fairytale tells us, it is only when the Beast is loved for his own sake that he can be freed from the spell and become the Prince.

—Liz Greene, Saturn: *A New Look at an Old Devil*

Saturn is sometimes a harsh taskmaster. Once his lessons are learned, however, he grants wisdom and an understanding of the earthly realm. During the approximately twenty-eight years it takes Saturn to transit all the signs of the zodiac, he points to the necessary ways a person must develop to achieve maturity. Saturn shows us how to live in harmony with ourselves, to take responsibility for our actions, and to act not only for our own benefit but for that of society as well.

Saturn represents the laws of limitation and conservation. Many people find it difficult to cope with the restrictions and structures imposed by Saturn, which is one reason the planet and The Devil card are linked. Often, Saturn's influence seems to correspond with painful circumstances that seem merely to happen, hence the planet's association with karma and fate. Ultimately, though, Saturn teaches us to face our own weaknesses, fears, and doubts—conditions represented by The Devil—so we can become our own authorities, rather than relying on external ones. He is the dweller at the threshold, the keeper of the keys to the gate, and through him alone we can achieve eventual freedom through self-understanding.

The Devil also symbolizes our lower instincts, obsessions, and indulgences. When we have freed ourselves and are no longer prisoners of those instincts and pass the tests Saturn sets for us, we become our own true, authentic selves.

The Tower

The Tower is related to the planet Uranus. Many Tarot decks show this card as a tower being struck by lightning and destroyed—both lightning and sudden destruction are ruled by Uranus. Astrologers also connect Uranus with change, especially the unexpected kind, and The Tower heralds major change of an unexpected nature.

The first outer planet in our solar system, meaning a planet that cannot be seen with the naked eye, Uranus is associated with transpersonal affairs. It rules Aquarius, the sign of humanity. In this role, Uranus sometimes instigates changes in our lives or in our society for the good of the whole, rather than the individual. Moving outward from the Sun, Uranus is the next planet after Saturn. Saturn represents structures, institutions, and social systems that may provide stability and security, but whose limits and rules can also imprison us. Uranus's role is to break up old structures and traditions that have outlived their usefulness, so that a new order can be ushered in.

The Tower illustrated on this Tarot card symbolizes protective, yet restrictive structures that must be destroyed. These may be outside influences—family or societal expectations, religious or political systems—or inner crutches that we have grown dependent upon. Many decks show one or more people being thrown from the crumbling tower in a haphazard manner. Indeed, we often experience Uranus's influence as unsettling and chaotic, and we may not be able to see where we are going while in the midst of the changes going on in our lives.

The end result, however, is freedom—one of Uranus's most distinctive attributes. Frequently the freedom brought by Uranus and signified by The Tower is independence from restrictive social conditioning and established ideas, which enables us to think for ourselves and make our own choices.

The Star

The Star is related to the zodiac sign Aquarius, which embodies the idea of the individual as a cooperative member of the larger whole, that we are all one big family—a concept which can be grasped only intuitively. Brotherhood or sisterhood is the ideal, for Aquarius sees everyone in the humanitarian spirit of friendship.

FACT

Astrology and astronomy are considered Aquarian vocations—an obvious link between the zodiac sign and The Star card. In a symbolic sense, The Star represents hope and a belief that the future will be a brighter, better place. Aquarius is the sign of the future, of all that is new and fresh and promising. No one is more idealistic than an Aquarian!

Aquarius is the eleventh sign of the zodiac, the fixed air sign. Aquarius experiments with all established structures and rebels against those it finds too restrictive. It freely crosses all man-made boundaries to experience the new and unusual. This sign's purpose is to bring about needed reforms by introducing innovative ideas.

The Moon

The Moon is related to the sign of Pisces, which encompasses the most ephemeral in human nature, the desire to unite with the cosmic consciousness. The twelfth sign of the zodiac, Pisces is emotional and intuitive. Ruled by Neptune, it is linked with creativity, psychic ability, empathy, illusions, poetic sensibilities. Pisces represents self-sacrifice for a higher cause. It also shows the soul's struggle with the imperfections of the material plane. Its symbol—two fish swimming in opposite directions—suggests the dichotomy between the material and spiritual realms.

The sign's dual image represents the finite consciousness on the one side, and the infinite consciousness of the universe, or cosmic consciousness, on the other side. The connecting point is our earth, where the spiritual and material aspects of being meet. One of the fish stands for the physical body, with all its limitations and mortality; the second fish is the soul and its invisible world where boundaries do not exist. Astrologically The Moon represents the Soul, which is the link between Spirit (Sun) and Matter (earth). Your lunar self is the channel for the flow of universal, or divine, energy.

The Moon not only illuminates the dark world, it also shines light into the nonconscious side of human life. In its diffuse light we can often see more clearly than in the glare of the noonday Sun. The Sun's light enables us to see the world around us—what is outside ourselves. But The Moon focuses light into our inner spiritual world, to reveal what springs naturally from inside ourselves. In moonlight we perceive the reality of our inner spiritual selves more clearly, we are more aware of the shadings and nuances of feelings and inner perceptions, and we tune in more accurately to the spiritual vibrations of others. Likewise, The Moon card represents the unconscious, the shadowy, hidden side of our natures, and the complex, emotionally driven, murky situations in which we find ourselves, as well as the deep well of intuitive knowing that cannot be accessed through intellect alone.

The Sun

The Sun card is related to the zodiac sign Leo, which is ruled by the physical Sun. Astrologically speaking, the Sun represents individuality, or the essence of Spirit. It is called the Light of the Soul. In metaphysical terms, it signifies each person's individual connection to the Divine. Psychologically, The Sun represents the archetypal father concept, which may or may not have a direct relationship to the actual parent.

In the Tarot, The Sun card represents clarity and vision, the brilliant light of day that illuminates the world and chases away the shadows of confusion. Under its bright rays, we can see the path before us. Thus this card signifies a release from a time of darkness as well as the light of reason shining like a beacon through the fog of the emotions.

Astronomically, the Sun is at the center of the solar system. In astrology, it is at the heart of the birth chart, showing what we are potentially, not necessarily what we will become. Why you think you are here on earth, where you are going in your life, what makes you feel important are all related to the Sun in your birth chart. It speaks to your purpose in life—the sense of "I am." In the Tarot, The Sun symbolizes individuality and self-confidence, your ability to be truly yourself regardless of what others think.

The Sun's glyph, a circle with a dot at the center, signifies the emanation of life-giving energy from the unlimited resources of the Divine. A perfect shape without beginning or end, the circle symbolizes the totality of the entire universe. The dot represents the point of Light that comes into the individual. As such, it is the aperture through which divine nature shows the unlimited possibility of growth that can be achieved through conscious attunement to the divinity within each being.

Judgment

The Judgment card is related to the planet Pluto, which symbolizes the transformative processes of both the inner psyche and outer form. Pluto is still a mystery of sorts. Astronomers aren't even sure of its true size. Some speculate that it is small and dense; others think that the central sphere we can see is merely the light-reflecting center of a much larger orb. Though not much is known absolutely, there seems to be no question that power resides there, power of a most potent sort. How we use power is one of the important lessons of Pluto and is depicted by the Tarot card Judgment. In this sense, both are connected with fate, or karma—the individual karma that is linked to the karma of the society into which we are born.

Pluto represents the bottom line in our lives. The planet of death and rebirth, it symbolizes the great collective, what C. G. Jung has called the collective unconscious, the point where we connect, for good or for ill, with the rest of our society—not just our local community but the totality of humanity.

As ruler of the Underworld, Pluto is a subterranean force to be reckoned with. Judgment, too, shows the inner forces that propel us, the larger societal forces that influence our personal lives, and the results of the interaction of these two forces.

The World

The World is related to the sign Capricorn—the world leader—which depicts father, authority, the social order, pragmatism, and the slow but sure ascent to the top of the heap. Ruled by Saturn, the planet of discipline, organization, limitation, awareness, and, most of all, time, Capricorn's principle is "I use." The tenth sign of the zodiac, Capricorn builds what is practical and useful to society. Then, while meticulously sticking to the rules of the game, Capricorn earns success and glories in its rewards.

The World, too, indicates success as the result of hard work. Rewards that are due to you, often after a long struggle, are represented by this card. Order, knowledge, stability, authority, and achievement are hallmarks of The World. It suggests that things are as they should be, not because of chance or dumb luck, but because the necessary steps have been taken, and the required effort has been invested to bring about a desired result.

Capricorn has always been regarded as a sacred sign, for within its boundaries the winter solstice takes place, bringing an increase of daylight to the Northern Hemisphere. Christmas and the winter solstice are celebrations of continued life amid the darkest, most barren time of the year, marking the return of the Sun and life. The World represents the cosmic order depicted by the seasons and the cyclic nature of life. A card of hope and promise, it also symbolizes light at the end of the tunnel, the sense of satisfaction and fulfillment that come from knowing you've done your best.

Chapter 7

Using the Tarot for Personal Growth

For centuries, the Tarot has been used to see into the future and to gain advice on practical matters, such as a job, a marriage, or economic issues. Even today, these are perhaps its most common uses. But the Tarot can also serve as a valuable aid to personal and spiritual growth—as a tool to deepen your understanding of yourself, to enrich your relationships with other people, and to strengthen your connection with your Higher Self.

A Path to Enlightenment

Encoded within the symbols and imagery of the Tarot are keys that can unlock the doors of perception, so that we may see our own lives and the path to higher knowledge more clearly. Many Tarot scholars believe the Major Arcana was designed as a course in initiation, presented in twenty-two stages: the trump cards. (In the next chapter, we'll look more deeply at these cards and the lessons they represent—a step-by-step process that is sometimes called The Fool's Journey.) But the Minor Arcana, too, is a rich body of information that you can draw upon for personal development.

You could think of both books of the Tarot as containing numerous chapters, one card being equal to a chapter. If you read these chapters in consecutive order, you'll notice a story unfolding. Each numbered card (the Major Arcana cards bear numbers, too) evolves out of the previous one and develops into the following one. In this way, they convey information much as any other course or textbook might.

For instance, the Three of Pentacles represents applying your abilities and resources in a productive way. The Four of Pentacles suggests securing your assets, stabilizing yourself, and making plans before moving ahead again. The Five of Pentacles shows changes in financial or practical matters that may require you to set new goals, develop additional skills, alter your plans, or seek different routes to make progress. The process described by the cards is fluid, orderly, and logical.

Whether or not you choose to study the Tarot in this linear fashion, however, is entirely up to you. There's no right or wrong way to seek truth, and as the old axiom states, all paths lead to the same place.

Daily Insights

Many people turn to the Tarot for daily insights. Each morning, you can shuffle your favorite deck, ask for guidance, and draw a single card. Sometimes this card will shed light on a problem, project, or issue you're dealing with in your life. Sometimes it may present the theme for the day. Or it may point to a matter you need to pay attention to. On and off throughout the day, you can think about the card you drew that morning and how it relates to what unfolds during the day. You can even place the card in a spot where you will see it often and reflect upon its meaning, letting its message guide you.

It may appear that you're selecting cards entirely at random, but there's nothing arbitrary or chance about it. Your subconscious and/or your Higher Self are presenting information in this elegant way, and the cards you pick each day are never irrelevant.

During particularly significant periods, you might draw the same card again and again over a span of a week, a month, or more. Like a dream that keeps repeating, this suggests that the same forces are operating in your life and that you need to keep working on the issues indicated by the card.

FACT

As you work on specific areas of your life, you'll see your growth reflected in the cards you draw. For instance, you might pick the Ace of Pentacles when you start a money-making venture. As the project bears fruit, you might draw the Seven of Pentacles, which shows you are beginning to see the results of your efforts.

It's a good idea to keep a journal or log of your daily readings. Note the date, what's going on in your life, and any particular concerns or areas of interest. Write down insights or questions that come to you in connection with the card or cards you draw each day. Periodically, you may wish to look back at the cards you drew previously to see how a matter has evolved or how your knowledge has grown over time. Something that was unclear to you before might make sense now. In this way, you can follow your progress and understand how the Tarot is guiding you along your path.

Daily Affirmations and the Tarot

You can also use the Tarot to inspire personal growth in much the same way as you would use affirmations. An affirmation is a short, positive statement that describes a condition or change you wish to produce. An example of an affirmation is: "My life is rich with abundance of all kinds." An affirmation may be a phrase you coin yourself, a quote by someone you respect, or a sentence from a book. By repeating the affirmation regularly, you reprogram your subconscious and, in time, bring about the desired result.

Tarot cards can function as visual affirmations. Let's say, for example, you want to find a romantic partner. Select the Two of Cups or The Lovers from your deck and gaze at it, while you contemplate your intention. If you like, you can display the card where you will see it often. Each time you look at it, you'll be reminded of your objective.

You can work on developing inner qualities in the same way. Choose The High Priestess if you want to improve your intuition. Strength can help you increase your personal power and confidence. The Queen of Cups is good for encouraging flexibility and acceptance.

Although you can work on more than one goal at a time, it's usually best to limit yourself to a few that you consider most urgent or important. Choose cards that represent the end result(s) you desire. Spend at least a few minutes each day contemplating the card(s) you've chosen, allowing the symbols to imprint themselves on your subconscious. If you wish, you can combine the cards with verbal affirmations—stare at the card while you repeat your affirmation aloud. You're more likely to get fast, effective results if you combine the two techniques.

Some Tarot decks are designed specifically for this purpose. The Tarot Affirmations deck, for instance, combines the imagery of the Universal Waite pack with selected affirmations and sayings. Each card is printed with several inspirational thoughts that relate to the meaning of the card.

Using the Major Arcana for Growth

It would be hard to find a more appropriate tool for spiritual and personal growth than the Major Arcana. For centuries, seekers have used this body of occult wisdom to access hidden knowledge and to connect with the higher realms. These powerful images portray archetypes that exist within the collective unconscious and that connect us to something larger than ourselves. At the spiritual level, each of the Major Arcana cards represents a state of being, or an inner truth about yourself.

The simplest way to understand the Major Arcana in spiritual terms is to think of it as an ascending staircase with twenty-two steps. Each card represents a lesson you must learn, a boundary you must cross in to move up to the next step. And you have to figure out how to do this yourself; there is no set system. Each step leads to the next and is a little different than the one before it. Each has a different lesson to impart. Some are wider or narrower than others; some are smoother or rougher. The time you spend on each step is up to you. You'll know when you're ready to move up to the next step because you will have understood the meaning of the previous one.

You can either study the trump cards in consecutive order, as in Chapter 8, or choose individual cards that represent areas or concepts you wish to work on, in whatever order suits your purposes. Or separate the Major Arcana from the entire deck, shuffle, and draw a card for study, letting your inner knowing guide you.

If, for example, you wish to discover the source of inner strength, pick the Strength card. Start by simply gazing at the card, without analyzing it. Let the colors, pictures, and symbols connect with your intuition and reveal themselves to you gradually, before you begin to examine the images more carefully.

You can recite this if you want to practice meditating on the Tarot with prayer: Everything that I believe to be true about the Spirit, I understand is also true about myself. Its Goodness is my goodness. Its Power is my power. Its Presence in me is my true self. There is only one True Self.

In her companion book to *The Sacred Circle Tarot*, Anna Franklin suggests you approach the card as if you were going to enter it, like walking through a doorway, and interact with the scenario depicted there. Don't just see the images, try to experience them. Allow your senses to come into play. Feel the sun on your face, the grass under your feet. Witness the murkiness and mystery connected with The Moon or the burning sensation of anger, jealousy, obsession, and fear depicted by The Devil.

Write down what you glean from your study—your insights, awarenesses, questions, impressions, and feelings. Notice how the energies represented by the cards are playing out in your own life—or how you would like to be able express them. Because the trump cards are quite complex, it's probably best to limit your study to one card at a time, until you understand it—even if it takes several days or weeks.

Using the Minor Arcana for Growth

The cards in the Minor Arcana represent everyday concerns and earthly matters. As discussed earlier, the suit of Cups represents the emotions and relationships, Pentacles stand for financial and physical conditions, Swords symbolize mental issues and communication, and Wands are linked with creativity, spiritual considerations, and willpower.

Working on a Specific Issue

Determine which suit covers the issue or situation you wish to work on first. Then, pick the card within that suit that speaks most directly to your objective. (See Chapters 13 through 16 for interpretations of the Minor Arcana cards.) For instance, if your goal is to rekindle the love and affection in a romantic relationship, select the Six of Cups from your deck.

FACT

The Six of Cups in the Waite deck has a large cup that rests on a pillar decorated with an X, which is the rune for love. Runes are ancient glyphs or symbols, often carved on stones, wood, or bone, and used as a tool for consulting the deities.

Begin by gazing at the card for a minute or two, without attempting to analyze it. Just let the colors, symbols, and so on impress themselves on your subconscious. Note any thoughts, feelings, or insights that arise into your awareness and write them down in your Tarot journal. Each person's responses will be different—and your own responses will vary from day to day—so simply jot down whatever comes to you without censoring yourself, even if it doesn't make sense immediately.

Next, examine the card more closely. Contemplate the symbols depicted on the card to ascertain their meanings. In most storytelling decks, for example, the Six of Cups shows a young man and woman (sometimes a male and a female child) in a pleasant setting—a peaceful village, or a sunny meadow in the country. Their youth is one of the keys to understanding the card—innocence and openness are necessary for love to flourish. The colors are cheerful and bright, signifying optimism. The image is one of generosity, comfort, companionship, and joy. Often the six cups pictured on the card are filled with flowers, a familiar symbol of love. Sometimes the male is portrayed offering one of the cups to the female as a token of affection, which indicates that sharing, giving of oneself, and being receptive—give and take—are essential in any partnership.

What symbols do you see on your own card? Some decks are more symbol-rich than others. What individual and universal meanings do they hold? It may help to make a list of the symbols you notice and your interpretations of them. Continue studying the card you've selected until you've uncovered all the information you feel is relevant at this time. After a day or two, revisit the same card to see if you can glean additional insights from it. If you own more than one deck, examine the same card in each deck. One card may reveal something that was not apparent in another.

One Suit at a Time

Working your way through one suit at a time is a good way to develop a deeper understanding of the four fundamental energies present in our world and the areas of life associated with them. Begin with the suit that represents the area in which you'd most like to expand your knowledge and select the Ace from that suit. Aces depict pure, primal, focused, core energies; each Ace contains the raw nature of the suit to which it belongs. Study the symbolism on the card. In the Waite deck, a disembodied hand extends from the clouds and offers you the Ace, as if a divine being were handing you a gift. What do the other symbols and images on the card mean to you?

Next, examine the Two in the suit you've chosen. The Two suggests polarity, duality, self versus other, and a need for balance, cooperation, and harmony. In some decks, the illustration on the Two of Pentacles shows a juggler trying to handle two balls. What do you notice in the card you've chosen? What feelings or impressions arise as you gaze at the card?

Continue in this manner until you've worked through the entire suit, progressing at your own pace. Some people are comfortable studying one card a day; others may move more slowly. Perhaps you'll prefer to famil-iarize yourself with several cards at a time, noting the way each builds on the energy of its predecessor. Allow your analytical mind and your intuition to inform you. Keep a record of your thoughts and insights as you study the cards, along with information about how the elemental qualities represented are being expressed in your own life.

Developing Intuition

In any kind of divinatory work, intuition is an important factor. Some methods such as tea-leaf reading or crystal ball gazing could be considered low data/high subjectivity, meaning there is little hard data to go on, and your intuition plays a major role in interpreting the results. In high data/low subjectivity systems, like astrology and Tarot, the use of a physical tool (i.e., the birth chart or the cards) provides a more clearly defined form of reliable information on which to base your interpretations.

However, even in the case of these data-rich systems, personal intuition is a vital component of an accurate reading. The symbolic nature of these systems allows for the possibility of interpretation on many different levels. Therefore, it is important to spend time and effort learning to communicate with your intuition. Meditation is a time-honored practice for developing a strong connection with your inner self. Dream work, too, can enhance your intuitive abilities.

It is precisely the holistic nature of intuition that gives it its power. In your unconscious, you have a huge data bank of experiences upon which to draw, even though you aren't aware of most of them. You know much more than you think you know, and your intuition can enable you to access this dormant knowledge.

Developing intuitive skills should be fun, not a chore. If your practice becomes monotonous, change the time or place for your meditations. Your sixth sense is part of who you are. Therefore, your moods, intelligence, education, interests, health, state of mind, past experiences, future aims, and ability to be open to the experiences and the time of day and setting—the "furniture of the mind" as author Willa Cather called it—can all affect how your intuition performs. Some people will naturally be more intuitive than others—psychic ability is like any other skill. And, like any other skill, it will improve with use.

How long it will take is up to you. Much depends on your personal goals, the quality and length of time you invest, individual aptitude, and factors as yet unknown. Sometimes people work diligently for a long time and nothing seems to be happening and then, bingo!—a portal appears. It's like walking along a dull, dreary street and suddenly passing through a gate into a beautiful, flower-filled courtyard hidden behind the facade of a building.

ALERT!

Using your cards regularly and trusting what they reveal to you, paying attention to your impressions, and noting how the information you glean from the cards plays out in your life will strengthen your psychic "muscles." In time, your intuition will be automatically activated when you lay out your cards for a reading.

As you learn to trust your psychic responses and let them operate on their own, success becomes automatic. You'll wonder how you ever got along without this valuable skill!

Using the Tarot to Improve Intuition

There are many ways to discover your own inner dimensions. One of the best of these is the contemplation of symbols, and the Tarot is full of symbols. Symbols speak directly to the unconscious. Meditating on the cards' symbols awakens the corresponding archetypal forms embedded in the unconscious, and that in turn allows you to arrive at the right interpretation, to see the truth in the heart of the matter. By reflecting on the deep meanings of the symbols on a regular basis, you set in motion an inward process that will reveal to you truths about yourself and enable you to look outward to grasp Universal Truth.

If you have a particular issue or concern about which you want advice, concentrate on that issue. Write it down in the form of a question, if you wish. Sit quietly, close your eyes, and hold the question or concern in your mind. Draw a card from your deck and look at it. Sit still and allow feelings, impressions, or ideas to bubble up into your consciousness. Focus on your breathing if your mind tends to wander. In the beginning, don't ask too much of yourself. Be patient and keep working. Intuition is a natural talent everyone possesses. You cannot fail.

If you want to build your predictive skills, try using the cards to predict the outcome of something that you will know tomorrow, such as the winner of a ball game or a political election. Keep track of your hits. Over time, your success rate will likely improve.

Other Ways to Develop Intuition

Accessing psychic data is a bit like tuning into a radio station. Sometimes you receive information clearly, at other times there's static. Trust and awareness are essential to developing your intuition. If you are not accustomed to doing internal processing in an aware manner, it may take a bit of time for you to get used to doing so. The important thing is to make a commitment to yourself and follow through on it. Don't expect immediate success, but don't rule it out either.

Notice coincidences and pay attention to signs. If you observe or experience something out of the ordinary, or with unusual frequency, take note of it. See if it ties into anything else. If any thoughts pop into your head in conjunction with the sign or coincidence, heed them, too.

During meditation, you empty your mind and allow it to be filled by something other than everyday, rational thinking. You relax into a light trance state and invite input from your higher self, subconscious, angels, guides, god, goddess, or whatever term you choose to use. Stilling the mind is easier said than done, however. Some people focus on their breathing, some listen to music, some chant or repeat mantras to quiet their minds. You can also gaze at a meaningful symbol, such as a tattwa or a Tarot card. The objective is to keep your mind and heart open, and to allow insight to flow into your awareness rather than permitting your thoughts to jump about like monkeys in a cage.

Prayer can also connect you with your intuition. Meditation is receptive, prayer is active. It's been said that meditation is listening to god, and prayer is speaking to Him. Praying puts us into an altered state of consciousness not unlike the ones used for self-hypnosis and visualization. When we pray, we are actually visualizing the result desired, even if we are not doing this consciously. It is a good idea to begin each Tarot session with a short prayer affirming your innate connection to Spirit and your faith in Divine guidance.

Spiritual Progress

Meditation on the cards activates your unconscious repository of images; these can be used for spiritual progress. Working with the Tarot opens a passageway between the material and the spiritual realms. The Tarot cards can be read at many levels, for they symbolize your unconscious understanding of your life experience—past, present, and future. From the esoteric point of view, the cards represent all possible experiences available to human beings.

ALERT!

If you are using the Tarot for spiritual development, keep a deck for this purpose only. Don't let anyone else touch this deck. It can be identical to the deck you use for readings, or a different design entirely. What's important is that the images on the cards speak to your higher consciousness.

Greater awareness of your own spiritual dimension and a deeper knowledge of your spiritual self are the rewards for concentrating on Tarot as a means of spiritual development. As one writer has commented, "Tarot cards are a step forward in our evolution to perfection." Though absolute perfection may not be possible in this world, in Spirit all is perfect.

Meeting Your Spirit Guides

We all have spirit guides, guardians, angels, teachers—divine helpers who lovingly guide us through our earthly lives. Sometimes these heavenly beings spontaneously appear to us. Sometimes they answer us when we petition them. If you haven't yet met your own guides, here's a method for making contact with a teacher you can trust and rely on.

- Form a question you want your guide to answer for you. The question should be as clear and succinct as possible. Vague questions produce vague answers.
- Do not ask a question that can be answered by a simple yes or no.
- Stick to the present and most pressing situation; avoid generalities.
- Do not ask for a prediction. Instead, ask for advice or guidance.
- Be willing to trust your guide. Accept what comes into your mind. If you draw a blank, try again later.
- When a guide appears, pay attention. Ask for a name, sign, or symbol by which you will know your guide in the future.
- Set aside a time and place when you can be alone and quiet, for at least half an hour.
- Relax, calm, and center yourself. Let go of the day's worries.

Imagine a peaceful place in nature—a forest, the seaside, a sun-dappled meadow, a sparkling waterfall—whatever appeals to you. In front of you, see a veiled object. Suddenly, a puff of wind blows away the covering and your guide is revealed to you. Begin a dialogue with the form you see before you. Ask your question and wait for an answer. You may hear words, see an image, or get an intuitive knowing. If a reply doesn't come at once, be patient. Your answer may even come in the form of a song, a book, or magazine article, something someone says to you, a scent or another sensation.

At every moment we are dying and renewing ourselves. Each moment we see that a new consciousness, a new thought, a new hope, a new light is dawning in us. When something new dawns, at that time, we see that the old has been transformed into something higher, deeper, and more profound.
—**Sri Chinmoy,** *Death and Reincarnation: Eternity's Voyage*

Whatever springs into your mind is the right answer, because you are accessing your own inner wisdom. Your guides are linked to you through the deepest part of your being, the part that is connected to all reality everywhere, at all times. If you don't get an answer or the answer seems to make no sense, accept that and try again another time. Remember, you are learning a new skill and it might take a while before you master it. Thank your guide for assisting you and tell him or her you look forward to further dialogue in the future.

Notice details of the place where you have met your guide, so you can return whenever you wish. Fix it in your memory. Before leaving and returning to ordinary reality, make an appointment to meet your guide again. At the designated time, repeat this meditation and continue strengthening your rapport with your guide.

Chapter 8

The Fool's Journey

The Major Arcana is also known as the Journey of The Fool, because its twenty-two cards represent the twenty-two steps on the journey that leads from innocence to enlightenment. The Fool, the first of the trump cards, symbolizes the emergence of consciousness. The World, the last of the trumps, signifies union with Self and the Divine. As a whole, the Major Arcana shows both the spiritual pilgrim's arduous sojourn toward wisdom and the soul's trip back to the Source.

8

Charting the Course

In the ancient study of numerology, twenty-two is considered a master number that resonates on the higher planes as well as the physical one. An extremely powerful number, twenty-two represents the master builder who can harness cosmic forces and use them to shape the world. The number of transformation, twenty-two also serves as a bridge between the earthly realm and the spiritual one.

FACT

Some Tarot researchers link the twenty-two cards in the Major Arcana with the twenty-two letters in the Hebrew alphabet. Others point to the twenty-two paths on the Kabbalistic Tree of Life. A few years ago, much was written about the significance of the number 11:11 as a gateway to higher knowledge, which relates because 11 + 11 = 22.

You could also look at the Major Arcana as being divided into three parts, with seven cards in each part (if you take on the role of The Fool yourself). Both three and seven are mystical numbers with many spiritual associations. Three represents a variety of trinities (mother–father–child, body–mind–spirit, Father–Son–Holy Ghost, maiden–mother–crone, unconscious–conscious–superconscious, above–below–within). Seven corresponds to the colors of the visible spectrum, the days of the week, the major chakras, the notes of the musical scale. Three times seven, or twenty-one, thus signifies wholeness and a totality of experience on every level of being.

Beginning the Journey

Each of the cards in the Major Arcana can be viewed as a lesson. Together, they describe all the possible experiences available to us during human existence. The individual lessons must be learned in order, and you must master a lesson before you can move on to the next. Another way to think of the trump cards is as chapters in a book. You must read the chapters in order, or they won't make sense.

As you begin your study of the Major Arcana, think of yourself as The Fool. Fool is not a derogatory term; it doesn't mean stupid or ridiculous, but refers to an innocent, childlike state in which you are open to receiving guidance and instruction. We often see The Fool depicted in myth and legend as the youthful hero who must go out into the world to seek his fortune. Along the way he encounters numerous trials and adventures that enable him to build his character. In many stories The Fool is the seemingly naïve, bumbling sidekick who ultimately saves the day. The dunce wearing a pointed magician's hat is actually a magus in training.

The Fool is the only unnumbered card in the deck. Zero is both a symbol of void and wholeness. Inherent in this symbol is the meaning of The Fool and his journey. He is pure potential, the seed that contains the entire plant, the as yet unmanifested—nothing and everything,

The Fool is followed by The Magician and The High Priestess. These two cards portray the two archetypal forces, the two opposite principles— masculine and feminine, yin and yang—operating in our universe. Throughout the rest of the journey, we see these forces interacting to bring about consciousness, alternating between the challenges of outer events and those of inner experience. Both dimensions must be explored and mastered for The Fool to achieve mystical knowledge. As you progress through the trumps, you, too, will meet outer-world challenges and inner struggles, connected with the lessons of the cards, and these tests will propel you toward achieving your goal of enlightenment.

The sacred is inside each of us, nestled at the core of our beings. Alas, our perception of our own divinity is too often buried by the dictates of others—family, teachers, and society and its institutions. But, no matter how faint the ember, we have only to go deeply within to find that eternal spark smoldering and fan it into bright flames.

One Card at a Time

Because the trump cards are complex and multidimensional, it's best to study them one at a time, beginning with The Fool and ending with The

World. Some people choose to examine one card per day and then go back to the beginning and review the cards in sequence again and again, until their understanding is complete. Some may reflect upon a single card for a week, a month, or longer before progressing to the next card. In her companion book to *The Sacred Circle Tarot*, Anna Franklin recommends studying the trump cards over a period of twenty-two months. She suggests meditating on one card at each full moon.

In your Tarot journal, allow at least one page per trump. You may wish to use a loose leaf binder so you can add pages as needed. At the top of the page, write the name of the card and its number. As you acquaint yourself with each card, write down your feelings about it as well as everything that comes to mind, even thoughts or impressions that may not seem logical or related. At a later date, those ideas will make more sense.

The unknown author of *Meditations on the Tarot* suggests concentrating on the cards without effort, by "fixing maximum attention on a minimum amount of space." Contemplate the imagery, first without applying too much analytical thought—just allow the symbolism to act upon your subconscious and let the impressions generated rise to the surface of your awareness. Focus on each card until you feel you know it intimately and have a feel for its energy.

Approach each card as if you were The Fool—the innocent, curious seeker—meeting a teacher or experiencing an event. How do you feel when you encounter The Magician? What does The Empress have to share with you? Imagine yourself embroiled in the chaos and shock of The Tower's destruction. Hear Judgment's trumpet calling to you. Try to keep an open mind and an open heart and let your awareness dip down into the well of archetypal imagery where truth resides.

Living the Journey

Exploring the Major Arcana is a bit like the journey of The Fool. As you take on the role of The Fool, open yourself to the adventures that are the gifts of any journey. See yourself as an empty vessel ready to be filled. You have no limits, no schedule, no plans. Stay open to serendipity. Take risks. Be willing to make mistakes. Have faith that your journey will lead you where you want to go, even if you don't know exactly where that is.

The Fool

The Fool represents a blank slate waiting to be written upon. This is the starting point, a symbolic and perhaps even a literal birth, for the Major Arcana represents your life on earth. Everything is new, wondrous, and perhaps a bit daunting, although in this state of innocence you cannot anticipate the challenges that await you. As you journey through the trumps, everything you encounter will imprint its message on your soul.

The Magician

This trump reveals one of the great secrets in life: You have the ability to shape your destiny. As the Buddha taught, with your thoughts you create the world. The Magician represents intellect and conscious thought. Here you discover how your attitudes, beliefs, and emotions manifest as the events in your life. You also learn how to use the power of your mind constructively. With this card, The Fool begins to take responsibility for his life.

The High Priestess

The counterpart to The Magician, this card awakens your intuition. You become aware that your intellect is only part of the mind and learn to reach into the instinctual, psychic, quintessentially feminine side of yourself. At this stage of the journey, The Fool begins to realize the duality of existence and the depths of his own psyche.

The Empress

The creative force that births all physical life is depicted by this trump. The Empress is the Divine Mother, Venus, the nurturing energy of the earth, the fertile power behind all creative forms. Encountering her, The Fool discovers another feminine archetype, one that is present in nature, abundance, harvest, love, and beauty.

The Emperor

Another of the male archetypes, The Emperor embodies the energy of leadership, strength, and organization. He is the Great Father, Divine Order, the form that materializes out of the creative forces operating in the universe. The Empress is receptive and unlimited, The Emperor is active and defined. Meeting him, you learn to direct your life, use your talents, and structure your world according to your own vision.

The Hierophant

The first of the societal cards, The Hierophant represents social order, hierarchy, authority, rules, and limits. Both spiritual and cultural laws fall under his domain. At this stage in The Fool's journey, you learn to accept limits as necessary for your growth. You also come to understand your place in the greater whole, the society in which you live and the universe whose laws govern earthly existence.

The Lovers

This card depicts the merger of male and female energies. Although it represents the urge to find a partner and unite with another human being, it also symbolizes union within yourself. This lesson teaches The Fool to blend emotions and intellect, left-brain and right-brain, inner and outer, yin and yang, anima and animus, to become whole.

The Chariot

Victory and vision are portrayed in this trump. At this point, The Fool has acquired quite a lot of knowledge and experience. Now it's time to use it. By learning to control your energies and direct your thoughts, you can make progress and achieve your purpose. Mastery, as you discover here, comes from aligning personal will with Divine Will.

Strength

Inner strength, not brute force, is represented by this card. Often illustrated as a young woman taming a lion, Strength depicts the struggle to overcome the ego and the impulsive, animal nature using patience, gentleness, and compassion as "weapons." The Fool becomes a spiritual warrior at this stage in the journey by learning to live from a place of faith, not fear.

The Hermit

The quest for truth often leads us into solitude. By retreating from the activity and distractions of the world, you can reflect upon your inner vision and learn the importance of silence. Here, The Fool's journey turns inward as he searches for his own inner light. Once you find it, you can hold a lantern as The Hermit does to light the way for others to follow.

The Wheel of Fortune

At this point in the journey, The Fool comes to realize the cyclic nature of life as shown in this trump. Change is the only constant, and we must learn to adapt to the ebb and flow of the universe if we are to find peace. We make our own good fortune by working with the times, rather than against them—if we want to reap a harvest in the fall we must plant seeds in the spring.

Justice

After learning to balance his actions with the cycles of life, The Fool now becomes aware of how actions are balanced by reactions. Actions don't exist in a vacuum. Justice is a card of rectification and adjustment, or in some schools of thought, karma. At this step in the journey, you realize you cannot escape the ramifications of your thoughts, words, and deeds. You reap what you have sown, according to Divine Law.

The Hanged Man

This trump teaches you to release attachments, rigidly held beliefs, and old patterns. Until now, The Fool has been proceeding on the path in a self-willed manner. Now it's time to let go and let god or the goddess direct your journey. Surrender and even sacrifice are part of the lesson of The Hanged Man, though what you are required to sacrifice is usually something that has outgrown its usefulness and is now limiting your progress. Seeing things from a different perspective—the figure on the card is depicted upside down—can help you find your way.

Death

Once The Fool has let go of self-limiting ideas, securities, and habits, the next step is to completely kill off the old to make room for the new. The journey now leads to the Underworld, where you must face your fears, recognize the defenses you've established to protect yourself, and strip them away so that transformation can take place on many levels—mental, physical, emotional, and spiritual. Major change is never easy, but it is necessary for continued growth.

Temperance

After the destruction and purging brought about by Death, The Fool arrives at Temperance. Often this card depicts an angel who represents rebirth and balance. Alchemy has occurred; the lead in your life has been transmuted into gold. Harmony and hope are renewed. But the only way to reach this place of peace is to merge your personal will with Divine Will, symbolized in the Waite deck by the angel mixing water that she pours from two chalices.

The Devil

The serenity symbolized by Temperance is not The Fool's final resting place. Even after much spiritual growth, fear and doubt still creep into our lives and block the path. The Devil represents deep-seated issues from childhood that may show up as confusion, obsession, and the misuse of power. At this stage, you must acknowledge your dark side—your inner demon— and do battle with it.

The Tower

In response to fear, we tend to put up walls around ourselves and hide behind old defenses and self-limiting patterns. Fear keeps us imprisoned in The Tower. At this stage of The Fool's journey, those old structures must be destroyed. This card represents breaking down the barricades that keep you separated from your true self and from others. As the walls come tumbling down, perhaps as a result of an unexpected event, you experience upset, insecurity, and confusion; however, the destruction ultimately brings freedom.

The Star

After the darkness, danger, and destruction of the previous two cards, The Star appears to light The Fool's path. The Star symbolizes hope, faith, and regeneration—like the rainbow after the storm, it promises that bad times won't last forever. As a result of having faced challenges along the way, you are now better equipped to make the best of new opportunities.

The Moon

Just as the moon lights the night sky, The Moon card illuminates the path into the deepest recesses of your inner being. Now The Fool journeys inward, to connect with the unconscious realm—both the personal and the collective. In this mysterious and shadowy world, you cannot rely on intellect. Instead, you must follow your intuition, emotion, and primal instincts to the center of the labyrinth and back out again.

The Sun

This trump follows upon the previous one just as daylight follows upon night. The bright rays of The Sun chase away the shadows, enabling The Fool to see the path clearly. After journeying inward to meet your dark side, you are now stronger and more capable. No longer driven by hidden motivations and unconscious energies, you can move outward into the world again with clarity and confidence.

Judgment

The Fool's long journey is nearing its end. As a result of the experiences you've had along the way, you are now ready to emerge into a new world, a new way of life. You understand how your thoughts and actions have led you to the place you are now. Perhaps you hear a divine call, symbolized on some cards by an angel blowing a trumpet. Even if you don't yet know what you are being called to do, you realize you have developed the skills and the faith you need to succeed.

The World

The Fool has reached his destination. The long, arduous journey is complete. A card of fulfillment, wholeness, and wisdom, The World symbolizes the state of contentment and inner peace that results from having united your personal will with Divine Will. You understand your place in the universe. Everything is as it should be, and all is right with the world.

Witnessing Your Own Journey

In *Meditations on the Tarot* (author anonymous), the Major Arcana cards are described as ferments or enzymes that stimulate our spiritual and psychic lives. Through our interaction with them, our awareness of the great truths is activated. As you study the Major Arcana, you'll awaken in ways you couldn't have imagined. The more you continue to work with the cards, the more they'll reveal to you. You'll begin to see your own life being played out in the cards. Let your Tarot journal become a travel log and write down the connections you experience as you journey with The Fool. How did The Hanged Man help you to see things differently? What old securities were you forced to shed with The Tower?

The whole world is an omen and a sign. Why look so wistfully in a corner? The voice of divination resounds everywhere and runs to waste unheard, unregarded, as the mountains echo with the bleatings of cattle.

—Ralph Waldo Emerson

You could liken your study of the Major Arcana to a spiral staircase. As you climb higher, you can look down at where you've been and see the lessons of each step from a different vantage point. It's the same in life. As you age, you can look back and see your experiences through the lens of maturity. Even though each step of the journey may have been a leap of faith at the time, you can now see how one step led to the next and brought you to the place you are today.

There are no shortcuts—in life or in the acquisition of knowledge. The journey takes as long as it takes. One of the purposes of spiritual study, however, is to become conscious of your path instead of meandering about aimlessly. Spend as much time with each trump card as you need to understand its meaning and see how it operates in your life. One trip through the trumps won't be enough. You could study this body of occult knowledge for fifty years and barely scratch the surface.

Trump Cards in Readings

As you begin doing readings for yourself, pay special attention to the appearances of Major Arcana cards. These cards represent spiritual, collective, or fated forces operating in connection with the subject of the reading. They show the partnership between you and the cosmos with regard to the matter at hand.

ALERT!

A reading that includes several trumps, or even a majority, describes a situation that is complex and multilayered. Sometimes the matter at hand has been developing over a long period of time and the trump-laden reading indicates a strong need for action or awareness. You might say the universe is trying to get your attention.

Trump cards can also be viewed as higher octaves of Minor Arcana cards. The Lovers, for instance, is the higher octave of the Two of Cups. Both cards symbolize partnership, however, at the level of The Lovers, the union represented is not only with another person, it's also a merger of the two sides of yourself. The Chariot is similar to the Six of Wands, taken to a more advanced, spiritually evolved level. Both cards are associated with victory, but the victory signified by The Chariot is mastery over your own lower nature, which then enables you to succeed in the world.

The pip cards indicate areas and energies over which you have conscious control. You bring about the events represented by these cards through your own efforts. The Major Arcana, however, reveals how your thoughts, having taken hold in the image world or what Dr. Wayne Dyer calls "the field of intention," are now manifesting in a way that seems destined or magical. Usually, the influences of the trump cards—and the situations they represent—will be felt more acutely than those of the Minor Arcana cards.

Some readings contain no trump cards at all. Most of the time, though, one or more Major Arcana cards will turn up in a spread. When they do, it's a signal to look more deeply at the issue and to discover what spiritual dimensions or unconscious archetypes may be operating.

Major Arcana Relationships

When two or more Major Arcana cards appear in a reading, notice the relationships between them. The cards can come up in any order, and they must be considered in terms of their positions in the spread. (You'll learn more about spreads in Chapter 10.) Consider where the individual cards fall in The Fool's Journey as well as where they turn up in the spread, for they'll suggest the developmental stages inherent in the situation and in the person for whom the reading is being done.

For example, let's say you're doing a reading for a young woman who's entering college. If The Fool appears early in the spread and The Empress shows up later, the reading is telling you that the student will acquire skills and knowledge through her schooling that will enable her to express herself creatively and successfully.

Sometimes the relationships of the Major Arcana cards reflect confusion or conflicts regarding the subject of the reading. This is most apparent when two trumps whose meanings are incompatible fall next to each other, or in the Celtic Cross spread when the second card crosses the first (see page 148).

For instance, if The Hanged Man turns up immediately after The Emperor, it could indicate that a situation or person might not be as stable and reliable as outward appearances suggest. Perhaps the queris isn't totally comfortable with an established matter and needs to look at it from a different perspective or let go of some controls or responsibilities. If, on the other hand, The Emperor follows immediately upon The Hanged Man, it's likely that an unsteady situation will become more secure. A person who isn't sure about a romantic relationship will make a commitment or a questionable business venture will turn out to be sound.

Although we usually think of The Fool's Journey as a lifelong quest toward self-discovery, the steps that comprise the journey can also be applied to any individual situation or undertaking. Let's say, for example, that you are beginning a new romantic relationship. You, in the role of The Fool, first must pay attention to how your thoughts, words, and expectations set the stage for the relationship to develop, as symbolized by The Magician. Next, you start to notice how your intuition and your emotions come into play and influence your interaction, as symbolized by The High Priestess. Work your way through the entire Major Arcana as the partnership progresses, observing yourself and the relationship in the Tarot archetypes. Let your experience be informed and guided by the cards.

Remember that when you consult the Tarot, you are asking your Higher Self for advice and guidance. Respect the answers you receive and try your best to enact them. If you are sincere, the Tarot will continue to speak to you and lead you toward greater wisdom.

Chapter 9

How to Do Readings

There are many reasons why a person picks up a deck of Tarot cards and begins to study this most elegant oracle, and no two people will have exactly the same motivation. Whether you choose to do readings for yourself or for others, to get advice about a pressing concern or for general guidance and personal growth, recognize that you are dealing with a power no one fully understands. Respect that power absolutely and don't fool around with the cards for mere amusement.

Attitude's Influence

Many factors affect the accuracy and clarity of a reading. The state of mind of the person being read for will profoundly influence a Tarot reading. If the querent doesn't take it seriously, or is skeptical, her doubt can set up a barrier between her rational mind and her intuition. If a querent is distracted, confused, or unclear about what he wants to know, the answers he receives from the cards will be garbled or vague.

Your Approach to the Cards

The more urgent your need to know is, the more likely you are to get a direct, definitive answer. That's because your entire consciousness is focused on the matter at hand, rather than being split up into several different areas. Your subconscious, higher self, spirit guides, and other levels of being long to make a connection with you and to impart their wisdom in ways that will help you. Most of us don't communicate very well with the different parts of ourselves. The Tarot provides a tool for opening up those channels of communication.

Our questions express our vision, lead us into the future, focus a light in the realm of the unknown. Zen masters do not teach by lecturing. They wait until the student asks a question; only then is the student ready to hear the answer and mature enough to use the knowledge.
—**Biochemist L. J. Shepherd,** *New Realities,* **May/June 1990**

A person's level of spiritual development influences the reading, too. Someone who is highly aware and in touch with his own inner knowing, as well as with the higher realms, is likely to derive greater meaning from a reading than someone who has a more linear, materialistic worldview. If you genuinely wish to acquire wisdom, if you see the Tarot as teacher and vehicle for transferring insights, you'll undoubtedly be offered a great deal of information.

It is also possible that if you approach a reading with a pessimistic mindset, you are more likely to get a discouraging reading than if your outlook is optimistic. That's because the future isn't fixed. Outside forces don't dictate what happens; we create our own futures. If we expect a negative outcome, that's usually what we'll get. On the other hand, if we keep an open mind and hope for the best, we'll have a better chance of attracting good fortune. Your life is a self-fulfilling prophecy, and you are laying the groundwork for your future right now!

Ability

The reader's level of ability to interpret the cards will also affect the depth, direction, and accuracy of a reading. Just as a physician's degree of experience and training enables her to diagnose a patient's problems, a Tarot reader's level of knowledge and sensitivity will allow him to bring forth information that is useful to the client. Each reader sees the cards in a slightly different way, based on personal experience, cultural background, mental aptitude, intuitive capabilities, and many other factors. A reader whose focus is primarily oriented toward material considerations and outer-world events will analyze a spread differently than one whose emphasis is on the spiritual dimensions of a situation. Both interpretations may be valid, but they reflect different perspectives. The Seven of Swords, for example, can mean leaving a job that you find stifling, or it can indicate a need to reach beyond a self-limiting philosophy to seek a higher truth.

ALERT!

As you do practice layouts, record in your Tarot journal what Major Arcana cards appear, whether they are upright or reversed, what position they occupy, and how you interpret them in relationship to each other. This is especially important for beginners, who may become confused by cards that seem to be saying different things in the same spread.

Remember, also, that people are at different levels of development in different areas of life. One person may be highly accomplished in his career (Wands) but have trouble dealing with emotional issues (Cups). None of us moves smoothly from one stage of development to another in all areas of life simultaneously. The captain of industry who controls the fates of thousands of employees may inside be a little boy who still wants his mama. A woman who does not have a job or career may be possessed of extraordinary maturity in matters of interpersonal relations.

Writing Questions

To get a lucid, meaningful response from the cards, you must be clear in your own mind and ask your question in a direct, unambiguous manner. One way to focus on your concern is to write the question on paper before you consult the Tarot. The physical act of writing your question pins it down and makes it more real. If you keep it in your head, you may allow other thoughts to intrude and convolute the original request.

Take a few minutes to think about what you really want to know. Relax, empty your head of all extraneous matters and distractions. Put all other considerations aside for the moment. Then write your question as concisely and precisely as possible. You can ask for a specific, straightforward, yes-or-no answer or simply request insight and guidance, depending on the situation and your intentions.

Let's say you are considering a job offer. If what you really want to know is, "Should I take the job I'm considering with XYZ company?" don't ask, "Is XYZ a good company to work for?" Even if XYZ is financially sound, highly respected, and fair to its employees, it still may not be the right place for you, or the particular position you've been offered might not be your best bet.

On a sheet of paper, write down exactly what you most want to know and the date, and then lay out the cards in the spread you've chosen. Record the spread on the paper, beneath the question, so you can keep a record of your query and refer back to it at a later date, if necessary. After getting an answer to your initial question, you can ask for additional information. If the cards have advised you to take the job, you now might ask, "What is the most important thing for me to be aware of in this new position?" or, "How can I best succeed in my new job?" or, "What will my relationships with coworkers and clients at XYZ be like?" If you simply seek general guidance, you could ask something like, "Please advise me about the job I'm considering with XYZ." If you have doubts or worries, address them, too. Again, write down each question and, underneath it, draw the spread you've laid to answer it. Continue asking related questions until you've received as much information as you desire.

Sometimes you may get an answer that seems incongruous or ambiguous. In such a case, you could try rephrasing the question. It's also possible that the situation you are asking about may contain conflicting or multilayered conditions. For instance, let's say you asked, "Will I be happy in the job I've been offered at XYZ?" and received a negative response, even though the cards had already advised you to accept the job. Perhaps other dynamics you can't understand at present may be in the works, so that both answers are true. Maybe you won't be happy in the job with XYZ but will make an important contact there that leads you to another job where you will be content.

FACT

It is human nature to be multifaceted; different strands of the person's life show up in the cards and open up issues for discussion. If, for example, The Hermit appears upright and The Devil appears also, it is an indication that the person needs to seek inner guidance (The Hermit) to resolve the problems or restrictions of The Devil.

The Tarot will usually respond to the most urgent matter on your mind or the one about which you feel most strongly—even if you ask something else. Therefore, if you are thinking about one thing and asking another, the reply might not make sense. Determine what's most important to you and write that down in the form of a question. From there you can make a list of additional questions, if you like, and work your way through the list in a logical, orderly fashion.

The Future, Fate, and You

As mentioned earlier, the future is not fixed. Every decision and action influences what happens from here on. Each choice you make in life is equivalent to turning down a path at a crossroads; where you end up depends on the paths you've chosen in the past. Thus, the outcome signified by a Tarot reading is based on the conditions that exist at the time of the reading. If a situation changes, so will the outcome.

When you do a reading, for yourself or someone else, it's a good idea to stress the fact that the indicators shown in the reading are conditional; they describe what's likely to happen if things continue as they are going along now. If you continue to act and think and feel the same way as you do at the time of the reading, you'll experience the outcome that's shown. But if you change anything along the way, the outcome could change as well. Therefore, it's a good idea to update a reading every few months or so.

Many spreads address the past, present, and future—sometimes the near future and the distant future. Near future may mean a few days for one person and a few weeks for another, whereas distant future could indicate a few weeks to a few months, depending on the situation and the person for whom the reading is being done. As you become practiced at doing readings, you'll come to understand your own time frames.

It's probably useless to ask a question about what will happen ten years from now—many variables can influence the outcome between the present and that date. Many outcomes do, however, occur as predicted—even over long periods of time. That's because most of us tend to behave and think in predictable ways and to follow prescribed, comfortable, long-standing routines.

Some spiritual philosophies hold that everything is happening simultaneously—past, present, and future are illusions. That's why psychics are notoriously poor at predicting exact dates. Now and future are relative terms, and although the cards are good at showing what's likely to happen, they aren't quite so good at putting a time limit on it. Therefore, if you ask if something will occur within, say, a year, you may have to allow a little leeway.

Reading for Yourself

Reading for yourself is one of the best ways to learn the Tarot. When you do readings for other people, you may not be able to follow up after the reading. You won't always know if what you saw in the cards was valid or if your predictions came to pass. But when you read for yourself, you can check the information you get from the cards for accuracy and compare it with actual events.

Objectivity can be a problem when you are reading for yourself, though. It's easy to project your hopes or expectations onto the cards, or to ignore things you don't want to see. Standard interpretations, such as those presented in this and other introductory books on the Tarot, can help you balance your intuitive impressions and subjective responses with the impersonal, commonly accepted views of other readers. You should study the ideas and opinions put forth by several different Tarot authors, rather than following only your own or only one teacher's interpretations. In time, you'll come to your own understanding, based on a blend of your experiences and observations, the work and writings of other Tarot readers, and your intuitive insights.

The Significance of a Significator

Many Tarot spreads include a Significator, a card that represents you in the reading. The Significator acts as a link between the person for whom the reading is being done (yourself or someone else) and the other cards in the spread, which describe the circumstances of the reading. When you read for yourself, the Significator brings you into the reading; it serves as your representative for the duration of the reading.

Because the Court Cards (King, Queen, Knight, and Page) depict people, they are popular choices for Significators. Often the Significator you choose relates to your sex, age, and astrological sign. It may also tie in with your profession, interests, physical characteristics, and other personal factors. For example, if you are a fire sign man over the age of thirty-five, who holds down an executive job or is active in the arts, and/or has light or reddish coloring, you would choose the King of Wands to represent you. If you are a sixteen-year-old Capricorn girl, you'd probably choose the Page of Pentacles as your Significator.

Astrological Significators

King of Wands	A mature man, born under the zodiac sign Aries, Leo, or Sagittarius
Queen of Wands	A mature woman, born under the zodiac sign Aries, Leo, or Sagittarius
Knight of Wands	A young male, born under the zodiac sign Aries, Leo, or Sagittarius
Page of Wands	A young female, born under the zodiac sign Aries, Leo, or Sagittarius
King of Pentacles	A mature man, born under the zodiac sign Taurus, Virgo, or Capricorn
Queen of Pentacles	A mature woman, born under the zodiac sign Taurus, Virgo, or Capricorn
Knight of Pentacles	A young male, born under the zodiac sign Taurus, Virgo, or Capricorn
Page of Pentacles	A young female, born under the zodiac sign Taurus, Virgo, or Capricorn
King of Swords	A mature man, born under the zodiac sign Gemini, Libra, or Aquarius
Queen of Swords	A mature woman, born under the zodiac sign Gemini, Libra, or Aquarius
Knight of Swords	A young male, born under the zodiac sign Gemini, Libra, or Aquarius
Page of Swords	A young female, born under the zodiac sign Gemini, Libra, or Aquarius
King of Cups	A mature man, born under the zodiac sign Cancer, Scorpio, or Pisces
Queen of Cups	A mature woman, born under the zodiac sign Cancer, Scorpio, or Pisces
Knight of Cups	A young male, born under the zodiac sign Cancer, Scorpio, or Pisces
Page of Cups	A young female, born under the zodiac sign Cancer, Scorpio, or Pisces

Keep in mind that you aren't limited to the Court Cards. You may prefer to select a Major Arcana card, such as The Hermit, The Empress, or The Fool to represent yourself. Or you might feel a connection to a card that depicts your state of mind at present—perhaps the artisan, shown by the Three of Pentacles, or the bored homemaker, depicted by the Four of Cups.

You can choose a Significator who will represent you in all readings, or you may decide to change Significators periodically, based on the circumstances surrounding the reading. If you've recently given up your corporate job to travel around the world, for example, you may decide the Knight of Wands now describes you better than the King of Pentacles. Another approach is to randomly draw a Significator from the pack before a reading—let your intuition determine who you are with respect to a particular reading. (In Chapter 10, you will learn more about Significators and the role they play in readings.)

Setting the Stage

Ideally, you'll want to designate a special place to study and read the cards. If you have an altar, a meditation area, or a separate room in your home that can be reserved for this purpose, so much the better, but any space you can make sacred will suffice. Some people like to enhance the space with candles, incense, flowers, crystals, icons, or artwork that holds meaning for them.

It is always a good idea to silently ask for divine guidance before using the Tarot cards. Some people like to meditate, pray, or engage in a ritual before doing a reading. When you feel calm and centered, begin shuffling your deck. Keep your mind open to receive information. Formulate your question and hold it in your mind while you handle the cards and write the question down if you wish.

One-Card Readings

Ordinarily, unless you choose a fixed pattern of shuffling, there will come a point when it feels right to stop. At this point, place the entire deck in a single stack and cut three times, to the left, using your left hand. Then, restack the cards in the reverse order.

If you are totally unfamiliar with the Tarot deck, begin by doing a simple, one-card reading. After shuffling and cutting, you can either draw a card from the top of the deck or fan out the cards and select one at random. In your Tarot journal, note the date, your question or concern, and the card you drew. Study the card, first allowing images and impressions to present themselves to your imagination. Consider how these insights relate to your question. Then, look up the meaning of the card you selected and compare your initial impressions to the interpretation given in this or another book. Engage your intuition and use your imagination.

At first, your reactions to the individual cards may vary from seemingly nonsensical to extremely profound, or anything in between. No matter what your response is, write it down. Later on when you review your journal (as you should do periodically) new significance will be revealed.

If one or more cards pop out of the deck while you are shuffling, consider them significant. You may choose to lay these cards to one side and view them as additional commentary on the reading to come. Or after considering them and how they apply to your query, insert them back into the deck and continue shuffling.

Continue this one-card process until you have worked through all seventy-eight cards in the deck. This may take a while, as you are likely to repeatedly select certain cards that relate to the concerns, questions, and issues currently operating in your life. In time, you'll develop a good sense of each card's meaning and how it can be applied to a given situation. Review your journal or notebook frequently. Compare your interpretations of the same card on different dates to see if, and how, they have changed. Examine your interpretations of the same card in different circumstances. Were your impressions of the Eight of Cups different when your question involved a romantic relationship than when you asked about a family matter? Your personal experience with the cards through doing readings for yourself will serve as your primary source of information about their meanings.

Once you have acquired a working familiarity with all of the cards in the deck, you are ready to do more complicated readings. Now you can progress to laying out three, four, or five cards and start to see how the individual cards relate to each other to present a more complete picture. Chapter 11 includes several easy spreads you may wish to use.

ALERT!

If a card seems especially unrelated to your question, look at it several times during the day, recording any feelings it stirs in you. Before bed, review the card and your notes. If you have a dream that is influenced by the images on the card, record it also. Often, dreams comment on your daily readings.

Reading for Others

When you are proficient at reading for yourself, you may wish to do Tarot readings for other people. Reading for others will expand your own understanding and present challenges you might not have encountered if you continued reading only for yourself. Different people bring different concerns and life experiences to the table, enabling you to see things in new and varied ways. A seventy-year-old woman, for example, will approach a reading in a different way than a twenty-year-old man. A homemaker with young children will have different concerns than a corporate executive. You can learn a great deal—about the Tarot and yourself—by reading for as many people as possible.

Keep the Future in Mind

If your primary reason for studying and using the Tarot is to do predictive readings for other people, be extremely careful about any pronouncements you make. Bear in mind always that many variables exist in the psychic world, that there is always a lot you don't know, even about your own psyche. Remember, too, that today's situation may well change in the future. Consequently, it's usually best to speak of trends and possibilities, rather than making absolute statements that apply to the future—especially when negative cards appear in a reading. You don't want to create a self-fulfilling prophecy by making a definite statement of future harm, ruin, disaster, or other ill fortune. It is much better to say something like, "It looks to me as if there might be a person around you who can't be trusted" or, "The indication is that you are experiencing anxiety and pain."

Let the person you are reading for give you feedback to confirm or deny your observations. If she or he can't relate to what you are saying, don't push it. The queris may not be able to hear or accept a negative interpretation, even if it is correct, and you have no way of knowing for certain that it is correct without the readee's validation. Always choose your words carefully when giving readings for others. You cannot know a person's inner state of mind, level of psychological savvy, or ability to receive information, especially if you are reading for strangers.

Whom to Read For

When you first start reading for others, it is best to stick to people you know well, such as family members and friends. One advantage is you'll already have some knowledge about the matter being addressed in the reading. You'll also be able to see how the information conveyed in the reading plays out in your friend or relative's life, which might not be the case if you were reading for a stranger.

When doing practice readings for others, it can be helpful to conduct a preliminary interview to determine what the querent hopes to achieve from the reading, so you can direct the reading accordingly. Sometimes it happens that the surface question is a screen for what's really on the person's mind. In such cases, the Tarot will almost always speak to the real issue.

If you are in doubt about how to interpret a card or a spread, be honest and say something like, "It appears to me that such-and-such may happen, but I'm not quite sure I'm getting this clearly." Have no reluctance to admit that the information flow is murky, blocked, or unclear. Remember that you are practicing and learning. A reading is not a performance. Never assume that you know it all or that you can make absolute pronouncements.

It's also important to choose your words carefully and keep interpretations as clear and simple as possible. Avoid esoteric references and metaphysical explanations; do not confuse the issue with the use of technical terms that might be unfamiliar to your readee. Stick to plain English and offer your insights with the other person's needs in mind. What you and the cards communicate to a querent is only valid if it provides useful information or a new perspective.

If you have friends who also read Tarot, you may enjoy reading for one another. This enables you to share insights and offer a variety of views and perspectives. Because each person's understanding is based on his or her experiences, a friend can provide information and ideas you might not have come up with on your own.

Be prepared for emotional responses, even tears. Reading for others involves certain responsibilities, including giving aid and comfort. The people who come to you for advice often reveal private, sensitive matters, and you need to respect their privacy. They may be confused or in pain, and their vulnerability should be honored and treated with compassion. They place their trust in you, so you need to be totally honest, yet diplomatic.

Sometimes, of course, you may want to do readings just for fun—that is to say, on relatively trivial matters such as whether a friend should go on a blind date or how a vacation trip will turn out. Regardless of how weighty the concern, be sincere and considerate. Be prepared, however, that when minor questions are asked, more serious issues may lurk underneath, and those issues could be revealed by the Tarot cards.

Practicing Readings

In the beginning, it is always best to do practice readings for yourself until you have mastered the interpretations of the cards and developed your own slant on them. The best method for practicing readings is to choose a particular layout, preferably a simple one (such as the Four-Card spread on pages 144–46), and use it each morning. Practice the same layout daily for two to four weeks or more, until it becomes second nature for you and you can easily put the pieces together to form a whole picture. Use the same layout to answer a variety of questions.

Once you have thoroughly familiarized yourself with a simple layout, pick a more complex one, such as the Celtic Cross spread on page 148 or another spread you like. Practice it until you feel comfortable with it and understand all the different card positions, their significance in the reading, and how they relate to each other as a whole. Be consistent, working with one spread until you have mastered it.

ALERT!

As you work with the cards and notice the juxtapositions that occur, you will begin to understand how they all relate to one another, enriching the information flow and giving substance to the reading.

Continue in this manner until you have learned to use several different spreads that appeal to you. (Chapter 11 contains sixteen spreads.) Some you'll like, others won't resonate with you. Some spreads are more appropriate to one type of question or situation than another. Do at least a few practice sessions with each spread just to find out how it sits with you. Which spreads to use is a matter of personal choice, but to choose wisely you need to have at least a working knowledge of many different ones. Later, you may enjoy creating your own spreads, as explained in Chapter 10. You can also develop your own variations on traditional spreads.

Timing Your Readings

Whenever you seek guidance, need advice or additional information, lack clarity, or have a decision to make, you can benefit from doing a reading. Some people like to do readings in connection with certain astrological energies. The new and full moons are good times to read for yourself or others. So are the days when the sun enters a sign of the zodiac. (You'll have to consult an ephemeris or specially annotated calendar to determine this.)

You should always do a reading on your birthday. You might also choose to do a reading each month on the date when you were born. If you were born on May 8, for instance, do a reading on the eighth of each month. Or you could do a reading each month when the moon reaches the same position it occupied at your birth. The moon passes through all twelve signs of the zodiac each month. (Again, you'll have to check an ephemeris to see when this happens.)

Samhain (pronounced *sow-een*) or Halloween is one of the best times of the year to do Tarot readings—or to work with any form of divination. On this night, it's believed that the veils between the worlds are thinnest, making communication between heaven and earth easiest.

How Often Should You Do Readings?

You should do readings as often as you wish. In the beginning, when you are learning the meanings of the individual cards and studying the Tarot, it's a good idea to do one or more simple readings for yourself every day. As you become more adept, you may decide to do readings only when you need advice about a particular issue or situation.

You might wish to do regular readings about a situation that is ongoing or rapidly changing in your life, to get direction and guidance, or to see how things are evolving. However, if a matter is stable or not particularly pressing at this time, there's probably no point in doing a reading about it. You'll know when you need to do a reading. Something inside you will nudge you to pull out the cards.

Usually it's not wise to keep asking the same question, day after day, unless you really need guidance, something has changed, new information has come to light, or the matter is urgent. Doing so indicates doubt. Nor is it a good idea to ask the same question again if you didn't like the first answer you received. Doing so indicates you don't believe what the Tarot is telling you and don't respect your own inner knowing. Instead, ask for additional illumination or advice. Ask a different, but related question. Or wait a week or more before asking the question again.

Chapter 10

Tarot Spreads

After you've learned the meanings of the individual cards, you can begin to combine them into significant patterns or spreads. Although we've already seen how a single Tarot card can answer a question and illuminate a situation, a grouping of several cards laid out in a prescribed pattern—what's known as a spread—will give you a great deal more information.

Acquainting Yourself with Spreads

Spreads are configurations or arrangements of cards—usually three or more, and up to more than a dozen—designed to convey certain types of information. You could think of a spread as a puzzle that presents a picture when all the pieces are in place. The next chapter contains sixteen different spreads, some simple, some complex. In a spread, each position within the overall pattern means something specific. The relationships between the cards become as important as the individual cards themselves.

FACT

By combining the meanings of the cards with the meanings of the positions in a spread, the insights provided are increased multiplicatively.

No one knows where the old favorite spreads, such as the Celtic Cross, originated. Some spreads, such as the Tree of Life spread on page 158 and the Feng Shui spread on page 161, are based on a particular spiritual or philosophical system. These layouts form designs that represent significant spiritual symbols, such as the Kabbalistic Tree of Life and the Chinese bagua, respectively. Other spreads are more open-ended and can be adapted to address a variety of possibilities. The cards in a three-card spread, for instance, may be viewed as signifying one of the following:

- The past, present, and future,
- The physical, mental, and spiritual aspects of a question,
- The situation, recommended action, and likely outcome.

You'll probably find that some spreads appeal to you more than others or are more useful for your purposes. None is better than another; the choice of which spread(s) to use is yours entirely. After you become experienced at working with the Tarot, you might decide to design your own spreads or adapt traditional spreads to suit yourself.

Choosing a Significator

One of the first steps in laying out many spreads is to choose a Significator. As noted in the previous chapter, a Significator is a card the querent selects to represent herself in a reading. This card usually is incorporated into the spread, although sometimes it is laid aside face up where it symbolizes the person for whom the reading is being done. In some cases, a Significator could represent a group or organization, a situation or event.

Choose a card that best describes the person or matter about which you are inquiring. You can either remove the Significator card from the pack or leave it in, according to the layout you are using. For instance, the Celtic Cross spread begins by the querent consciously picking a Significator, removing it from the deck, and placing it as the first card in the spread. Here, the Significator serves as the center, or grounding point, of the layout. If the Significator is left in the deck and it turns up in the spread, the position it occupies becomes particularly important.

If you like, you can use only the Major Arcana cards in a spread. In this case, your Significator will also be a trump card, and it plays a key role in your reading. Below are descriptions of the Major Arcana cards with suggestions for using them as Significators.

The Fool

The Fool can stand for a child or young person, or for an innocent, naive individual who lacks experience in life. It can also be used to represent an adventure of any kind, such as when the reading involves a life change or a trip. Or The Fool can signify a decision that needs to be made, especially if the decision involves risk.

The Magician

The Magician can represent someone who has latent talent that he or she wants to bring to manifestation. This is a card of potential and describes a person with mental or magical power. Because its energy is masculine in expression, it can stand for a mature man who wields power of any kind. The Magician could represent someone in the field of applied sciences,

THE EVERYTHING TAROT BOOK

such as engineering, medicine, or chemistry. He might also signify a man or woman with artistic ability who wants to put that talent to a practical use.

The High Priestess

As a Significator, The High Priestess represents secrets, intuition, and mystery. She could stand for a very private and mysterious person, or someone who is keeping a secret—or who wants to reveal a secret. It is a good Significator for anyone who is dedicated to the pursuit of knowledge, such as a scholar or researcher. Because The High Priestess represents a feminine archetype, this card can represent a mature female with psychic ability or a wise woman.

The Empress

This card signifies a woman of substance, someone who is mature and capable at handling life's challenges. She occupies a position of authority, wealth, and power. She could be a politician, corporate executive, or someone aspiring to public office. The Empress can signify a creative person who is in command of her resources and expresses her talents productively, or someone with an earth mother personality. Also, she can represent a pregnant woman or one who has many children.

The Emperor

Use The Emperor to signify a man of authority, wealth, and power. He could be your boss, father, or leader. A man in a profession that commands respect, such as the law or medicine, might also choose this card. The Emperor represents any male authority figure, such as a politician, a military officer, someone in law enforcement, a CEO of a corporation, or a government official.

The Hierophant

This is the card of a teacher or mentor figure, especially someone who is in the clergy or member of an established institution, such as a university professor. The Hierophant can also represent a ceremonial figure with public duties, such as the head of an awards committee or grant-giving institution.

The Lovers

This card can represent two people or a situation involving two people who have to cooperate with each other. This may mean a married or engaged couple, or a business partnership between two individuals. Issues concerning a love relationship, a friendship, or any one-on-one situation between two people could also be signified by The Lovers card.

The Chariot

This card can signify a messenger, or someone who is waiting to receive a message. A person who is involved in the transportation industry or the military service might also choose this Significator. Use The Chariot to represent any situation where conflicting elements are involved or need to be controlled, such as a group of people with different views or objectives.

Strength

Use this card to signify someone who is strong and in control—male or female. It can also symbolize a person with charisma and charm. Strength represents any situation where physical strength is required, such as athletics or exploration, or where inner strength and perseverance are factors.

The Hermit

The Hermit is a good card to use if guidance is needed. He can symbolize someone who either seeks knowledge or possesses it—a wise man, professor, guru, or elder. The Hermit may be someone who prefers solitude to company, a recluse or monk, or a situation in which isolation is called for. A person who has retreated from ordinary life, or who desires to do so, might choose this card as a Significator. It can also signify anyone who is concerned about the past and delving into it, such as a researcher or historian.

Wheel of Fortune

This card is not used to represent a person, but it can be chosen to signify a situation that has already been put into motion and is playing itself out.

Justice

Use this card to represent someone who is in the process of weighing a decision, or who is looking for information to help him/her make a decision. Justice can also signify someone involved in the law, such as a judge, attorney, or arbitrator, or it may stand for the legal and jurisprudence system. Choose it as a Significator for someone who is involved in a lawsuit or other form of arbitration.

The Hanged Man

This card represents a querent who is at a crossroads. It can be used to signify someone who is at a turning point in life or who feels he or she is at a standstill. The Hanged Man can also refer to someone who is in a hospital, or for whom an illness has provided the chance to embark on a new course.

Death

Many people shy away from this card, and it is not usually chosen as a Significator. However, it is a good card to use when a situation involves a major transformation, such as the end of a relationship, the loss of a job, relocation, or any crisis that leads to a transformation.

Temperance

Use this card as a Significator for a healer or caretaker—a nurse, doctor, psychotherapist, chiropractor, massage therapist, etc. Temperance can also be used to signify resourcefulness and conservation, or someone who manages resources wisely.

The Devil

This card can be used to signify someone who is depressed, engaged in obsessive/compulsive behavior, addicted to alcohol or drugs, or in a destructive state of mind. The Devil can also represent a person who feels trapped and can't see the way out. It refers to any restrictive situation that is limiting the querent's progress.

The Tower

The Tower can be used as a Significator to depict an explosive situation or to represent the presence of forces beyond one's control. It is not generally used to signify a person.

The Star

The Star can signify someone who is of a humanitarian bent, offering aid to others without expectation of recompense or reward. It can also stand for a person who entertains others, such as an actor or musician, or someone who is an inspired artist. A beautiful person of either sex could be indicated by The Star, too.

The Moon

The Moon can be used to represent someone who is moony, or loony. There are many associations with the moon in life—the maiden or virgin, the mother, the wise woman—and this card could depict any of them. The Moon is linked with Artemis, the "Lady of the Beasts," and all in nature that is wild and free. Use The Moon card to signify anyone who strongly relates to the inner feminine.

The Sun

The Sun card is the usual Significator for children, or situations concerning children. It can also be used when you want to throw light onto a situation, or to bring something into the light of day. Someone with a sunny, radiant personality might also choose this card as a Significator.

Judgment

Use this card when the querent is either in the process of becoming more aware of what he needs to do, or who should be developing this awareness. Judgment represents someone who is seeking the truth about a particular situation or who must make a clear judgment in a situation.

The World

This card represents a self-actualized and fulfilled person. It can also signify a situation that is going especially well. Use it as a Significator for someone who is involved in the natural sciences or environmental work.

The principle of synchronicity suggests that meaningful coincidences create the impression that there is a sort of foreknowledge of a coming series of events available to the person who works with divinatory tools such as the Tarot, astrology, or runes. The Tarot spread is a picture of the moment.

Laying Out a Spread

If a Significator is called for, select it from the deck. Then choose a spread you feel is suitable to the question or issue at hand and lay out the cards according to the instructions in Chapter 11. Different spreads are designed to answer different sorts of questions or to comment on certain types of situations. If you don't know which spread is best for your question, you can use the Celtic Cross spread, shown on page 148. This versatile pattern was recommended by Arthur Edward Waite as "the most suitable for obtaining an answer to a definite question."

Next, proceed with whatever shuffling method you have decided to use (as discussed in Chapter 3). Many readers encourage the querent to shuffle the cards, to put his or her vibrations on them. Other readers prefer not to let anyone else touch their cards. The choice is up to you. No matter how you shuffle, or who shuffles, the cards will automatically arrange themselves as they should be. Count on it! The order in which they come up is never an accident.

The querent (you or someone else) then cuts the cards. After cutting and reassembling the deck, begin dealing the spread from the top of the deck. Some readers lay the cards face down; others, face up. Again, the choice is yours. Regardless of whether the querent sits across from or beside the reader, the cards are always read as they face the reader. If you deal cards face down, be sure to turn them up from left to right so that you don't reverse upright cards or turn reversed cards upright.

Some writers on Tarot insist that the rest of the deck be kept face down at all times. Once a layout is dealt, the remaining cards may be laid aside and left out of the reading. Or if you prefer, hold the unused part of the deck as you read and, when it seems appropriate, for elucidation or to answer further questions regarding the matter, draw cards at random from the deck. As you continue doing readings, you will develop your own methods. There is no right way.

FACT

Reading Tarot is like playing a piece of classical music. The score is written by the original composer, but every performer plays the music slightly different, according to his or her own interpretation.

Interpreting a Spread

It's important to look at any spread first as a whole. Before you start interpreting the individual cards and their placements, look at the overall picture. What colors are most evident? Are the images powerful and dramatic or peaceful and benign? Is the general tone one of contrasts or of harmony? How do you feel when you gaze at the spread?

Next, check for similarities, voids, preponderances, or weaknesses. Does the spread contain many Major Arcana cards or mostly Minor Arcana ones? Are Court Cards present? Aces? Are there many cards from the same suit? Is any suit absent? Do several of the numbered cards bear the same number?

Time Lines and Levels of Awareness

If the spread indicates a time line, as is the case with the Past-Present-Future spread and the Celtic Cross, notice which cards appear in the beginning and at the end of the time period represented. If the "past" includes negative cards and the "future" shows positive ones, you can see definite progress being made and better days ahead. If the opposite is evident, it could indicate that you aren't handling the situation appropriately or that things may get worse before they get better.

If the spread is designed to describe various levels of awareness, such as the World Tree spread, note whether the different levels are harmonious or incongruous. Are the images shown in one section calm, the other disturbing? Or do they seem to flow together in a coordinated manner? In a spread such as the Horoscope spread or the Feng Shui spread, which describe different areas of your life, check to see if positive cards turn up in some areas while negative ones appear in others. Do the cards fall into positions that seem to correspond to or conflict with their basic natures?

Numbers in Spreads

Pay attention to the numbers shown on the pip cards and where they fall in the spread. Do you see lots of fours and eights, indicating stability, or fives suggesting change? In a time-oriented spread, do low numbers turn up early in the spread and higher numbers later on? This can show development with regard to the subject of the reading. Consider the numbers on the trump cards as well as those on the Minor Arcana cards.

After you've assessed the spread from a broad perspective, you can zero in on the meanings of the individual cards in their respective positions. By combining the meanings of each card with its position, you can gain highly personal and detailed information.

What Different Spreads Can Tell You

As you study the spreads in Chapter 11, you'll notice that each addresses an issue in a particular way. Some offer practical advice; others focus on the spiritual or psychological dynamics underlying the situation. Some offer quick-and-easy answers; others go into great depth and analyze many facets of a matter.

The Horoscope spread, Feng Shui spread, and Tree of Life spread incorporate concepts from other esoteric traditions. These layouts are particularly good to use for life readings, when you want to understand the big picture, rather than when you seek insight into a specific concern. Spreads such as these address many parts of the querent's life—work, health, relationships, and so on—and show the energies operating in each of these areas.

ALERT!

In some cases, you may wish to examine an issue from more than one perspective. Laying two or more spreads can give you a breadth and depth of information that couldn't be achieved with a single spread. Many professional Tarot readers lay out several different spreads during the course of a reading, especially when the querent's concern is complex.

Spreads such as the Four-Card spread and the Quick Answer spread provide guidance about specific issues. They focus on a single matter and cover the various angles of the situation. The advice they offer is usually of a practical nature, although spiritual influences may come into play. By contrast, the Tree of Life spread and World Tree spread deal mainly with the spiritual aspects of a situation or describe the querent's psycho-spiritual development.

Deciding Which Spread to Use

Which spread to use depends on the nature of your question and what you want to know. Let's say you've recently met a man who interests you, and you are curious about the possibilities of a relationship with him. If you simply want to know whether you should consider him as a prospective partner, you could use one of the Yes-No methods on pages 140–42. Or you could try the Single Card technique (explained in Chapter 11), which will give you some clues to the man's character. Or pick a single card from the deck. A positive card suggests pursuing things further; a negative card says don't waste your time.

If your initial indicators are good, and you'd like to know how to proceed with this man, you could use the Four-Card spread. This describes the situation, an obstacle or opportunity you may encounter, what action you should take, and the likely outcome to the relationship. The Immediate Situation Three-Card spread could be useful, too.

Once you've entered into a relationship with this man, you might feel a need to get more advice or information about him and your situation. The Horseshoe spread or the Practical Advice Five-Card spread can reveal some of the hidden influences at work and recommend how to address them. After you've been together a while, you might choose the Thirteen-Card Story spread, which explains the progression of the relationship and provides insight into the situations that have occurred between you.

You can do the Horoscope spread on your birthday to gain an overview of the coming year, but it can also be useful if you want to see how a particular decision or matter will affect your entire life.

Although the simpler spreads can be used on a regular or even daily basis, the more involved ones, such as the Tree of Life spread and the Feng Shui spread, deal with larger areas of life and longer periods of time. It's probably best to use these only once or twice a year, unless a significant change has occurred.

Trumps in a Spread

Major Arcana cards represent spiritual or universal forces, higher consciousness, the collective, and archetypes. When they turn up in a spread, they could be considered messages from the Divine. This may indicate that you are being helped or influenced by powers beyond your own immediate everyday awareness, or that aspects of the reading (or the subject of the reading) have implications beyond the obvious, physical ones—even beyond your own personal existence. A spread with many trumps in it shows that the matter is complex and involves different levels of being. It can suggest that to handle the issue, you need to ask for assistance from a higher power and trust that power to guide you.

Some people view the trumps as indicators that fate or destiny is operating with regard to the subject of the reading. To other readers, the presence of Major Arcana cards means you are seeing the results of past actions starting to manifest in your life.

Trump Position

Notice the positions of the Major Arcana cards. Do they appear in the early or past portion of a spread or toward the end or future part? Do they represent opportunities or obstacles? Do they show areas you are aware of or hidden influences? Whenever a trump card turns up in a spread, pay extra attention to it, for it can reveal a great deal.

You will notice as you do readings that shuffling the cards can cause some of them to get turned upside down. When cards appear upside down in a spread, they are said to be reversed. Some readers simply turn reversed cards upright again. Others interpret cards differently when they are reversed than when they are upright.

Importance of Reversed Cards

Much disagreement exists concerning the significance of reversed cards. Many Tarot readers consider a reversed card to be weakened, so that it has less impact than it would if it were upright. Another popular view suggests that reversed cards depict more negative, dark, or malevolent energies at work. In her book *Tarot Reversals*, Mary K. Greer offers an interesting opinion: "Reversals reveal the esoteric or hidden components, the shamanic perspective of the world, and a place known as the dream-time or inner planes versus so-called 'reality.'" Reversals encourage us to see beyond and through the obvious, and to consider a matter's underlying dynamics as well as its apparent ones.

Whether you choose to interpret reversed cards in a spread or read only upright positions is up to you. You may wish to work with the Tarot for a while before you decide whether to interpret reversals in a different manner, and if so, how.

Creating Your Own Spreads

After you know what the cards mean and have experimented with a number of different layouts, you can feel free to design your own spreads. A spread is like a blueprint of the reading you are going to do; through its pattern, you build the reading. You can include as many or as few cards as you like in a spread. You can expand on standard layouts, or you can design a completely original layout pattern. You are limited only by your imagination.

FACT

An example of an expansion of a pre-existing layout, the three-card spread can be expanded into a nine-card spread by using three layers of three cards each and designating each layer as past, present, or future.

Begin by identifying exactly what it is you want to know and what you want the spread to convey. Then organize those issues into an ordered plan, marking each card's position according to what it will signify. By doing this, you are telling your unconscious that you want specific answers to your questions, and you are determining the method you will use to access the information you seek.

Let's say a person has had an auto accident and thinks there is some deeper reason than bad driving for what's happened. This individual wants to explore that issue in depth by consulting the Tarot. By having a dialogue with the readee, you go through a process of clarification by asking questions, such as "What role is this accident playing in my life now?"; "How did I participate in this accident?"; "What purpose are the accident and its results serving in my life?"; "Why did I have this accident?"; "What am I getting out of having had this accident?"; "Am I avoiding something by having had an accident?"; and so forth.

You then organize the questions into a card plan. Draw your layout and designate a card position that corresponds to each question. Number the card positions on the plan. You decide how many cards to use, depending on how many questions or facets of the issue you wish to have answered.

Then choose a layout pattern that appeals to both you and the person for whom the reading is being done. The visual pattern of the spread can be varied according to your personal inclinations: Some people work best with linear shapes, others with circular patterns, and still others with rectangles or star shapes. You can combine both your concept and your aesthetic sense in the layout, for this invites your intuition to speak through it.

As you order the questions and place the card positions in the plan, you may decide to drop some questions and add others. Include the readee in the entire process. You might, for example, want to add to the above list such questions as, "What are the past influences that led to the accident?" and/or, "How will this accident affect my future?"

You can also design multipurpose spreads that can be used to address a wide range of issues and questions. Base them on your personal belief system or a special interest, if you like. Use your creativity, experiment, and have fun!

Chapter 11

Sixteen Spreads

Spreads are configurations of Tarot cards that have been designed to convey information in a particular way. The simplest spreads use only a single card; complex patterns may involve more than a dozen. A reading can include one or several spreads, depending on the situation and what you want to know. The sixteen spreads here offer a variety of approaches. You should experiment with all of them to see which ones work best for you. Each explanation is followed by an example to help you understand when and how to use each spread.

Single Card Method

This is the easiest and most basic of all spreads, and it can be used to answer all types of questions. Although you won't get as much in-depth information as you would from a longer, more complex spread, this method can be surprisingly helpful—especially in answering straightforward questions for which you need an immediate answer.

Shuffle and cut the cards while thinking about your question. Then draw a single card from the pack. You can either pick the top card from the deck or fan out all the cards face down and select one at random. The card's meaning will shed light on your question.

An Example of the Single Card Method

Ellen felt that a friend was angry with her, but when she asked what was wrong her friend said, "Nothing's wrong." Ellen turned to the Tarot and asked for insight into the tension she experienced between herself and her friend. She drew the Four of Swords, which she interpreted as an indication that her friend was tired and needed some time alone to rest and relax. As it turned out, the friend had been under a lot of stress at work, and the pressure was causing her to behave in a brusque, impatient way, even though she wasn't really angry at Ellen.

Yes/No Method

To use the Yes/No method, you need only decide which cards will represent yes and which no. After the usual shuffling and cutting, draw a single card from the deck, either from the top or at random. Consider the card's meaning, too, for this will provide further information. There are no firm rules, but here are some guidelines:

Designating Yes/No Cards	
Major Arcana	
If you are willing to work with the concept of the card.	Yes
If you are unwilling to do the work.	No
Minor Arcana	
Even Numbers	Yes
Odd Numbers	No
Court Cards	
King	No
Queen	Yes
Knight	No
Page	Yes

Once you have decided which cards mean yes and which indicate no, you should also consider whether your chosen card is upright or reversed.

Upright

If it's a Yes card, the upright position represents a definite Yes.

If it's a No card, the upright position indicates a definite No.

Reversed

If Yes, there will be a delay.

If No, there will be obstacles to prevent you.

You may use these guidelines or you may opt to create a system of your own for determining which cards signify yes and which ones signify no for you.

An Example of the Yes/No Method

John was thinking of buying a house in the country and unexpectedly found exactly what he was looking for, but the price was higher than he wanted to pay. However, someone else had put a bid in, and he had to make an immediate decision. He opted for a Yes/No reading—should he buy the house? The card that came up was the Ten of Pentacles, upright—a definite Yes. Since the Ten of Pentacles signifies acquisition of a home and success in money matters, John was being advised to buy the house in confidence, that he would have the financial wherewithal. The card also indicated it was the right choice and that he would be happy there.

Either/Or Method

Use this spread when you have two options and can't decide between them. After shuffling and cutting the deck, select two cards either from the top or at random from the pack. The first card represents one option, the second card signifies the other choice.

An Example of the Either/Or Method

Jennifer had two job offers. To determine which she should accept, she used the Either/Or Method. To represent the smaller and less well-known of the two companies, she drew the Queen of Swords, which suggested that they would respect her as an employee and treat her well. Her work was likely to be well-publicized if she contracted with them and she could gain recognition. Jennifer drew the Four of Pentacles to stand for the larger, more established company. This card indicated that although she would receive a larger amount of money from this company, she couldn't expect as much potential growth, fame, or satisfaction if she accepted their offer.

Past-Present-Future Method

This three-card spread lets you see the past influences or conditions regarding a situation, the present state of the matter, and what's likely to occur in the future. After shuffling and cutting the deck, select three cards either from the top of the pack or at random. Lay them out side by side. The card on the left represents the past; the middle card shows the present; the card on the right indicates the future.

An Example of the Past-Present-Future Method

Tom had reconnected with an old girlfriend after many years and wondered what their chances were now for a happy relationship. He shuffled and cut the cards, then dealt three from the top of the deck. The past card was The Fool, which suggested he'd been too young when the couple first met and had not been ready for a serious commitment. The Six of Cups turned up in the present spot, showing renewed affection. In the future position, Tom laid the Seven of Cups, an indication that many possibilities existed and that his own attitude would play an important role in the outcome.

Immediate Situation Three-Card Spread

This simple, quick layout focuses on what's happening now and provides insight into the matter at hand. It's a good spread to use when you want to focus on a particular situation, clarify what's happening, and receive insight or a new perspective.

Card 1: The nature of the present situation

Card 2: Your attitude toward what's happening

Card 3: The key element for you to consider

An Example of an Immediate Situation Three-Card Spread

Imagine the following results for a reading for Irene, a married woman with two young children, who requested a reading because she suspected her husband wanted a divorce, even though he did not actually say so.

Card 1: The Chariot

In the position of the nature of the present situation, The Chariot indicated that Irene needed to stay centered and not get overly emotional about her suspicions, which were unproven. She had to steer a middle course between her conflicting thoughts and emotions and get them both moving forward in tandem, instead of pulling her in opposite directions.

Card 2: Three of Swords

The Three of Swords in the attitude position indicated that Irene had already made up her mind that she and her husband were going to separate. She was depressed and angry and in pain but felt no hope for mending the situation.

Card 3: The Empress

The Empress card in the key position advised her to be mindful of herself as a mother as well as a wife. She needed to address issues of communication with her husband, which were at the root of the problem. The Empress told Irene to be more loving and nurturing and less critical of what she considered his shortcomings. She had Venus in Virgo, which indicated her tendency to criticize her partner. The Empress is related to Venus, which rules marriage, a sign that the marriage would survive if she shared her feelings and learned to give and receive love uncritically.

Four-Card Spread

This spread offers advice for dealing with a specific concern. Its strength is its simple, direct approach to dealing with practical, everyday problems. Shuffle and cut the cards, then lay them out side by side in a horizontal line, from left to right.

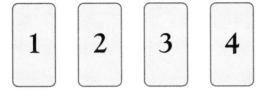

Card 1: Situation

Card 2: Obstacle

Card 3: Action recommended

Card 4: Outcome

An Example of the Four-Card Spread

Mark had held his present job for nearly three years. Despite his abilities and efforts, he had been overlooked for several promotions and wondered why he couldn't seem to get ahead.

Card 1: Four of Cups

This card described Mark's present situation. He was bored and felt stuck in a rut. He no longer had any enthusiasm for his job, but he couldn't muster the courage to make a change.

Card 2: The Devil

As the obstacle card, The Devil suggested that Mark's own fear and doubt, as well as his excessive concern with security, were blocking his progress. Even though he was a reliable and hard-working employee, he lacked self-confidence. As a result, his employers were reluctant to promote him to a position of greater authority and responsibility.

Card 3: Knight of Wands

Knights often represent movement, and in Mark's case, laying this card in the action spot advised him to seek another job with another company where he'd have more opportunity for advancement. This card also recommended that Mark be more adventurous and willing to take the risk involved in changing jobs.

Card 4: Ace of Pentacles

As an outcome card, an Ace indicates the likelihood of a new beginning—in this case, one that involves money or material resources (pentacles). Thus the reading strongly shows that Mark would benefit from finding a new job.

Practical Advice Five-Card Spread

As the name suggests, this simple spread is good for gaining insight into practical matters. After shuffling and cutting, lay the cards out from left to right in a single row.

Card 1: Past influence

Card 2: Present influence

Card 3: Major influence

Card 4: Advice

Card 5: Outcome likely if advice is followed

An Example of a Practical Advice Five-Card Spread

The querent was Joshua, a young man only a year away from graduating college. He was considering taking off a year after graduation before going to work and wanted advice.

Card 1: Ten of Wands

This card in the position of past influence indicated that Joshua had been shouldering a heavy load for a long time, working a part-time job in addition to carrying a full load of course work.

Card 2: Two of Pentacles

This card in the position of present influence revealed that Joshua was receiving money from more than one source. His parents helped out, and he had a student loan as well as his part-time job. It further indicated that he was constantly juggling money matters, which put both external and internal pressure on him to join the work force immediately after graduation.

Card 3: Four of Swords

This card appearing in the major influence spot indicated that Joshua was overtired and badly needed a rest. He needed time for respite and meditation, to be alone and get in touch with his inner self instead of being pushed about by outside circumstances and the expectations of others.

Card 4: The Fool

The appearance of The Fool in the advice position recommended that Joshua should have the experience of freedom and enjoy his youth, at least for a while, before buttoning himself up in the corporate world. This card advised him to go out and experience the world as a free spirit, to put aside his fears and worries about making the right career moves as soon as he graduated. He was being advised by The Fool to have faith, to take a leap into his unknown future, to go adventuring with a carefree attitude before settling down to the serious business of a lifetime of working.

Card 5: The World

The World card in the position of the likely outcome, if he follows The Fool's advice, is that he will travel and see the world. In the end all will be well, and success will be his. In other words, the world's his oyster if he goes willingly where The Fool leads.

Traditional Celtic Cross Spread

This popular and versatile spread calls for a Significator. Place it on the table to bring you (or the person for whom the reading is being done) into the reading and lay Card 1 on top of the Significator.

Card 1: This covers you and describes your immediate concerns.

Card 2: This crosses you and describes obstacles facing you.

Card 3: This crowns you and describes what is known to you objectively.

Card 4: This is beneath you and describes the foundation of the concern or past influences affecting the situation. It can also show what is unknown about the situation.

Card 5: This is behind you and describes past influences now fading away.

Card 6: This is before you and describes new circumstances coming into being—the near future.

Card 7: This is your self and describes your current state of mind.

Card 8: This is your house and describes the circumstances surrounding the situation.

Card 9: This is what you hope or fear, perhaps what you both want and fear.

Card 10: This is what will come and describes the likely future outcome.

An Example of a Celtic Cross Reading

The querent was Sue, a middle-aged woman with a Pisces sun sign and an emotional nature, so the reader chose the Queen of Cups as her Significator.

Card 1: Seven of Pentacles

She was concerned about money because she had lost her job due to ill health and was totally dependent on her husband for financial support.

Card 2: King of Pentacles

Sue's husband was well-off and owned his own business, but he was a dominating man who held on to money tightly. Naturally timid, Sue was afraid of him. His obvious masculine power and the financial advantage he held over her made her feel powerless in his presence.

Card 3: The Moon

Her unconscious creative forces were suggesting she could, despite her ill health, work to develop her artistic creativity, which she had all but squelched. In astrology, the moon represents the public, so this card showed that she might eventually make money with her talent.

Card 4: Justice

Sue was involved in a class-action lawsuit regarding her illness, which had been caused by ruptured breast implants. She was hoping for a hefty financial settlement, which would free her from dependence on her husband, whom she wished to divorce.

Card 5: The Nine of Swords

This card suggested that Sue's pain and travail were coming to an end, and that a solution to her emotional problems and financial worries would be found.

Card 6: The Wheel of Fortune

This card indicated that forces she had already put into motion—the lawsuit—were continuing and that there would be a favorable result that would allow her to make significant changes in her life.

Card 7: Strength

This card clearly indicated that underneath her seeming passivity and timidity Sue had inner strength that would see her through this difficult time.

Card 8: Knight of Cups

This card showed Sue was receiving loving support from her son who had recently suggested she leave her husband (his stepfather) and move to another state to live with him and his wife.

Card 9: The Chariot, reversed

The Chariot reversed indicates that Sue was afraid of losing control over her life and that her lack of self-confidence had stopped her from extricating herself from her unhappy marriage.

Card 10: The Nine of Pentacles

This card shows that Sue will become financially independent, probably through the success of the lawsuit, and be able to live alone.

General Life Conditions Spread

This spread can be used to answer just about any question. It provides insight into the querent's psychological state while shedding light on practical matters.

Card 1: Who you are right now

Card 2: What is affecting you

Card 3: What you value

Card 4: What's bothering you

Card 5: The short-term

Card 6: The long-term

An Example of a General Life Conditions Spread

The querent was Janice, a married woman with a learning disabled child and an unemployed husband.

Card 1: Ten of Wands

The Ten of Wands in the "Who are you?" position said that Janice was carrying a full burden of responsibility on her shoulders, but that she was managing the situation successfully and working hard toward bettering her life.

Card 2: Five of Pentacles

The Five of Pentacles in the "What's affecting you?" position, indicated money difficulties as a major concern. Due to her husband's unemployment, Janice was the only earner and had applied to receive food stamps.

Card 3: The Hierophant

In the "What you value" position, The Hierophant indicated that her deeply felt religious belief was the glue holding Janice together during this time of trial and difficulty.

Card 4: Two of Pentacles

In the position of what is bothering her, we find the Two of Pentacles, indicating that she had been juggling finances to make ends meet since her husband had been out of work. Still, it is a positive card that could indicate extra income, perhaps from part-time work.

Card 5: Ace of Pentacles

In the position of the short-term, the Ace of Pentacles said that new money was on its way to Janice and would arrive soon. She had a settlement pending as a result of an accident, and this Ace indicated it would be adjudicated quickly, and that the money received would ease her situation.

Card 6: Ten of Cups

In the long-term position, the Ten of Cups was a strong indication that Janice's family would soon be moving into a new positive cycle of emotional well-being and happiness in family matters.

Quick Answer Spread

After shuffling and cutting the deck, lay out the cards in a horizontal row, from left to right.

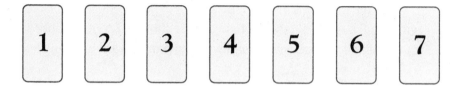

Card 1: Concern

Card 2: Immediate past

Card 3: Immediate future

Card 4: Querent's state of mind

Card 5: Obstacle

Card 6: Help

Card 7: Outcome

An Example of a Quick Answer Spread

Debra was a single woman in her late twenties who had always lived with her parents. She wanted to get out on her own and live in a warm climate and was thinking of moving from New York to Florida.

Card 1: Four of Wands

This card in the concern position indicated that leaving her family and the happiness and security it had always provided for her was a major issue. Being on her own for the first time, she knew she would miss her close-knit family life.

Card 2: Queen of Pentacles, reversed

This card represented Debra's mother, who had always indulged her daughter with material things but was a domineering, controlling woman. She was angry that her daughter wanted to move away and they had recently quarreled bitterly about it.

Card 3: Eight of Wands

This card in the immediate future suggested that Debra would take a trip, probably soon and by air. The cards indicated that she should take her vacation in Florida. She could check out the job market and see how she felt about making her home there.

Card 4: Five of Pentacles

This card showed that uppermost in her mind was her fear of living on her own. She worried that she would not being able to make it financially, which her mother had brought up during their quarrel.

Card 5: The Fool, reversed

This card in the obstacle position indicated that Debra was afraid to take chances. She feared risking making a fool of herself by not being able to manage on her own, having to return home, and admit failure.

Card 6: Ace of Pentacles

This card appearing in the help position suggested that new money and opportunities for making money were coming to her, and that her fears of poverty were unfounded.

Card 7: The Sun

The Sun card in the outcome position was an indication that she would be successful—in a sunny climate! The move to Florida would free her from the oppressive sense of guilt and obligation she felt to her parents for their support. The Sun card clearly said, "Go for it; I'm with you!"

The Horseshoe Spread

Each card position in this spread represents a specific area of life. After shuffling and cutting the deck, lay out the cards from right to left. There is also a ten-card version of the Horseshoe spread, but the seven-card layout is a bit more simple.

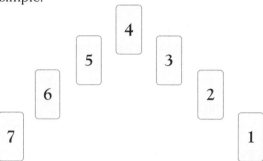

Card 1: The past. Describes what past events, emotions, and actions pertain to the question being asked.

Card 2: The present. Refers to what's happening now or the querent's current state of mind regarding what has just occurred.

Card 3: Hidden influences. This position indicates unexpected influences, occurrences, or expectations about which the querent is unaware.

Card 4: Obstacles. Describes what is standing in the querent's way of attaining her desires. The obstacles may be outer conditions or problems in the querent's attitude.

Card 5: The environment. Describes other people, or another person, and their attitudes toward the querent and her issue.

Card 6: What should be done. This position shows action to be taken or recommends a change in attitude.

Card 7: The most likely outcome. What's likely to occur, assuming you follow the advice given by Card 6.

An Example of a Horseshoe Spread

The querent was Kim, a young woman who wanted to know if the romantic relationship in which she was involved would develop into marriage.

Card 1: Three of Swords

This card indicated that the relationship had already been plagued by separation. The on-again off-again affair had caused Kim much pain and anxiety.

Card 2: Knight of Cups

This card revealed that Kim had recently had a communication from him indicating he wanted to get back together, suggesting he might be ready for commitment.

Card 3: The Empress, reversed

This card warned that Kim was thinking of accidentally getting pregnant to force a marriage, a course of action that would doom her to failure.

Card 4: Queen of Pentacles

This card represented Kim's mother, who strongly opposed her daughter's choice. Her family was well-off and socially well-connected; the young man was from a blue-collar background and was working his way through college.

Card 5: Strength

The appearance of this card indicated Kim was ready to declare her independence and marry her lover.

Card 6: Temperance

This card counseled patience and self-control. It cautioned Kim not to rush into anything but to work to reconcile the opposing forces, to allow her mother to realize the young man's good qualities, and to have the maturity to accept that things often take time.

Card 7: Ten of Cups

This card indicates that if Kim follows the advice given and does not use any trickery or deceit to get her man, the result will be a happy marriage blessed with children and prosperity.

The World Tree Spread

This pattern is based on the Celtic Pagan concept of a World Tree, a sacred oak that connects the three realms of existence. The roots reach into the underworld, which is not the same as the Christian Hell, but rather is the primal source from which life emerges. The trunk crosses through the earthly realm as we know it, and the branches stretch into the heavens or realm of the spirit. Use this spread when you want to understand the relationship between the three layers of reality or the three levels of the querent's consciousness.

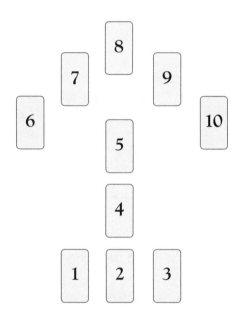

Cards 1, 2, and 3: Influences in the subconscious or underworld. These three root cards describe the source or roots of the situation. They may exist in the querent's subconscious, or they may be hidden spiritual forces, perhaps conditions stemming from past lifetimes.

Cards 4 and 5: The present situation. The two trunk cards show physical or conscious conditions, and they may also indicate how the querent is working with the forces described by the root cards.

Cards 6, 7, 8, 9, and 10: Influences in the spiritual realm or higher self. The cards that make up the branches represent spiritual forces and the querent's higher consciousness.

An Example of the World Tree Spread

The querent was Alice, a woman artist in her thirties whose parents were alcoholics. Through her personal growth work and spiritual studies, she was attempting to release the fear and anger stemming from her childhood and to develop more faith and self-confidence.

Cards 1, 2, and 3: The Devil, Five of Pentacles, Nine of Swords

The Devil in this position reveals the deep-seated doubt, rage, and self-loathing Alice was holding onto, destructive emotions that had a crippling effect on her. The Five of Pentacles told of the poverty in which she'd grown up, as well as the insecurity that still plagued her in adulthood. The Nine of Swords showed that Alice's fears and disappointments, although based on real conditions in the past, were now only memories that she was allowing to continue causing her pain.

Cards 4 and 5: High Priestess, Three of Cups

The High Priestess shows that Alice was very intuitive and imaginative and was using these qualities in the present to try to heal the suffering from her childhood. At present, she is working on a series of paintings that express the difficulties in her youth and her growth through her current Buddhist spiritual practice, which is helping her to release the past. The Three of Cups represents a group of fellow artists whose encouragement and friendship bring Alice much happiness and whom she views as her new family.

Cards 6, 7, 8, 9, and 10: Queen of Wands, Three of Pentacles, Six of Cups, Strength, Nine of Pentacles

These cards show the guidance and help that Alice's higher self offers and the spiritual forces that are present in her life. The Queen of Wands shows the creative talent she possesses. The Three of Pentacles represents benefits from putting her abilities to use. The Six of Cups suggests renewed love and joy in her life, as a result of her group of artist friends and her spiritual path. Strength says that Alice has powerful protective forces operating at a spiritual level, and that she is inwardly much stronger than she believes herself to be. The Nine of Pentacles also points out that she is capable of making her own way and reaping the rewards, self-confidence, and security she desires.

The Tree of Life Spread

Based on the Kabbalistic Tree of Life, this spread provides insights into the querent's spiritual nature as well as the outer conditions that are related to the matter at hand. The card positions correspond to the ten sephirot (which represent the ten characteristics of divinity) on the tree. (Note: The Tree of Life Spread is read from the bottom up, from card 10 to card 1.)

Card 1: Light (outcome)

Card 2: Wisdom (goals, changes, power)

Card 3: Understanding (receptivity, creativity, limitations)

Card 4: Mercy (abundance, generosity, memories)

Card 5: Severity, strength (struggle, activity, destruction)

Card 6: Beauty (love, compassion, new insights)

Card 7: Victory (romance, emotions, desires)

Card 8: Glory (knowledge, analysis, discrimination)

Card 9: Foundation (sexual issues, illusions, fears, the unconscious)

Card 10: Kingdom (physicality, money, practical matters)

An Example of a Tree of Life Spread

The querent was Kyle, a man of thirty with musical talent and ambitions. He wanted to quit his "day job" to devote himself to developing his talent and wondered if this was the right choice.

Card 10: Eight of Pentacles

This card in the money and practicality position signified that Kyle would be learning new skills, becoming an apprentice at a new trade or career. It augured well for his being able to make money with his music, especially considering that he was full of enthusiasm and determination and practical enough to manage his limited funds until his new career took off.

Card 9: Queen of Wands, reversed

This card represented Kyle's wife, a beautiful and ambitious woman who was against him risking their financial security. He wanted her support but feared her disapproval and worried that if he didn't make enough money she might leave him despite their strong sexual attraction to each other.

Card 8: Three of Pentacles

This is the card of the craftsman, which indicated Kyle had the knowledge needed to practice his art and will keep developing his abilities in a discriminating way. It also suggests that he will make money with his creative talents, for he is good at what he does. His success will come through his own faith in himself.

Card 7: The Moon

The Moon in the position of romance, beauty, and desire indicated that Kyle has a strong feminine side to his nature, which makes him sensitive and creative in addition to having a practical side. This was corroborated astrologically by the fact that in his chart Venus was found in the sign of Taurus, an extremely practical earth sign that grounded his love of beauty (Venus) while his Moon was in the extrasensitive sign of Pisces, which is linked with creativity, art, music, and compassion.

Card 6: Six of Wands

In the position of new insights, this card indicates Kyle will triumph over adversity and be victorious in his endeavors. He will overcome what opposes him, and his self-doubt will be resolved, indicating success and recognition.

Card 5: The Chariot

In the position of struggle and activity, The Chariot indicated that Kyle was going to have to work hard to harness both sides of his nature, the practical and the dreamy. This card also shows that he'd have to put effort into convincing his wife that his plans would eventually benefit her so that she would become his partner and not oppose his wishes, which would be destructive to him.

Card 4: Four of Pentacles

Money has always been an issue for Kyle, as shown by this card appearing in the position of abundance and memories. He came from a modest background where each penny had to be carefully counted, and there were none to spare. He worked his way through school with great difficulty and still has painful memories of frugal living. To solve his issues of abundance, he has to have faith in himself, as was already indicated by card 8, and perform daily affirmations to strengthen his inner belief in his value as a musician.

Card 3: The High Priestess

In the position of creativity, receptivity, and limits, The High Priestess indicates that Kyle has much talent that is yet to be developed. At the moment, he is suffering limitations because he has not delved deeply into himself to discover what he can do, but he is receptive to the idea of uncovering and utilizing his creative abilities to the greatest extent possible. As the moon rules The High Priestess, this card is an echo of card 7, The Moon, and encourages him to express himself fully.

Card 2: The Wheel of Fortune

This card appearing in the position of goals, changes, and power indicates that Kyle has already put the wheel of change into motion by his intense desire to pursue his musical career. Whether he is fully aware of the process or not, his vivid fantasies of the kind of life he wants to live have already served to get his subconscious mind to work to make it happen. Kyle is going to make this change and reach his goal—because his inner self is directing him and has already taken charge. There is no turning back now.

Card 1: Ace of Wands

In the outcome position, the Ace of Wands indicates that Kyle is starting in a new work/career direction and that all will turn out well. All kinds of new opportunities will come his way, and new contacts will be helpful. His excitement about making this life-changing move will carry him to success.

Feng Shui Spread

This pattern represents the eight-sided octagon called a bagua, used by feng shui practitioners to examine the connections between a person's home and his/her life. The cards show the energies and influences operating in each area of the querent's life.

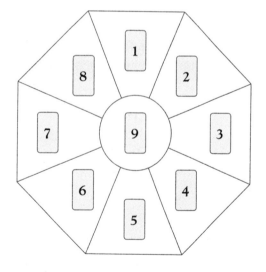

Card 1: Fame, future, career

Card 2: Relationships, marriage, partnerships

Card 3: Creativity, children

Card 4: Helpful people, friends, agents/associates/colleagues, travel

Card 5: Self, identity, image

Card 6: Wisdom, knowledge, spirituality

Card 7: Family, community, neighbors

Card 8: Wealth

Card 9: Health

Example of a Feng Shui Spread

The querent was Eric, a software designer in his midthirties who had just relocated to California after living in the Midwest for most of his life. He wanted to know what he could expect as a result of this move.

Card 1: Eight of Pentacles

In the fame/future/career position, this card indicates that Eric could succeed if he was willing to work hard and sincerely pursue his goals.

Card 2: Three of Swords

This card reveals part of the reason for Eric's move—a divorce. He had decided to start over by putting distance between himself and his former wife, but the separation was causing him pain, and he felt lonely and alienated from the people he cared about.

Card 3: Ace of Wands

The Ace of Wands indicates that Eric is starting a new job that excites him and stimulates his creativity. He'll have many interesting and challenging opportunities available to him in this new position.

Card 4: The Hermit

The card of isolation and introspection, The Hermit in this spot showed that Eric might have a hard time making new friends and could find himself alone much of the time. However, he needed to get in touch with himself, do some soul-searching, and discover his real path in life, rather than surrounding himself with family and friends as he'd done previously.

Card 5: King of Swords

Although Eric knew he was intelligent and creative, he hadn't yet had a chance to show what he could do in his field. This card suggested that the move to California and his new job would enable Eric to express his knowledge and skills and gain self-confidence as a result.

Card 6: Page of Pentacles

This card in the position of wisdom/knowledge indicates that Eric could benefit from taking classes or improving his practical skills. Shortly before this reading took place, he had enrolled in a financial management course.

Card 7: Seven of Swords

A card of movement and intellectual freedom, the Seven of Swords shows that Eric had left his old home and family to strike out on his own in an area that would allow him more independence. As a result of his relocation, Eric hoped to find like-minded people and opportunities that weren't available to him in his former location. However, this card also reminded him not to make waves in his new community.

Card 8: The Magician

In the wealth position, this trump suggests that Eric needs to use his intelligence, skills, and willpower to accomplish his financial goals. Much depends on his attitude and how he utilizes his knowledge to earn money.

Card 9: Four of Swords

This card, in the position of health, shows that Eric has been under a lot of stress due to his recent divorce and relocation. He needs to rest and recuperate, or he could run the risk of illness.

Horoscope Spread

In this spread, twelve cards are laid out in a circle and each card corresponds to one of the twelve houses of the astrological chart. A thirteenth card, a Significator, can be placed in the center if desired.

Houses

House One begins at the nine o'clock position, and the cards are dealt counterclockwise. Each house refers to a specific area of life; thus, the cards are read in reference to the house in which they fall. This spread is not generally used to answer specific questions—it provides an overview of the person's life at the time of the reading. The querent's sun sign or birth chart are not factors in a reading that uses this spread.

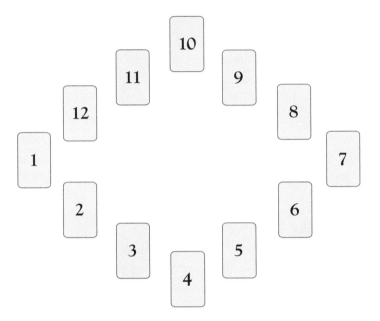

The First House: The Self

The first house refers to the physical body and appearance, as well as the querent's vitality, identity, sense of self, and the immediate impression he makes on others.

The Second House: Personal Resources

The second house shows what the querent considers valuable. This includes money, personal possessions, resources, earning ability, and the person's identification with what he owns.

The Third House: The Near Environment

The third house covers three areas of life that at first may not seem related, but taken together represent normal daily life, what astrologers call the near environment—communications related to the routine of everyday life; involvement with friends, neighbors, siblings, and the community at large; and short-distance travel in one's near environment.

The Fourth House: Roots

The fourth house represents the foundation of one's life—home, family, parents (especially the mother), tradition, heritage, the past, one's homeland—in short, the querent's roots.

The Fifth House: Self-Expression

The fifth house shows the querent's creative and self-expressive side, which may play out as artistic endeavors, romantic relationships, hobbies and amusements, or children.

The Sixth House: Health and Service

The sixth house relates to health, health-oriented routines including nutrition and exercise, and the link between work and health. It also describes the querent's daily work or chores, duties, job-oriented relationships, service to others, and the capacity for self-sacrifice.

The Seventh House: One-on-One Relationships

Traditionally the house of marriage and partnerships, the seventh represents all one-on-one relationships—business and personal, including relationships with enemies.

The Eighth House: Transformation

The eighth is the house of the past, transformative change, death, inheritance, and other people's resources. In this case, death usually refers to the end of something old so that something new can emerge. The eighth house also shows how another's resources affect you.

The Ninth House: Higher Knowledge

The ninth house represents the higher mind, philosophy, religion/spirituality, the law, and advanced education, as well as long-distance travel, especially to foreign lands. This house shows the querent's search for meaning and how he goes about expanding his or her horizons and knowledge of the world.

The Tenth House: Life Task

The tenth house represents social or professional status, career, public image, and parents (the father especially). Authority, responsibilities, honor, and reputation are tenth-house matters, too.

The Eleventh House: Friendships

The eleventh house refers to the querent's friends and groups with which he is affiliated. Goals, hopes, and wishes are shown by this house, too.

The Twelfth House: The Hidden Realm

The twelfth house represents that which is hidden, or not yet revealed, including our dreams and fantasies. It also reveals the querent's latent talents as well as fears, weaknesses, secrets, and unknown enemies. Because matters associated with this sector are often unknown to us, the house is sometimes connected with self-undoing.

An Example of a Horoscope Spread

The querent, Alison, was a woman in her midforties, married with a four-year-old daughter. She worked full-time in an academic job at a university, appeared healthy, and was of a cheerful disposition. Her husband's work required him to travel, and he was away from home much of the time.

House 1: The Sun, reversed

This card showed that Alison's natural optimism and sunny disposition were being affected by her life situation, which was yet to be revealed by the remaining cards. She was suffering from low self-esteem but trying to maintain a façade of cheerfulness and normality. However, something was clearly wrong.

House 2: Page of Cups

This card referred to her daughter, who had been asking questions about why daddy was never home. Alison replied that her father was away working (which was true), but the child was nonetheless delivering a message to her mother that she sensed in her heart (Cups) that the family situation was amiss. Her child was the most important person in Alison's life, and her welfare was essential.

House 3: Eight of Swords

This card indicated that communications were being blocked, and Alison was in a quandary as to what to do about the situation. She and her husband hardly ever talked about anything important; he had withdrawn from communication with her, and she felt helpless.

House 4: The Tower, reversed

The appearance of the reversed Tower indicated that Alison was trying to hold on to the crumbling structure of her home life. The situation was exacerbated by her husband's constant traveling, which Alison thought was a means to avoid confronting their marital problems for the sake of her daughter.

House 5: Ten of Wands

This card suggested that Alison was carrying a burden that was preventing her from enjoying life. She had shouldered total care for their daughter and resented her husband's absences and lack of concern for the little girl, which made her feel like a single parent. She felt alone with heavy responsibilities and had little time for socializing or fun.

House 6: Three of Swords

This card indicated some kind of separation from a work situation that was unsatisfactory. It turned out that Alison was in the process of changing jobs, to a new department within the university, which would be less stressful than her present position.

House 7: King of Swords, reversed

This card represented Alison's husband, who was an Aquarius, the fixed air sign. It showed his rigid mental attitudes toward the marriage and his unwillingness to open up and talk to her due to his desire to avoid messy emotional scenes. This card illustrated that the marriage was over and existed in name only. Alison confessed that she and her husband had been using separate bedrooms for several months.

House 8: The Empress, reversed

This card suggested that a past issue involving pregnancy or a maternal figure was involved in the situation. Alison admitted the only reason she had married was that she had become pregnant. When she discovered herself pregnant, her husband did the right thing but subsequently was not much interested in the child he hadn't wanted or planned for.

House 9: The Star

This card indicated Alison would have great success in her academic career and/or that she would pursue other forms of consciousness-raising. She said she was very happy with the prospect of the new job, which carried much prestige, but also she was interested in pursuing a study of metaphysics, such as astrology and Tarot, and learning one of the healing arts, Reiki.

House 10: The World

This happy card in Alison's tenth house of career assured that the job change was a smart career move and that she would be happy and successful with it. She verified that the new job was the single really bright spot in her life at the time.

House 11: King of Wands

This card represented the head of Alison's new department who had asked her to lead a task force in her specialty, which meant she would be involved with group activities. The King indicated her leadership style would be forthright and masculine rather than subtle and feminine. Success was assured.

House 12: The Moon

The Moon appearing in the twelfth House indicated that Alison needed time by herself to get in touch with her deepest feelings, to access her intuitive self, to step back from the pressures of work and taking care of her daughter to process her feelings about her marriage situation before deciding what action to take. She needed to consult her own inner feminine wisdom rather than relying on an intellectual, rational approach to her marriage problem.

Thirteen-Card Story Spread

This method describes the evolution of a situation over a period of time. After shuffling and cutting the deck, lay out thirteen cards in three rows, as shown in the following illustration.

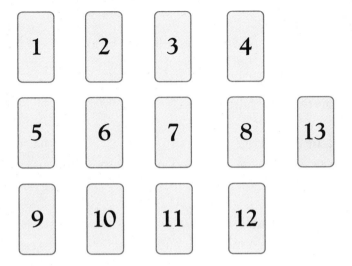

Card 1: The birth of the subject of the reading.

Cards 2 through 11: The development of the situation—positive and negative conditions, opportunities and obstacles, progress and setbacks. The linear pattern lets you see how each step has led to the next and how they influence the current concern.

Card 12: The near future.

Card 13: The more distant future.

An Example of a Thirteen-Card Story Spread

Harry, a man in his early sixties, was considering retiring, but he had concerns about turning over the family business to his son.

Card 1: Two of Pentacles

This card represents Harry's business, a printing company, which he and his brother had started more than three decades ago and built into a successful company.

Card 2: Five of Swords

During the early years of operation, the two brothers had often disagreed about how to grow the business. Harry, being more conservative than his brother, wanted to move slowly and at times he felt they'd taken too many risks and overextended themselves.

Card 3: Five of Pentacles

At times, money had been tight and had caused cautious, security-conscious Harry much distress.

Card 4: Eight of Pentacles

Through hard work, determination, and conscientious business practices, Harry and his brother had managed to make their printing company a stable, reputable operation.

Card 5: Knight of Wands, reversed

Harry's brother, a salesman and optimist, had convinced Harry to branch out into other areas and to open new locations. However, their plans failed when the economy took a dive just as the brothers had invested heavily in a new plant, equipment, and staff. It took years for them to recoup their losses, which left Harry feeling very wary about making changes. The lingering memories of loss and failure were at the root of his present fears about giving the reins to his son.

Card 6: Ten of Swords

This card reveals a period of difficulty and stress, as Harry and his brother struggled to hold onto their company and pay off debts.

Card 7: Death

This card shows the death of Harry's brother, due to a heart attack. Harry believed that overwork and stress had contributed to his brother's early demise. Because Harry was beginning to experience health problems himself, he wanted to retire, before he was too old to enjoy himself.

Card 8: King of Pentacles

This card represents Harry, now the sole head of the family business.

Card 9: Page of Swords

After the death of his brother, Harry brought his son into the company. Swords suggest the nature of the business—communication—but this card also reveal the son's sense of insecurity and inexperience.

Card 10: The Chariot

Harry still feels a need to control the business. His son has some good ideas for updating the company by adding new equipment and techniques, but Harry is reluctant to take risks. This card shows the two men need to work together cooperatively for the good of the company.

Card 11: The Hanged Man

This card signifies the present and advises Harry to let go and allow his son to take over the business. Harry needs to learn to trust that all will be well.

Card 12: Nine of Pentacles

As the card of the near future, the Nine of Pentacles clearly indicates that the business is sound and will continue to prosper.

Card 13: Ten of Pentacles

The more distant future looks bright, too. The Ten of Pentacles represents family money and security, so this reading assured Harry that he could feel confident in his son's ability to run the company successfully.

Chapter 12

The Major Arcana

You now know about the significance of the Major Arcana as a journey to self-discovery and a course in enlightenment, and you are aware of the importance of these cards as archetypes, symbols of spiritual forces, and collective energies. Now examine each of the trumps individually to understand their symbols and the meanings of specific cards when they appear in a reading.

The Fool   0

Description

The Fool is a fascinating figure, yet he can be an ambiguous symbol. Related to the jester or the joker of the ordinary playing deck, which is often used as the wild card, he seems beyond ordinary cares and concerns.

In the Waite deck, The Fool is shown as a male figure standing on the edge of a cliff, as if about to step off into thin air, yet his gaze is brightly upward as if he expects the heavens to support him. In some decks, he is looking back over his shoulder, but he is always unconcerned—or unaware—of any danger lying ahead. Usually The Fool is youthful, but sometimes he is an older traveler who has obviously been on the road a long time.

Like a hobo, he carries all his worldly possessions tied in a small bag on a stick over his shoulder. Behind him, the Sun, symbol of the source of all life, is shining on his enterprise.

He may carry a rose, symbol of love, or a traveler's staff. Often he is dressed in bright colors, and the card's general impression is cheerful and sunny. Sometimes he is wearing the parti-colored costume and cap and bells of a medieval court jester, or he might be dressed in the plain garb of a wanderer.

Often he is accompanied by a dog, which is a symbol of your natural instincts, for a dog has the uncanny ability to follow an invisible trail, using his nose and other senses. The little dog gambols about The Fool, sometimes pulling him back from the danger ahead, suggesting that our instincts, if followed, do provide us with guidance on our life journeys.

Ordinarily, The Fool is shown as a person full of confidence—often the confidence of youth—and trust in the beneficence of the universe. He symbolizes that blind leap of faith that we all must take upon entering the journey of life itself, especially if that journey is spiritual.

Interpretation

When The Fool appears in a reading, depending on its position in the layout, it symbolizes someone who is about to embark on a new way of life. This may involve a physical journey, moving to a new place, starting a new job, or getting married or divorced. Often, the appearance of The Fool indicates a person who is ready to start on a spiritual path, who has made peace with the need to experience absolute faith and trust in the universe. In such a case, the person has no sense of worry or fear and feels that she is protected and that everything will turn out well. The person may be consciously in touch with the intuitive realm of his being, or she may simply be naive about what the future will bring. The Fool represents a state of openness and faith that she'll be supported in her adventure.

Mythologically, The Fool is linked to Dionysus, the early Greek god of sacred revels in honor of the Great goddess. In medieval courts, the king's fool, or jester, was given great license to make fun of everything and everybody with no threat of punishment or recrimination. His was a special role in a time when simpletons, or fools, were thought to possess divine madness, and irrational behavior was thought to be the result of possession by a god or spirit. Silly meant to be blessed. The Fool is also associated with Parsifal, the Arthurian knight known for his innocence, and with the Green Man of the Celt tradition, a god of new life and fertility and Nature's ability to restore itself.

Upright

At this time, you are out of sync with the rest of the world, but in a positive way. You may want to go out on your own, "Full speed ahead and damn the torpedoes." Or you may feel somehow isolated from the general group, a loner. Your experience of the current situation is different from those around you, which may make you feel as if you are marching to a different drummer, and you probably are. You need to listen to that different drummer, for this is the beat of your authentic self trying to get your attention.

Reversed

The time for independent action may not be right. You must discriminate between your personal fantasies—of going off on an adventure or chucking it all for a new track—and reality. The advice given to people who want to become writers or artists may apply here: "Don't quit your day job." This is not to say that what you want to do is invalid, only that you must consider all of the pros and cons carefully in the light of present reality.

The Magician

Description

The Magician is powerful, representing worldly wisdom and the control of unseen forces that operate in human lives. A deeply complex symbol, he is usually depicted as a male figure who stands alone before an array of the traditional magician's tools. In most decks, these are the symbols of the Minor Arcana suits, each of which corresponds to one of the four elements: a pentacle for earth, a sword for Air, a cup for Water, and a wand for Fire. To possess knowledge of these elements is to gain mastery in the world.

In the Waite deck, The Magician holds a wand, a phallic symbol, aloft in one hand toward the heavens, or the upper world of divine power, while his other hand points downward to the earth, the base of life. Above his head floats the symbol for infinity. He knows how to use his tools to connect the two worlds of spirituality, or metaphysics, and physicality, or the mundane plane of existence.

In the Waite deck, above him are trailing vines, like grapes, symbol of wine, a sacred drink in many cultures. At his feet is a garden of roses, lilies, and greenery. These represent the vegetable kingdom in general. Roses refer to desire and the five senses; lilies refer to purity and proper use of arcane knowledge.

The totality of these symbols tells us that The Magician is in possession of knowledge that enables him to manipulate the material world through aligning it with the spiritual plane, to create the desired circumstances.

Interpretation

The appearance of The Magician in a reading indicates latent powers, yet to be taken up and brought into manifestation. Also known as the Juggler, this card suggests that everything in the universe is spread out before us, and if we learn to use them correctly we can manifest the results we desire. These are literally the basic materials of creation, and it is the task of The Magician to handle them well, to manipulate and control them for beneficent purposes. This is mental work that affects the material realm.

Thus, The Magician shows us that what we consider to be illusion is another form of reality, and what we consider to be reality can be mere illusion. This is not trickery, but a deep understanding of how we must learn to use our intellects, our intuitive abilities, our personal talents, and our practical skills to mediate between the two worlds, both of which affect us simultaneously.

The Magician is a card of power, for just as a mage, or true magician, stands at the center of the universe with the tools and ability to manipulate it for his purposes, so does each of us create, or recreate, our own universes within ourselves, first in our minds, and then in our manifest realities. This card tells us that our nature is one with the nature of the universe. It suggests that we have the ability to control our own lives, that we can manipulate people, things, and events—so long as we go about it the right way and for the right ends.

The Magician's costume varies with different decks—from Egyptian to Greek to medieval—but he usually wears a belt. In the Waite deck, this is a coiled snake, the ourobouros, or snake biting his tail, an alchemical symbol for wholeness. This represents the power to heal through connecting the two worlds within one's self.

This card is primarily about self-development; as Tarot Arcanum One, it is the beginning of the road to spiritual enlightenment, the starting point. It does not say that we are already able to control our universes, but that we must learn what mode to use to gain our ends and reach our goals, whether they are spiritual or mundane.

Mythologically, the Magician corresponds to Hermes-Trismegistus, messenger of the gods and guide of souls in the underworld. As messenger of the gods, he has the ability to communicate between the celestial and earthly realms. As a guide, he mediates between our conscious daylight world and the unconscious, hidden recesses of the psyche, often in dreams. The Magician suggests the use of higher intuitive forces, which may appear as a flash of insight. The Magician can serve as an inner guide who, if we listen carefully, will prompt us to develop and fulfill our potential—from within.

Also know as "Le Bateleur," the Magician corresponds to the number One and to the first letter of the Hebrew alphabet, Aleph.

Upright

This is a situation of new beginnings and new choices. It indicates someone who is willing and able to manipulate the situation to achieve the desired ends. It suggests leadership potential, ambition, desire for action, and new relationships coming into being. The tools for whatever action you desire are already at hand, as is the knowledge for using them correctly. It is a time to evaluate the tools you have at your disposal and relate them properly to your aims.

Reversed

Now is not the time for change. It may be that you are not ready internally, or that you are not fully prepared in an external way. New directions are in the making, but patience is required for them to work out properly. You may be experiencing self-doubt about a new venture, or your spirits and vitality may be too low to accomplish the action required. Creativity abides in the latent stage, like a caterpillar in its cocoon, and there is no sense in rushing things prematurely. Wait until the time is ripe.

The High Priestess

Description

The High Priestess is a most mysterious card, representing that which has yet to be revealed, secret knowledge, the duality of life on earth. She symbolizes feminine spiritual power, or the goddess from whom all life comes and to whom all returns in the ever-cycling round of earthly existence.

She is depicted as a serene-faced female figure, sometimes seated with a book on her lap. In the Waite deck, this book bears the word Torah, but in other decks it is merely an open book or scroll suggesting the divine law that underlies the manifest universe. The scroll or book represents the Akashic Records, the divine repository of our lives past, present, and future. Sometimes, she is standing, holding a staff and pointing toward an unseen object in the distance, another indication of something yet to be revealed.

THE HIGH PRIESTESS

She sometimes sits or stands between two pillars, which represent the opposites of the dual nature of our world: good and evil, light and dark, truth and deception, positive and negative. She promises reconciliation of these opposites to those willing to follow the spiritual path of understanding universal law. In the Waite deck, The High Priestess sits at the doorway to the temple, which symbolizes the body, as if welcoming students to enter and learn her secrets. However, the crescent moon at her feet warns of the danger of releasing higher knowledge to those unprepared to handle it.

In the Waite deck, two pillars represent a doorway to the interior of life's mysteries, with The High Priestess as the guardian of the entryway. Also in the Waite deck, she sits against a background of pomegranates, a reference to Persephone, daughter of Demeter, who leaves the daylight, or upper world, for six months each year to tend to the dead in the underworld. In some decks, she carries flowers or is depicted against a background of vegetables and vegetation, another reference to the goddess, or Grain Mother.

On her breast, The High Priestess wears a cross, symbolic of the four elements—Fire, Earth, Air, and Water—held in balance. She wears a crown, usually a crescent, the horns of the moon, or a variant of it. In the Waite deck, between the horns sits a sphere, representative of the full moon, while the horns echo the images of the waxing and waning moon. The three lunar phases symbolize the three stages of womanhood: maiden, mother, crone. This particular card is reminiscent of the Egyptian mother goddess Hathor, who wears a similar headdress. Hathor can be considered a forerunner of Demeter/Persephone, as one who gives life and takes it back in due course.

Interpretation

When The High Priestess appears, she indicates that something hidden, or interior, is preparing to come forth or that the person needs to pay more attention to his inner world of dreams, imagination, and intuition. She advises you to develop awareness of the totality of yourself, the night side, so to speak, as well as the daylight personality and activities. Usually, the person is ready to accept the importance of developing this part of his life but may have been holding back out of fear or inertia.

The High Priestess may indicate that the person is attempting to hide something that needs to be revealed. Or she can mean that the person is too much involved in an isolated inner world and needs to reconcile the inner life with the outer one.

Psychologically, the underworld refers to the unconscious, or what is in the process of coming into being. In this twilight realm, of which dreams are a component, we encounter our inner selves through intuition and fantasy. The High Priestess is an image representing our potentials that have yet to be discovered and brought forth—our secret selves longing to be recognized.

The High Priestess is linked to the Egyptian goddess Isis, queen of the intellect, in her veiled form. Isis understands fully the workings of the universe and is familiar with both the upper world and the underworld, where her husband Osiris reigns. Her essence is divine wisdom and a deep knowledge of the laws that underlie and unite both realms. She knows the secrets of regeneration after death, of the transformative powers inherent in secret knowledge.

Upright

You are experiencing a high degree of awareness of the invisible world, where inner change takes place before it manifests in the outer, material world. Your attunement to these inner, invisible sources is acute now, and you are in a position to take advantage of this fact. You may want to remove yourself, literally, from your day-to-day life to go deeper into your inner core. Tune in to your inner voice and spiritual awareness.

Reversed

Something within you is seeking greater recognition of your inner needs, which you may have been neglecting, although at a deep level you are aware that something is stirring. You may be tuning in to yourself in a very private way, not wanting others to know about this activity. Those around you may notice that you seem vague, or not quite yourself, and you may be fending off comments about your not being here. Ignore them. You are in the process of finding your own personal way into your inner world and the riches it contains.

The Empress

Description

The Empress is a card of beauty and creativity, the matriarch incarnate, symbolic of the Universal Mother as monarch. She represents the social concept of the feminine in the maternal role: procreation, nurturing, the security and comforts of home, and domestic harmony.

The Empress is always a mature female figure, often seated on a throne. In some decks, she is standing in a field, surrounded by flowers and vegetation representative of the bounty of Mother Nature and her harvest. Full-breasted and sometimes pregnant, she symbolizes fruitfulness and earthly abundance.

As a symbol of The Empress's royal position, she sometimes holds a scepter and wears an imperial crown of great magnificence. In many decks, a shield or coat of arms leans against her throne, at her feet. In the Waite deck, this is heart-shaped and bears the astrological symbol for Venus, which also appears in many other decks. Venus is the planet of love, beauty, desires, and pleasure—the quintessential traditional feminine symbol.

Interpretation

When The Empress appears, a strong feminine energy is at work. As a mother figure and representative of the traditional female role, The Empress is a creative force that works for harmony. She brings disparate things together, reconciling differences, like a mother running a household must do. This is a card of emotional control and making things work congenially toward a common social goal.

The Empress also refers to the person's emotional and physical resources—for nurturing, healing, feeding, and supporting other people. Often, there is a situation in the person's life where love and nurturing are required—sometimes by the person herself, sometimes by others in the environment. This card is related to the caretaking process and may refer to the way the person was mothered, for the first and most significant relationship you form is with your mother, and this relationship has a direct bearing on all subsequent relationships. Sometimes The Empress indicates that the person either had an overbearing "smother mother," or is acting out that role.

As a female authority, The Empress's appearance may signify, depending on its place in the spread, the person's need to become that female authority, especially if the person is a woman. In a man's reading, the indication is that he needs to recognize the feminine component of himself and acknowledge its power to unite opposing forces.

The Empress is linked to all of the mother goddesses of antiquity, but especially to Greek Hera, the wife of Zeus and the quintessential matriarchal maternal figure. She is called Juno by the Romans and has an asteroid named after her. As a primary symbol for feminine fertility, she is associated not only with Demeter, Ceres, and all of the great fertile mother-goddesses of the pagan religion but also with the Virgin Mary of the Christian tradition.

Also called "L'Imperatrice," The Empress corresponds to the number three and to the Hebrew letter Gimel.

Upright

You are in a position of nurturing someone else, or several others. This could be caring for children or the sick or being supportive of a spouse or friend in need. This card could also refer to a pregnancy, or the desire for a pregnancy. It is appropriate for you to be nurturing now, for you have the inner strength and the ability to do so without harming or depleting yourself.

Reversed

This is a time for you to be nurturing yourself. You may have been spending too much time caring for others (or you may have recently had a child whose demands have worn you out). This is an indication that you need to take time out for yourself instead of neglecting your own personal needs. This is a call for self-love and the awareness that you deserve the same care and attention you give to your loved ones. Maintain a balance between the needs of others and your own, equally valid, needs.

The Emperor

Description

The Emperor is a figure of supreme authority, as his title suggests. He is usually shown seated on a throne, sometimes flanked by animals. In the Waite deck, these are ram's heads, symbolic of masculine power. He wears robes over a full suit of armor, holds a scepter in the shape of the Egyptian ankh, and is crowned elaborately. In some decks, his shield, bearing the symbol of the imperial eagle, leans against the throne. He is clearly a figure to be reckoned with. Often he appears outdoors, against a backdrop of mountains, another reference to worldly power. His age and position of

authority speak of experience and wisdom gained. Although he is depicted as a warrior, his attitude is one of kindness as the beneficent ruler of his empire.

While at rest, The Emperor's attitude suggests he is willing to fight for what is right and what is his duty to protect. He is the executive, or leader, who has reached the summit of authority and achieved worldly power.

Thus, The Emperor is a father figure, as The Empress is a mother figure. He lays down the ideals, morals, and aspirations for the entire family to follow.

He is the builder in the material world who strives to make constructions of lasting value and importance.

Interpretation

When The Emperor appears in a reading, look for issues related to authority. Although The Emperor represents worldly power and wisdom, he is not simply a figure who gives commands to others. His achievement is to understand that peace and security require a willingness and ability to defend it. "The price of freedom is eternal vigilance."

The Emperor is related to Zeus, the father-god of the Greek pantheon. The Romans called him Jupiter; the Norse called him Thor. All these deities were known for throwing thunderbolts, or lightning. In some decks The Emperor carries lightning instead of the ankh.

The Emperor is a teacher figure, and what he teaches is the meaning of power and how to use it in this world. Though not overtly aggressive, he tells us that it is necessary sometimes to take up arms against evil forces. With The Emperor, there is no waffling about what is right and good, no rationalizing that the ends justify the means. As a protective male force, especially of the home and of domestic harmony, he personifies the ideal that what is worth having is worth fighting for.

The Emperor in a reading can also indicate issues concerning one's biological father, or authority figures in general. He can show that the time has arrived to become the authority figure, rather than depending on others to provide protection. The Emperor often appears when the person is struggling to achieve personal independence, to overcome the inner parent tapes, to become his own person. The Emperor says that one must, often late in life, come to terms with what father means in his life, and reconcile related issues.

When The Emperor appears, he can be an indication that the individual's real father has either recently died or may die soon, a situation that can bring up feelings of being abandoned by a protective father figure. Even if the personal father was a negative factor, there is always a yearning for someone else to take care of us, protect us, and advise us. It is important to remember though that separation from the parents is a crucial stage in human development and must be accomplished. It's also possible that someone in the person's life is acting as a father figure, perhaps a boss or a husband. Whether this is positive or negative will be indicated by the placement of the card in the layout.

From a pagan perspective, because The Emperor follows The Empress, he represents the Horned god who always accompanied the Great Mother goddess, of which Pan is the most common figure. As consort to The Empress, he represents parenthood and masculine creativity.

Also known as "L'Empereur," The Emperor corresponds to the number four and to the Hebrew letter Dalet.

Upright

This is an indication that you are involved with the established order, or with someone who represents the establishment. You may have a need to identify with a powerful group, whether religious, ideological, intellectual, economic, or political—to be one of them. Or you may be associating with someone else who has this need.

Reversed

You may be in conflict with the established order—perhaps at your job or with your family, religion, or ethnic group. Perhaps you feel pressured to accept responsibilities you don't want, or don't feel capable of handling. You may have recently experienced a loss of power, such as through downsizing, or you may lack the energy required to reach your goals. A need for more experience, drive, or improved health could be indicated.

The Hierophant

Description

The Hierophant is a figure with authority and power, like The Emperor, but The Hierophant's power is of a spiritual nature whereas The Emperor's is temporal. Often, he is shown as a religious leader, such as the Pope of Roman Catholicism. Some decks title him The Pope. He is usually seen seated on a throne, dressed in priestly raiment, crowned, and holding a scepter. His implements will vary according to the religious theme of the deck.

THE HIEROPHANT

His scepter symbolizes the three worlds—the physical, the astral, and the etheric. His free hand is held aloft in a position of blessing. Two or three acolytes may stand before him, either as participants, supplicants, or students, deferring to his wisdom and understanding him as a representative of religious authority.

Like The Emperor, he contains within himself the wisdom of a spiritual calling, and like The High Priestess, The Hierophant frequently sits or stands between two pillars, which signify the duality of matter and spirit.

In this role, The Hierophant can be seen as a teacher to those who seek the keys to the sacred Mysteries. The Waite deck shows two crossed keys below him, representing the intellect and intuition and the need to use them in tandem. He is responsible for making spiritual decisions for others and for blessing them. Unlike The High Priestess, whose world is primarily internal and ephemeral, The Hierophant's influence is of this world, and his spirituality can be achieved through conscious choices made on an intellectual basis.

Interpretation

The Hierophant suggests that the person has chosen a religion or philosophy with which to guide his or her life. In such a case, there is usually a great deal of loyalty to it, whatever the person's concept of god may be. Sometimes the card indicates disentangling yourself from such an association.

In some organized religions, the supreme deity does not speak to the individual directly, or to the general populace. Therefore, institutionalized religion makes use of human interpreters who convey the word of god (the Divine Will) to their followers.

The Hierophant symbolizes any organized institution—be it religious, philosophical, educational, spiritual, or temporal—that exerts authority over its followers or participants, a kind of mind control. In such groups, there is always a person, or a group of people, who insist that their way is the only way, that theirs is the ultimate truth.

Therefore, when The Hierophant appears, the idea of choice is being presented. At this stage of your spiritual development, you are challenged to remain a follower or to break out and find your own individual truth. This card suggests that you have the opportunity—and often the desire—to choose your own road to salvation, to interpret the word of god in your own way. The Hierophant asks, will you continue to depend on an outside authority, or will you learn to think for yourself? The answer is yours alone, and there may be considerable conflict concerning the issue, but what you decide will affect the rest of your life.

FACT

As a spiritual teacher whose task it is to connect the world of humans with that of the gods, to forge a link between the material and spiritual worlds, The Hierophant is a pontifex, an ancient word that meant maker of bridges, and that is used to designate a priest.

The Hierophant is linked in myth to the Centaur, or Chiron, teacher of Apollo, the sun god and healer. Half man, half horse, the Centaur represents the quest for meaning in life. Related to the sign of Sagittarius, which represents higher learning and the dissemination of knowledge, the Centaur is a teacher figure who guides the spiritual seeker to find a connection or bridge between the two worlds—the inner and outer, the material and immaterial. The Hierophant's understanding goes beyond organized religion and is not based on any rigid dogma but on the truth of the unconscious inner world of the psyche.

Also known as "Le Pape," or "The Pope," The Hierophant corresponds to the number five and to the Hebrew letter He.

Upright

A traditional factor is active in your life, whether it is a religion, a philosophy, a social organization, or another authoritative group. You feel a great deal of loyalty to this tradition or group and find it supportive. You choose to live in accordance with the beliefs you share with the group or organization.

You may aspire to become a leader, or you may have a close relationship with the leader. This group or tradition serves you in many ways, inspirationally, as a teacher, as emotional support. There may also be a judgmental quality involved. You are expected to follow a certain set of beliefs, and if you fail, you are called to account.

Reversed

You may wish to overthrow an old tradition—religious, ideological, intellectual, or cultural—that you feel is suffocating you or simply no longer serves your needs. You want to live by whatever philosophy or belief structure resonates with your true nature. You want to direct your actions your own way, even if this puts you into conflict with some established tradition. Perhaps your faith is being challenged in some way and you must re-evaluate tenets heretofore taken for granted. You want to be accountable to yourself alone.

The Lovers

Description

One popular image on The Lovers card shows a young couple either nude or clothed, standing apart or touching. Above them is an angel-like figure with its wings spread out over them, its hands held above their heads in a gesture of blessing. The Waite deck depicts them as Adam and Eve, standing respectively before the Tree of Eternal Life and the Tree of the Knowledge of Good and Evil. Imagery in other decks suggests choice is involved as well as the possibility of union.

THE LOVERS.

Some decks include three people, as if the third party—who might be another young person or an older parental figure—were an influence in their relationship. In decks where three figures are shown, a winged, cupidlike figure on a cloud may appear and point an arrow in the direction of one of the women.

Interpretation

Although many readers interpret this card as representing romantic love, it is allegorically a statement about union of opposites, whether those are a man and woman or inner conditions of conflict. The Lovers refers to discrimination in making choices. The male and female figures are symbols not only of human love and marriage but also of the dual nature within ourselves. We all have opposite traits and inner dichotomies that need to be reconciled. Partners of any kind often experience conflict that requires making choices, sometimes tough ones, and effecting reconciliation.

When The Lovers card appears, it points to the need to heal an inner rift. Although it can herald a romantic involvement, it most often turns up when a critical life decision must be made, sometimes in connection with a love relationship. There are obstacles to be overcome, both within and without. This card suggests that you are at a crossroads. You have to consider all of the ramifications of the situation and choose carefully to further your own development and to accommodate the needs of others in the situation.

ALERT!

In decks that show one young man and two young women on the Lovers card, the implication is that he must choose between them, another indication that this card is as much about choice as it is about partnership.

In mythology, The Lovers card reflects Eros, the son of the great goddess of love and beauty, Aphrodite. Eros was named Cupid by the Romans, and it is his job to shoot the arrows of love, which was considered a form of madness, at unsuspecting youths. Thus, Eros was often depicted blindfolded to represent that love is blind. But Eros has another role—to guide us toward our true destiny, which is to say, "Do what you love and everything else will follow naturally."

Also called "L'Amoureux," The Lovers corresponds to the number six and to the Hebrew letter Vav.

Upright

This is a card of cooperation, of working together in coalition with others to accomplish joint purposes. It stands for attraction of any kind, not only the romantic variety, and for any venture requiring harmony, union, and cooperation. A choice between two factors of equal worth may be required, but the choice you make will be the right one. Two or more forces or people may have come together in your life in pursuit of a common goal. This may be a temporary conjunction for some specific purpose or it might be a long-term relationship.

Reversed

Your own disparate parts are in cooperation with each other, and warring factors of your personality are coming together. You might realize you can be beautiful and brainy at the same time, or strong and gentle simultaneously. Whatever the case, you are finding a way to bring together what was causing conflict before and melding these differences into a system of mutual support for yourself. Sometimes this card indicates a delay of some project that needs mutual cooperation or that you are trying to force cooperation among basically incompatible elements.

The Chariot

Description

The Chariot is usually depicted as a strong male figure holding the reins of two Sphinx-like beasts, one black and one white. Sometimes the beasts are unicorns or other mythical creatures like Pegasus, the winged horse, or griffins. The charioteer is fully armored and carries a scepter suggesting royalty or that he is in the service of royalty. In some decks, he wears a belt and a skirt decorated with zodiacal glyphs, symbolic of time. On his shoulders are crescent moons indicating emotional factors and unconscious habit patterns that need to be changed.

THE CHARIOT.

In some decks, the charioteer holds no reins—he uses sheer willpower to keep his steeds moving together in a forward direction. The beasts pulling the chariot signify the opposing forces, which were reconciled at the stage of The Lovers and represent the person's mastery of these opposing forces and control over inner conflicts. This card suggests that before taking on outer enemies or obstacles, it is essential to be in charge of the inner opposites and stop fighting yourself. The Chariot is a symbol for the self and its direction, as is any vehicle, such as an automobile, that appears in a dream.

Interpretation

When The Chariot appears, there is a need to be in control of competing forces, whether these are inner conflicts, people, or a situation in your life that requires you to take command to reach your goals. Like the celebrated but seldom achieved bipartisanship of government, the solution to the problem at hand is to take the middle road between the conflicting elements.

You may feel unequal to the challenge of controlling the multiple factors of a given situation, but if you choose to just go with the flow and make the best of where it takes you, you will succeed. Once you have resolved the conflict within your own mind, even if that requires considerable struggle, you will be able to move forward. To do this, you need firm resolve— self-mastery. With a strategy determined by clear thinking and a sense of purpose, you will overcome all obstacles.

Receiving The Chariot in a reading, depending on its position in the spread, is generally favorable. It indicates you have the means to triumph over all obstacles and stay the course you have set for yourself. It can also mean that assistance is on the way as a result of your own strength and determination. It may suggest you are in the process of transforming yourself and your ways of thinking and behaving to create a firm foundation from which to go forward and achieve your desires. At this time you are keenly aware of how to use your past experience to reach a major goal and you are in touch with deep inner resources.

At a literal level, The Chariot relates to travel and transportation and could mean changing your mode of transport, such as buying a new car or traveling by rail or some other form of wheeled vehicle.

The Chariot is related to the myths in many cultures. Helios, the Greek sun god, drove a chariot of fire across the heavens. In the Hindu culture, the Lord of the World drives his chariot along the road of time. In ancient Rome, the god of war, Mars, was depicted triumphantly riding to victory in his chariot. These mythic images suggest that the charioteer has triumphed over all conflicting forces, found his true path in life, and is now being guided by intuition and a sense of clear and unambiguous purpose.

Also known as "Le Chariot," The Chariot corresponds to the number seven, which is linked with the hidden rhythms of the universe, and to the Hebrew letter Zayin.

Upright

Victory is assured! Things are moving fast, and transition is occurring rapidly. You are holding things together successfully, uniting opposite energies to stay on track. This is a situation where you are completely, totally involved, and happily so. Whatever task is at hand can be accomplished. Though the pace is faster than usual, you are attuned to the rhythm of it and keeping up with the changes that are happening—at your job, in a relationship, or in some community or worldly involvement. You are sensitive to the minor adjustments you must constantly make to keep things going in the right direction.

The wheels of the chariot signify the ever-changing life cycles. The animals are pulling in opposite directions, and the charioteer is holding the reins taut to keep the beasts in tandem—a symbolic statement of the need to master and reconcile conflicting forces, both inner and outer.

Reversed

When The Chariot is reversed, the changes and transitions are happening internally, but at a rapid rate. Things are moving so fast that you feel out of control and seem to be struggling to keep your head above water. It may seem that you are being pulled in two directions at once and are stressed out by the pressure. It's time to choose a direction carefully, to accept the process of inner transition as a positive one, but to do so with clarity about your direction in life. The more you can tune in to your own transition process, the more control over it you can exert.

Strength

Description

The Waite and Grey decks show Strength as number Eight; many other decks, however, show Justice as Eight and Strength as Eleven. This book follows Waite's ordering of the cards.

Most decks depict Strength as a woman in relationship to a lion. Some writers see this as a struggle, but in many decks there does not appear to be any conflict. In fact, she seems to be controlling the lion and may even seem affectionate toward him. A few decks show a strong young man wrestling with the lion. The man is bare-handed, which suggests that he needs no weapon.

In the Waite deck, the woman is bending over the lion in a gesture of gentleness, closing his jaws as if she expects no resistance to her touch. She is garbed in a flowing garment and wears a garland of flowers in her hair. Above her head is the symbol for infinity. In other decks, she caresses the lion, rides atop him, or stands beside him.

Although many interpreters view this card as emblematic of the struggle with one's inner animal nature, others see it as symbolic of self-confidence and inner strength, of being in harmony with one's instinctive nature. The woman is taming or making friends with the powerful force represented by the animal nature. Though the lion is clearly the more physically powerful of the two, the woman represents human courage and willpower that masters the instinctive realm not by force, but by cooperation.

Interpretation

When Strength appears in a reading, you are exhibiting moral courage and fortitude. You have learned to work in harmony with your own instinctive nature, to listen to it and hear its whisperings. As in tales of the hero's journey, the seeker often meets with animals, representative of the instinctive realm, who guide and help him on his way. Strength indicates that you have come through difficulties and learned to rely on inner strength to solve your problems.

FACT

Strength relates to the pagan goddess known as the Lady of the Beasts, who possessed understanding of the ways of nature. In ancient pagan times, this goddess reigned supreme. Later, she was personified by the Greeks as Artemis, goddess of the hunt, and by the Romans as Diana.

This is a time when faith in yourself will pay off, when your position is strong because you have made yourself strong through suffering trials and tribulations without being defeated by them. It is a time to let people around you know who you are—especially anyone who has been dominating you.

The indication is that it is the feminine principle that does the work of reconciling the mental-rational facility with that of the intuitive-instinctive nature. The feminine is always in closer touch with nature than the masculine. Whether the reading is for a man or a woman, the same meaning applies. The lesson is that we do not conquer our animal natures by brute force (which is the typical masculine mode of approach to obstacles) but by gentleness and feeling our way into rapport with the instinctive side.

Depending on the placement of the card in the spread and the question being asked, Strength indicates that what is required in the situation is for spiritual strength to replace or overcome physical strength.

Also known as "La Force," Strength corresponds to the number eight and to the Hebrew letter Chet.

Upright

You have come through severe trials and triumphed. You have found your deep inner strength, and it will see you through whatever comes your way. You are firmly connected to the instinctual world (represented by the lion) and you are able to make friends with it and control it for your own benefit and that of others. Your positive connection to your animal self will protect and care for you. Your inner drives are in harmony with your outer needs, and your instinctive nature is supporting all that you do or hope to do. At this time, your logical mind—if it is in conflict with your intuition—is not as important in making decisions as is what you feel to be right for you. Whatever decisions you make, or actions you take, will be successful.

Reversed

You are struggling to gain your own in a situation that is difficult and that may be harmful to your ultimate good. As a result, you are experiencing an upsurge from your inner, instinctive nature that is calling upon you to pay attention to your own needs instead of following the orders of others. It is a time of travail, but you will eventually overcome the difficulties and come out on top. Others may think you are behaving in a way that seems to them illogical or contrary to what is normal or generally accepted. Regardless, your basic instincts of survival say this is a time for change and expressing your individuality.

The Hermit

Description

THE HERMIT.

The Hermit is a guide figure represented as an old man, often bearded, holding a lighted lantern aloft in one hand and a staff in the other. He is usually dressed in the long robes of an anchorite or monk, plain and unadorned except for, in some decks, a knotted or tasseled cord around the waist. He radiates the wisdom of the archetypal elder figure, the sage of myth and legend.

The Hermit is generally standing, sometimes walking, looking ahead at what only he can see— your future. He is an ancient who is experienced on many levels and now functions as a teacher and guide. Mountains in the distance suggest he has reached the heights and returned to our plane to assist us in our development. He is wise in the ways of all the worlds, visible and invisible, material and immaterial.

The Hermit's slightly bent posture and serious expression link him to Father Time, or Saturn—the planet that symbolizes boundaries and limitations, the obstacles and lessons that appear on everyone's life course. His solitude suggests the periodic need to withdraw from the hectic everyday world to regain perspective through silent reflection.

Interpretation

When The Hermit appears in a reading, it can mean that a guide figure is at hand, offering help. The querent must make an effort to connect with this guide or consciously begin a search for the truth. A second interpretation is that the questioner must voluntarily withdraw from contact with the outer world for a time to search her soul for the meaning of life. The implication is that the inner work needs to be done now, and that Spirit cannot speak to you if you are distracted by the noise of everyday life. The answers lie in silence, and the work can only be done alone.

The Hermit travels alone, a seeker after truth, lighting the way ahead for those who follow. He needs no trappings of rank or royalty, wears no adornment, and carries no baggage. His goal is to search and to show others their true direction. His wooden staff symbolizes his connection to the forces of nature and the instinctual realm.

Whichever interpretation seems to suit the querent and the question being put to the Tarot cards, the overall meaning is the same: the time has come to reunite with the Source, whether for guidance or inner balance. Sometimes, the guide figure may represent a person, such as a counselor of some sort—a therapist or clergy person—but usually it refers to inner guidance, or getting in touch with a guide from the other side.

The Hermit is linked to Uranus and Cronos, the god of time. The myth of these two fathers—both deposed by their sons because they refused to face up to the facts of their inevitable ends—warns us to accept the reality that all must grow old and die for new life to emerge. The death may not be a physical one but the shedding of life-denying ideas that serve as limitations on the Spirit, that we may renew ourselves in rebirth.

Also known as "L'Hermite," The Hermit corresponds to the number nine and to the Hebrew letter Tet.

Upright

The Hermit is a guide figure, waiting patiently for you to turn to him for advice. Usually, you are aware of his influence, but you may be ignoring it. At this time, you may be involved actively in seeking guidance from the invisible world. You may be isolating yourself in some way, seeking solitude, wisdom, and inner peace. You want to gain some perspective on your life, and you are open to the inner guidance that is available to you upon request.

Reversed

You have been putting off giving yourself the solitude you need to sort out your life and the issues you are currently confronting. Keeping busy can be a form of denial. It is time—or long past time—for you to engage in some self-evaluation, to reflect on your aims and goals, associations, relationships, career, and life path. You may find yourself wanting to withdraw to think things through; stop avoiding it.

The Wheel of Fortune

Description

Invariably, The Wheel of Fortune card shows a wheel—often with eight spokes, a reference to the eight Pagan holidays that mark the ever-turning cycles of life, death, and rebirth. The Wheel is also a symbol for the sun's path across the sky. Human or mythical figures may also be attached to the wheel.

The Waite deck shows a sphinx holding a sword at the top of the wheel, calmly watching as the karmic wheel revolves. Around the wheel are letters that spell "Rota," a reference to the "Royal Road of the Tarot." The ascending figure on the right is a jackal-headed man, called Hermanubis, who is known for keen eyesight. A serpent descending on the left side represents the earth and the sexual energy that arises from it. Above and below, at the four corners of the card, are winged creatures holding open books. These correspond to the bull, the lion, the eagle, and the man, symbols of the fixed signs of the zodiac, Taurus, Leo, Scorpio, and Aquarius respectively. In the Christian tradition, these refer to Matthew, Mark, Luke, and John.

WHEEL of FORTUNE.

Other decks show monkeylike figures caught on the wheel, or people in flowing robes wearing garlands in their hair, or eight young women between the spokes wearing expressions that range from joy to despair. The suggestion is that the figures are rising and falling through the various life cycles as the wheel turns. Occasionally, the wheel stands alone, obviously turning, or it is a disc decorated with symbols suspended in the sky. Sometimes a blindfolded woman is turning the wheel.

Interpretation

When The Wheel of Fortune appears in a reading, it means that something has been put in motion over which you now have little or no control. You are being forced to accept the action of the forces of destiny, to get in tune with them, and to align yourself with their aims. Generally, however, the outcome is considered favorable.

These forces already set in motion foretell of changing circumstances, usually for the better, beneficial changes that will promote your growth and advancement. Balance may be an issue if you are resisting change, but you now have no choice but to go along with whatever process is working in your life. The Wheel of Fortune is a reminder that every period of intense activity must be followed by a fallow time of rest and inactivity. Where you are in your own personal cycle will be shown by the other cards in the spread. This card almost always heralds good fortune coming as a result of what you yourself have put into motion, even if you aren't totally aware of what you have done to initiate the process. You may have applied for a new job, met a new person, begun a romance, decided to take a college course, or had a chance encounter that got the ball rolling—or the wheel turning. It means a new phase, possibly the need to make an important decision, or even a totally unexpected circumstance developing that will change your life.

Also called "La Roue de Fortune," The Wheel of Fortune corresponds to the number ten and to the Hebrew letter Yod.

Upright

You have done something—quit a job, made travel reservations, begun or ended a relationship, or opted out of a friendship or other situation. Destiny has been set in motion, and all will turn out as it is intended. There's very little more you have to do except to go with the flow. There may be unexpected turns of events—such as meeting people while you are on a journey or receiving an offer of some sort—but they too are part of the grand plan for your life. This card is the precursor of good fortune.

FACT

The Wheel of Fortune is linked to the three Fates. One spins the thread of life, the second weaves it, and the third cuts it. Thus, The Wheel of Fortune is a reminder of the mysterious cycles of life, death, and rebirth and of the invisible forces that measure them out to each of us.

Reversed

You are holding back your own destiny by your refusal to make the necessary changes or take the required actions. Refusing to set things in motion is causing stagnation and frustration. Although you rationalize the fact that you are standing still, you are uncomfortable with the situation. You think you are waiting for the propitious time, but fear of the unknown is blocking you. You may be fantasizing about what you want to do, but you have to take action before anything can happen. You may experience delays in your projects because of lack of commitment. Ask the universe to show you the way and fearlessly follow the direction you are given. It's time to quit being wishy-washy and get on with what you already know you need to do.

Justice

Description

The Justice card usually depicts a female figure, robed, sometimes armored, and crowned. She holds an upright sword in one hand and in the other perfectly balanced scales. In some modern decks, she is either a nude figure with arms outstretched in absolute even balance, or she is shown standing between a large set of scales while holding a smaller set.

Unlike the contemporary image of Justice as blindfolded, this Justice is open-eyed, suggesting that divine justice rather than the laws of man are at work here. She stares straight ahead, suggesting that divine justice is not bound by human limitations and that divine law is not subject to error and bias.

Interpretation

When the Justice card appears in a reading, it can indicate that an actual legal matter is pending or being considered. Whatever the situation, you must weigh many factors to make a reasoned and factual assessment, i.e., judgment, of the matter at hand. The Justice card warns you to receive guidance from your inner self, not to rely solely on human advisors. Also, it cautions prudence and care, the need to deliberate calmly and carefully before taking action or concluding an outcome.

If other people are involved, you would be wise to take their point of view into consideration, for issues of fairness are paramount now. You can expect legal matters, if a part of the circumstances, to proceed smoothly, fairly, and in a dispassionate manner. Be confident that Justice will prevail as a result of your own temperate behavior and rational thought. Depending on what other cards appear in the spread, a third party could come to your aid and help you get the fair outcome you deserve. This card can also represent anyone involved with the legal profession—a lawyer, a judge, witnesses, law enforcement officers, and the like.

ALERT!

Justice may describe a matter in which some sort of rectification is necessary, where wrongs must be righted, in a spiritual or personal sense, regardless of whether any laws have been broken. This is a card of karma and suggests you are reaping what you have sown. The card may be advising you to become more balanced or fair-minded.

Justice is related to a mythic lineage that stretches back to ancient Egypt. In Egyptian mythology, the goddess Maat—whose name means truth and justice—stood in the underworld. She held a pair of scales upon which she weighed the newly dead person's soul against the Feather of Truth to decide if the soul was worthy to pass into the realm of Osiris, god of the underworld.

Also known as "La Justice," Justice corresponds to the number eleven and to the Hebrew letter Kaf.

Upright

You are concerned with external circumstances, waiting for the right time to act. You may be seeking justice in personal or business affairs, or you may be involved with a lawsuit. In any case, it is important to resolve the situation in a way that is fair to all participants. You must create a balance, not only of power but in terms of your emotional reactions to the situation at hand. This is a time for moderation in all things, for creating harmony to facilitate relationships. You may be called upon to arbitrate for others, or may be subject to arbitration yourself. Your judgment is good at this time, and you are not swayed by personal considerations or bias.

Reversed

Justice in reverse indicates delays in legal matters or unfairness in some other situation, and you might become angry and hostile. If you are the person in power, you may be unduly severe in meting out punishment. If you are in the powerless position, you may be festering with resentment over being treated unfairly. Your state of equilibrium is out of whack, and you may be swinging from one extreme to another. The antidote is to balance your own life and become less dependent upon outside influences.

The Hanged Man
Description

The Hanged Man is a tantalizing figure. Usually a male, hanging upside down by one leg, The Hanged Man's expression is serene, as if he is thoroughly enjoying his state. Suspended as he is by one foot, he appears to be engaged in a rather bizarre form of meditation or ritual.

THE HANGED MAN.

In the Waite deck, The Hanged Man is shown hanging from a tree. Its roots are in the ground and the crosspiece that supports him sprouts leaves. Some authorities say this is the Tree of Life itself. Around The Hanged Man's head is a golden halo, like the rays of the sun. Yellow is the color of Mercury, the planet of the mind. Other decks picture only the horizontal beam, but it too has leaves on it, showing that it is living wood.

Interpretation

Many writers see The Hanged Man as a card of self-sacrifice and martyrdom, but others view this tantalizing card as voluntary surrender to the process of achieving enlightenment. It may require giving up superficial pleasures and trivial activities in pursuit of a more spiritual way of life. The word sacrifice derives from the Latin *sacra fice,* which means to make sacred. Therefore, The Hanged Man may represent a sacred pursuit.

When this card appears in a reading, depending on its position in the layout, the person has usually received a call to follow a less materialistic way of life. You are ready for whatever personal sacrifice is needed, or you are preparing to make such a gesture. You may need to pause momentarily and suspend ordinary activities to better realize where you are headed spiritually.

FACT

Often, The Hanged Man signifies going through a major transformation, perhaps caused by illness or some loss. The result has shaken up your old way of life and made you realize that there is more to life than money, material goods, and physical reality.

This card can indicate that a new commitment to the development of the inner self is demanded. You might need to spend time alone to re-evaluate just what is and what is not important to you. It may be very difficult to let go of old patterns—a relationship, a job, a worldview, a lifestyle, or a group of other people—but letting go is essential to your continued growth.

The Hanged Man is related to all of the dying and resurrected gods of mythology, of which there are many. Odin was the Norse god who voluntarily hung for nine days from the windy tree called Yggdrasil, another form of the World Tree, to achieve knowledge of the runes and magic. Attis was a Greek who bled to death under a pine tree. The pagan world was filled with corn gods who were sacrificed annually so that their blood, sprinkled on the cornfields, would produce an abundant harvest. Later on this sacrifice became ritual instead of literal, to symbolize that we die to be reborn in Spirit. In the Christian tradition, Jesus' death on the cross depicts this sacrifice.

Also known as "Le Pendu," The Hanged Man corresponds to the number twelve and to the Hebrew letter Lamed.

Upright

You are suspended between the past and the future; a new direction for your life is in the making. It is a time for a new perspective. Look at things from a different angle to make necessary readjustments. You need to make a clean break with the past and concentrate on becoming spiritually attuned. Readjustment is needed, but the good news is there's no hurry. Take your time and make the right decisions about where you truly want to take your life at this time and for the long term. Pay attention to your inner development and be prepared to dance to a different drummer in the future.

Reversed

You are at a crossroads but are at a standstill because you have become stuck on the material plane and are neglecting your spiritual development. You may be in denial about your real needs, which could be causing depression, dissatisfaction, or apathy. You feel that any effort will be futile. This is because you are not being true to your inner Self. You may be sacrificing some part of your life unnecessarily because of a martyr complex and a refusal to make decisions. It's time to end such behavior and commit yourself to a worthwhile goal that will lead to your higher good. This may require turning your world upside down.

Death

Description

The Death card tends to frighten people who see it come up in a reading, but despite its grim depiction it symbolizes the transforming powers of life, death, and rebirth. Many decks picture a skeleton with a scythe grinning toothily and wearing a black hooded robe. The Waite deck pictures Death as a man in black armor riding a white charger, suggesting the perpetual movement of the cycles of life and death.

The knight carries a banner on which is embroidered the mystical white rose, symbol of pure and true love. The rose with five petals represents the five senses of material life combined with the immortality of the heart, or soul. Greeting the knight with hands outstretched in blessing or supplication is a priest figure wearing a mitered cardinal's hat. Two children look on in awe. In the background, the sun is rising, a sign of resurrection, over a body of water representing the unconscious realm.

Other decks show barren backgrounds; sometimes severed body parts are lying about randomly. One deck features the four horses of the Apocalypse riding through a stormy sky. Another presents a black-robed and hooded faceless figure standing in a woods, who appears to be supporting with one outstretched arm a huge white rose that dominates the card visually.

Death is related to such figures as the Hindu goddess, Kali, who wears a necklace of skulls, and to the Greek Hades, god of the underworld, renamed Pluto by the Romans. Also called "La Mort," Death corresponds to the number thirteen, which is the number of lunar months in a year.

Interpretation

The Death card in a reading rarely foreshadows a physical death. What it means is the end, or death, of a cycle. Whenever a stage in one's life ends, there is a need for mourning. It is only the refusal to accept that something is ending—trying desperately to hold on to what is clearly over—that causes trouble. Employing cosmetic means to stave off the approach of age, for instance, is a useless effort to avoid the inevitable. What gives importance and meaning to this card is the querent's acceptance of the change that cannot be avoided. Thus, in essence, the ultimate message of the Death card is the promise that new life follows disintegration.

Upright

Contrary to the grim illustration, the Death card is actually positive, for it indicates a transformation for the better. It does not portend actual physical death. Usually, the person is experiencing a metamorphosis of some sort, a destruction of the old, outworn circumstances that have been holding back new development. Patterns you once found workable are no longer effective. The old ways must be destroyed to make room for the new that is coming into being.

Reversed

You are putting off making necessary changes, usually out of fear. You feel that others are standing in your way, but it's really yourself who's blocking you. You're stuck in old habit patterns that you know need to be changed, but you don't want to put forth the effort to alter them even though you are unhappy with the current situation. Whether you recognize it or not, you are going through some internal changes that will eventually lead to external reforms. But at the moment you would rather not participate. You may be depressed or in a state of apathy, the result of refusing to accept the necessary process of psychological death, which leads to rebirth. The way out is to face up to your stagnation, frustration, and unhappiness. Jettison any relationships that aren't working. Begin to make the decisions that will throw out the old and ring in the new.

Temperance
Description

This lovely card often features a winged angel—male, female, or androgynous. In the Waite deck, the angel is standing in a stream bordered by flowers, with the rising sun shining in the background. In most decks, the figure is pouring liquid—the elixir of life—from a golden vessel into a silver one in a continuous stream, suggesting the interplay of the material and spiritual worlds and the eternal flow of the waters of life. The word vessel is related to the great Mother goddesses of antiquity, and the body is often referred to as the vessel of the soul. Thus, both the angelic figure and the cups are symbolic references to the feminine principle of cooperation, balance, harmony, receptivity, and creativity.

Interpretation

Temperance, as its name suggests, is about moderation in all things. When Temperance appears in a reading, depending on its position in the spread, you are being cautioned to have patience, which may be difficult under the circumstances. However, the circumstances of your situation will teach you to wait calmly when it seems like nothing is happening.

The person who receives Temperance in a reading is not in a position to hurry matters along. The only course is to sit and wait for things to move in their own time. The trick is to make the waiting constructive. This is one of the great lessons of the Zen masters. Learning to do nothing mindfully is a milestone on the spiritual path. It's of vital importance to know that there are times when nothing can be done and nothing needs to be done. Therein lies the state of grace.

FACT

The word temperance is derived from the Latin *temperare*, which means to moderate, blend, or mix together harmoniously. Interestingly, this card was earlier named Time, which is a key to its underlying meaning.

Temperance is linked to the Moon and corresponds to the Hebrew letter Nun. Its number is Fourteen and on the fourteenth day after the New Moon the lunar orb is at the exact midway point of its monthly cycle.

Upright

You are being asked to blend things in a harmonious way, and you have the ability to achieve this goal. You are learning to temper your ego needs with the legitimate needs of the spirit within. This is a time of inner growth and outer harmony. With patience, you can blend disparate elements— whether they are raw materials, resources, personnel, or ideas—into a harmonious whole.

Reversed

Things seem to be stalled. There's not much you can do at the present except to let things work themselves out, which they will in time. Patience is the key, for trying to force inharmonious elements together will only cause bad feelings and poor results, like mixing oil and water. This is a time to concentrate on blending the different parts of yourself together into a new form—of combining your psychological, emotional, and spiritual elements into a new you. Temper whatever inner conditions you have that make you feel out of balance.

The Devil

Description

Many decks picture a medieval Christian-type devil, complete with horns, hooves, a hairy tail, and a pitchfork. Usually at the devil's feet are two small, humanlike figures, one male and one female, with chains around their necks that are attached to the block upon which The Devil sits. However, it is important to note that the chains are loose and the people could easily slip them off, suggesting self-imposed limitations.

Whatever form The Devil takes in various decks, he is usually pretty scary looking. Occasionally, he is batlike or stylized depending on the theme of the deck and its designer's inclinations toward the figure. The Gilded Tarot portrays him as a muscular young man, whose face is half-hidden beneath a helmet-mask. In some decks, he has an inverted pentagram over his head or on his brow. In one deck, there is no devil at all, only two nude figures chained to a symbolically decorated block, straining toward an open doorway at the end of a long tunnel.

The variety of illustrations implies widely differing opinions of the card's meaning. For some, the devil is a creature of consummate evil; for others the devil is a mythical creature. Many psychologically-oriented people see the devil as a symbol of human indulgence, ignorance, egotism, greed, and irresponsibility. Thus, the illustration appearing on the card represents a point of view as well as the traditional meanings associated with the card.

Interpretation

Superficially, The Devil appears to be one of the more alarming cards of the Major Arcana. However, he does not represent satanic forces with evil intent, and it is important to remember this when doing readings. He is the Horned god of pagan times, connected to the fertility rites banned by the Church, which feared the power of pagan rituals, especially those including sexual activity.

When The Devil shows up in a reading, depending upon his position in the spread, he is telling you that you need to re-evaluate your relationship to material things, which are keeping you chained. It's time to look at whatever is limiting you and holding you back from personal growth, especially abusive, obsessive, or harmful relationships. You are being called upon to confront your fears about financial security and social and material success—the things of this world. The Devil is a reality check.

You need to recognize and acknowledge things you don't like about yourself—your personality, body, or temperament. It's time to let go of old fears, hangups, inhibitions, and ways you manipulate others to satisfy your needs instead of taking responsibility for yourself in a positive manner. Often there is a sexual component involved that is having a harmful effect on your whole life. Or there could be a nonsexual relationship that binds you and that must end before you can grow further.

ALERT!

The Devil is related to the old pagan god Great Pan, a god of nature and the natural processes of the physical world, including sex. The Greek form of Pan was Dionysus, who was known for cavorting with satyrs and in whose honor wild and uninhibited rituals that included a sexual free-for-all were held annually.

Whatever the situation, you are the only one who can change it. The two chained figures on the card represent bondage to the material realm. Their loose chains indicate your potential for attaining freedom by relinquishing obsessive ambition and excessive attachment to the things of this world.

Also known as "Le Diable," The Devil corresponds to the number fifteen and to the Hebrew letter Samech.

Upright
The Devil is a mythical creature with no real substance, but symbolically it represents the bondage that we create and maintain for ourselves.

There may be obstacles in the environment that you find frustrating, or you may feel your options are narrowing. Someone else may be involved, but you have the ability to free yourself from the situation by using your will-power.

Reversed

You feel trapped in a situation over which you feel you have no control, but close examination will reveal that your own attitudes and beliefs are causing the problem. The solution is to carefully examine your beliefs to learn how they are restricting you. Be careful of any quick fix to your problems, which are structural and not superficial. If you are willing to do the hard work, both on the inner and outer planes, you can solve the issues and achieve success on your own. Remember that Saturn rules The Devil card, and Saturn's influences are long-term.

The Tower

Description

The Tower usually depicts a stone tower of fortresslike construction, such as those still remaining from medieval times in Europe. The Tower is in the process of falling down or being destroyed, most often by fire or lightning.

In the Waite deck, and some others, The Tower's crown is being blown off by the fiery impact. The blast catapults human figures out of the windows. The implication is that the forces of heaven are angry and attacking the structure, causing flaming debris to fly out in all directions.

THE TOWER.

Interpretation

Like the Death card and The Devil, The Tower tends to strike alarm and fear into anyone in whose reading it appears, and indeed many writers assign a fully negative meaning to this card. The Tower does not necessarily represent ruin and devastation, although its appearance usually does herald swift and dramatic change—sometimes shocking and extremely upsetting change.

FACT

The Tower parallels the Old Testament story of the Tower of Babel, which was a massive structure intended to reach all the way up to god in His heaven. Also known as "La Maison Dieu" (The House of God) and the Falling Tower, or the Tower of Destruction, The Tower corresponds to the number sixteen and to the Hebrew letter Ayin.

It is important to keep in mind that the querent has usually brought the situation on herself by ignoring or denying that something is rotten and needs restructuring or deconstructing. Most likely, the querent is already well aware of a pressing need to make changes, but she is steadfastly refusing to take action. Then along comes a circumstance, such as losing a job or getting a divorce, having an accident or a financial setback, that forces the person to face reality.

There's no question this card signifies the crumbling of an old and outworn structure. It demands that you begin to deal seriously with your life collapsing all around you instead of, like the Roman emperor Nero, fiddling while your house burns. Any number of possibilities exist—breaking off an unsatisfactory or destructive relationship, quitting a stifling job, casting off false materialistic values, confronting long-buried issues of guilt and shame, shucking the social conventions that limit your progress, selling your over-mortgaged house and living more simply, or ridding yourself of burdensome possessions. The list is endless, but the querent nearly always knows what the issue is and that she is imprisoned by a self-created fortress, whether for protection, safety, or from fear of facing the unknown.

The message of The Tower is that you must destroy the old structures before they destroy you, so you can become free. Otherwise, they may be shattered by seemingly outside influences (which you have actually created yourself). In the wake of the chaos, a new order will grow. What was unsound will come tumbling down. You can pick and choose among the rubble to decide what is worth saving, and from that, rebuild your life in accordance with who you truly are.

Upright

Many people interpret The Tower as representing catastrophe, but whatever disruption or adversity it heralds is for the best. The Tower represents the overthrow of false ideas and old habit patterns that need to be gotten rid of. In this sense, it is not a negative card but a positive one. Sometimes, there is indeed some kind of loss—personal or financial. But careful examination of all of the factors will generally show that the catastrophic event could have been foreseen if you had only been aware and willing to face facts. The Tower is related to Uranus, the planet of unexpected, lightning-fast events. What is destroyed in conjunction with this card has served its purpose and needs to go.

Reversed

You are refusing to change old habit patterns, and you will suffer continued disruption in the form of unforeseen difficulties until you finally get the message that it's time to make some changes in your life. You may be confused about just who and what you are. At a deep level, you are being prepared for the changes that must eventually take place, but you are resisting what your inner self knows already. It is possible for you to alter fixed beliefs and limited ideas about your identity. Once you do, there will be far-reaching ramifications and a new sense of freedom in your life.

The Star
Description

This lovely card usually portrays a nude female figure in or beside a pool of water, pouring from two jugs, one held in each hand. In the Waite deck, she kneels and pours the contents of one pitcher into the stream and the contents of the other into the ground, showing the connection between the two feminine elements: earth and water.

The background of this card always displays stars; often, one directly above the figure's head is much larger than the others. Many decks show

THE STAR.

seven subsidiary stars, sometimes arranged to reflect the portal or two-pillar theme, sometimes set in a circle or a halolike form around her. The stars sparkle above a pastoral setting—trees, mountains, birds, flowers. If trees appear in the image, they may be configured on either side of her, another echo of the portal or pillars. The colors are usually bright, often with yellow (the color of optimism) predominating, although some decks depict a nighttime scene.

The naked woman represents unveiled truth and purity. The jugs she holds contain the waters of life. Some of the water is being returned to the Source, some is being used to infuse the land with new life.

Interpretation

The Star is a universal symbol of hope. Its appearance can signal the end of the travails represented by some of the earlier cards, symbolizing that a new and happier phase of life is coming into being. We see shooting stars as harbingers of good luck. From earliest times humans have been awed and fascinated by the star-spangled sky and the constellations.

The Star in a reading is like looking up at the bright starry sky on a clear night and seeing all the magnificence of the universe. It stimulates us to ponder the great potential of each and every human being for growth, inspiration, intuition, inner wisdom, and happiness.

Although The Star does not usually point to any specific planetary transit, as do some of the other Major Arcana cards, it does have a strong connection to astrology in general, for the zodiac signs relate to constellations. When The Star appears in a reading, it is a good time to have your horoscope read or to begin studying astrology yourself. A gate has opened for you to new possibilities. This card portends good fortune, creative inspiration, spiritual growth, help from unseen forces, and wishes come true. It marks a time of fulfillment.

The Star is linked to all the great goddesses of love and beauty from many cultures. The Greek Stella Maris, "Star of the Sea," was one of the titles bestowed upon Aphrodite. The Romans renamed her Venus. It is Venus who appears to us as the morning and evening star.

Upright

At this time you are experiencing a new flow of energy and self-confidence. You feel good about yourself and your place in the universe. You have arrived at a significant place, for which you have been preparing yourself. You are receiving assistance both from the invisible world and from the material world. Good things are in the offing—money, possessions, love, recognition, or assistance—because you are freely flowing with the pure energy of the universe. Full of faith and trust in life and its many processes, you are setting new goals for the future and opening the door to new opportunities in your career or relationships.

Also known as "L'Etoile," The Star corresponds to the number seventeen, which in old numerological systems was connected with immortality, hope, intuition, and self-expression.

Reversed

When The Star is reversed, it says that you are seeking your own path in a private way, without regard for the outside world and its benefits. You may be feeling alone, withdrawn, even resentful of outer obligations at this time, because your inner need is great. You may recently have experienced some disappointment, and this might have brought on a mood of pessimism that has caused you to turn inward for comfort. This is a necessary step. You need "repair time," including silence and solitude to attune yourself with your inner needs. When you do, you will begin to re-energize yourself in concert with who you truly are.

The Moon

Description

The Moon is a magical, mysterious card emblematic of the unconscious and the invisible realm of dreams, imagination, and psychic impressions. Usually the moon occupies the top half of the card, sometimes shown in both its full and crescent phases with the crescent enclosed in the full circle. In the

Waite deck, drops of water fall from the moon, raining down on two canines, a dog and a wolf, who bay at the moon. Two towers, one on either side, reflect the portal theme. At the bottom of the card is a pool or pond of water from which crawls a crab (symbol of the astrological sign Cancer, which is ruled by the moon), crawfish, or lobster. The water suggests the moon's link with the tides, the earth, the emotions, and the unconscious realm.

THE MOON.

Some authorities say the animals represent our opposite tendencies—the wolf, the untamed inner animal nature; the dog the domesticated, daily persona we show to the world. But canines and the moon have deep mythological roots that relate to the underworld. In addition, the dog indicates psychic ability as it is able to follow an invisible trail and locate what cannot be seen.

Interpretation

Astrologically, the moon represents the soul, which is the link between spirit (sun) and matter (earth). The moon is feminine: It symbolizes what we feel and how we respond. Therefore, it is emblematic of all that is receptive in human nature: the subconscious, the emotions, the instincts, and the automatic functions of the body. The lunar self is the channel for the flow of the universal, or divine, source, and as such, the moon has great power. It affects everything and everyone on earth, from the ocean's tides to the moods and reproductive cycles of humans.

Therefore, when The Moon appears in a reading, it suggests that you should be paying more attention to your inner self, your lunar self. It advises you to illuminate your deepest nature. In its diffuse light, we can often see more clearly than in the glare of the noonday sun. The light of the sun enables us to see the world around us, but the moon allows us to illuminate what springs naturally from inside ourselves.

During the hours of night, our subtle senses are more open and receptive to our inner spiritual harmony. When The Moon appears in a reading, it is time to attend to your dreams, feelings, instincts, and intuition.

Although traditionally The Moon card can indicate deceit and self-deception, confinement and undoing, these conditions are usually a result of ignoring your own inner promptings. If you get "taken"—especially emotionally—it's because you were letting your rational mind override your feelings. The Moon card's appearance also notifies you to take care of loose ends connected to the past, especially to your mother or other females.

ALERT!

The Moon card can point to a need to nurture yourself or to care for your health. For artistic people, its presence in a reading may mark a time of increased imagination and creativity.

The Moon is the symbol for the goddess, whose three aspects represent the three faces of the Great Triple goddess. As the newborn crescent, the moon is the maiden, the virgin—not chaste, but belonging to herself alone, not bound to any man. At the full moon, she is the mature woman, sexual and maternal, giver of life. At the end of her cycle, the waning moon about to turn dark represents the crone whose years have ripened into wisdom.

Also called "La Lune," the Moon corresponds to the number eighteen and to the Hebrew letter Tsadeh.

Upright

The Moon says that you are aware of the need to tune in to your lunar energies. You are now perceiving the reality of your inner nature more clearly, becoming more aware of the shadings and nuances of feelings and inner perceptions. The Moon also suggests psychic ability. You can tune in to other people's vibrations because you are connected to the information network of the invisible world. Pay attention to hunches and dreams. This is also a good time to develop your psychic skills.

Reversed

Your soul is calling for help, trying to get your attention. You may have been ignoring your lunar needs—self-nurturance, artistic expression, and receptivity. The demands of the day—the masculine side—are overwhelming you, and you need time out to reconnect with the feminine side of life. You have allowed the pressures of the outside world to throw you out of balance, and you feel disconnected from your true self. It's time to rest and reflect.

The moon's energies change continually, segueing from one phase into the next. After the night of the dark moon, for example, the energy of the new moon begins increasing, and two weeks later culminates in the full moon. The energy of the full moon can usually be felt two days before total fullness is achieved and continues for another day or two afterward, diminishing as the waning phase takes over.

> The Moon, as the luminous aspect of the night, belongs to [the goddess]; it is . . . an expression of her essential spirit. [It] appears as a birth— and indeed as rebirth. Such processes are the primordial mysteries of the Feminine . . . from which all life arises and unfolds, assuming, in its highest transformation, the form of the spirit.
>
> **—Erich Neumann, *The Great Mother***

To increase your sensitivity to the moon and your lunar self, sit facing the direction of the visible moon. If possible, position yourself in front of a window or go outside where the rays of the moon can shine on you. If you cannot see her, acknowledge her by closing your eyes and imagining the beautiful silver crescent or disk in the dark sky. Sit quietly for several minutes until you can feel the moon's energy contacting you. Imagine her vibrations entering your body, connecting your soul to her. Feel the magnetic pull of the moon on your sensitivities, just as they pull the tides, and allow yourself to be touched within by her softly glowing light. Let the moon illuminate your dark night of the soul, inspiring and uplifting you.

The Sun

Description

The Sun card features a blazing sun, sometimes with a face, with sunbeams radiating out from it. Beneath the Sun, in the Waite deck, a smiling nude child is riding a white horse. Behind him, a banner unfurls, held up by a winged staff. In the background, huge sunflowers grow against a stone wall.

THE SUN .

Some decks show two children with their arms around each other; other decks picture a young couple holding hands. The child, or children, are clearly very happy. The Sun's planetary ruler is Leo, which is linked with children, pleasure, and creativity. The astrological sun also rules the heart, the center of the body and the personality. The Sun card represents life itself, for the Sun gives life to everything on earth. The Sun suggests vitality, confidence, achievement, ego-attainment, and success in all endeavors. It is emblematic of the proverb, "May the Sun shine on all you do," the implication being that sunshine brings joy.

Interpretation

When The Sun card appears, it is an indication that your past work is now bearing fruit, a concept that is symbolized by the child or children. Along with The Moon, it implies the union between the unconscious realm of creativity (moon) and the conscious realm of manifestation (sun). Whether the birth represented is a biological child or a creative project, the outcome is a happy one. It is a time when good things come into your life—success, optimism, achievement, health, general good fortune, and happiness.

When The Sun turns up, it brightens any negative cards in the spread—no matter where The Sun appears in the spread. His influence is always beneficial, suggesting prosperity, enthusiasm, honors, public recognition, and attainment. You are happy to be alive because you feel it is the dawning of a new day. Any special efforts or ventures, such as taking a test or making a presentation, will turn out favorably.

In the wake of the demise of the Great Mother goddess as the sole divinity, the Sun, which represents the masculine principle, came to be worshipped as the central deity in many cultures. The ancient Egyptians, after eons of a pantheon of goddesses and gods, under the leadership of the pharaoh Akhenaton, were persuaded, albeit reluctantly, to accept a single god—known as Ra, Amun-Ra, or Aton (all of which were names for the Sun)—which Akhenaton believed was the god of all gods. The Greeks called their sun god Helios, whom the Romans named Apollo.

Also called "Le Soleil," The Sun corresponds to the number nineteen and to the Hebrew letter Qof.

Upright

Generally considered a positive card, The Sun relates to energy, vitality, confidence, success, and good times. It signifies a time of new beginnings, of things going well, of accomplishment, success, and contentment. You feel cheerful and self-confident, full of life and vitality, ready to undertake new projects and make changes for the better. Whatever you are planning, you feel a great deal of enthusiasm for it and aren't worried about the outcome. You may be starting more than one project, or upgrading something in your life, such as moving to a better-paying, more satisfying job, remodeling your home, or moving to a sunnier climate.

FACT

The appearance of The Sun in a reading can foreshadow a reward for your previous striving and suffering with a day at the beach. The Sun card can indicate you are going to take a wonderful vacation in the Sun where you can relax and let go of your worries.

Reversed

All of the above apply to the reversed Sun, because it is never a negative card. However, the reversed position indicates that there will be delays or that you will have to make some adjustments you hadn't planned on. Maybe you need to spruce up your appearance for that new job—get a new haircut or a new wardrobe to show yourself at your very best. Now is the time to explore new and more effective ways to express who you are to the outside world.

Judgment

Description

The Judgment card visually seems rather negative. In the Waite deck, a winged figure, whom some call the angel Gabriel, emerges from a cloud and blows a trumpet. Beneath him are several nude figures of men and women looking up, hearing the trumpet's blast. Their arms are outstretched, and they seem to have risen from coffins or the earth itself. Their expressions reveal awe tinged with fear.

Of all the allegorical symbolism of the Major Arcana, this is the most purely Christian, suggesting the feared Day of Judgment, when god will judge all souls and apportion out rewards or punishments accordingly. However, this is not a totally Christian idea; the Egyptians and other cultures also expressed the notion of the soul being judged. The goddess Maat, for instance, weighs the soul against her Feather of Truth.

Whether seen from a Christian point of view (which these medieval images represent) or from a universal one, the idea behind the symbols is that of an awakening.

Interpretation

When the Judgment card appears, what is being awakened is a sense of a Higher Self within. Sometimes the card coincides with a person turning away from a traditional set of beliefs toward one that better suits his personal philosophy of life. Judgment represents the end of something—an old way of life, a cycle that is finished. It is a time to seek new direction, to make adjustments that reflect who you truly are—perhaps by breaking away from your conventional way of life and believing.

Generally speaking, this is a positive card symbolizing regeneration and rebirth into wholeness after a period of confusion and a sense of confinement (shown by the coffins). You may have been feeling "dead" in your old life. When Judgment appears, you have the unique opportunity to relive, to enliven yourself and your environment by making the appropriate changes. What is ending is doubt and indecision, depression and despair, fear and inhibition. It's a time of new freedom to be yourself.

The Judgment card relates to classical Greek Hermes-Trismigistus in his role as psychopomp, or guide of souls. The activity of Hermes refers to alternatives of life, to the dissolution of fatal opposites, to clandestine violations of boundaries and laws. In other words, the overturning of the rational world and the discovery of the magical powers of the inner world.

Hermes was called Mercury by the Romans. The deeper expression of Hermes-Mercury's role as messenger of the gods is that which mediates, or delivers messages, between the conscious mind and the unconscious realm.

Also called "Le Jugement," the Judgment card corresponds to the number twenty and to the Hebrew letter Resh.

Upright

You've had a wake-up call from the universe and are now ready to step into a new phase of your maturing process. Your life is fairly settled now, and you are letting things grow and mature at a steady pace, not trying to hurry the process. A new phase in your life is coming into being as the natural result of your maturity—like a tree that has gone through the flowering stage bears fruit as the product of its maturity. You may get important news that will prove beneficial, or you may acquire new knowledge that will bring you joy and a sense of fulfillment. Health improves, and problems are easily solved.

Reversed

Interior biological and psychological factors are at work, and you have little or no control over them. You may be thinking about making some changes, which are being signaled by these inner timing mechanisms. This process may be throwing you into a state of confusion as you aren't sure just how to handle what's happening. Nonetheless, you are facing a new phase in your life and must make your peace with it. Emotionally, you may be called upon to grow up. Judgment reversed can also indicate frustrating delays or postponements, a materialistic view of life, refusal to take charge, possible loss or separation, and the need to cope with these life changes.

The World

Description

In many decks, The World card shows a young woman, sometimes nude or wearing a long scarf. The scarf covers her genitals but leaves her breasts bare. In each hand, she holds a double-ended wand that points both upward and downward, suggesting, "As above, so below." In the Waite deck, she is surrounded by an oval-shaped wreath.

THE WORLD.

As with The Wheel of Fortune card, to which The World is related, the four corners of the card feature a bull, a lion, an eagle, and a man—representing the four fixed signs of the zodiac: Taurus, Leo, Scorpio, and Aquarius. These elemental figures also depict the four directions. In the Waite deck, the wreath is bound at the top and bottom by ribbons in the shape of the infinity symbol that is found on both The Magician and Strength cards.

Interpretation

This is the last numbered card of the Major Arcana. It represents balance and support by unseen forces and symbolizes the end of the spiritual journey begun by The Fool. To embark upon the spiritual journey is to invite unseen forces to interact with us. These creative energies manifest in many ways, and often serve as guides. Guides bring us into grace and show the way. To encounter a guide—and they come in many guises—is to enter another realm, a place of great powers and, sometimes, great secrets. This realm belongs to the invisible world, although its denizens can, like angels, assume human or animal form. To interface with this world is to be impacted in a way that is life-changing. With guides, we enter a world of supreme power—

not the power of the material world but of the invisible order that supports and nourishes our world and our lives here. It is the realm of the sacred.

When The World card appears in a reading, it is a signal that you have been guided to the successful conclusion of your spiritual journey. At this, the final stage, you will receive what is rightfully yours because you have earned it. Now you are and feel whole, complete. You are refreshed from your long journey and ready to begin anew at a higher level.

The World card can be linked to Shiva, the Hindu god who dances the world into being and then destroys it only to once again dance it into being, in the eternal dance of life, death, and rebirth.

Upright

Success in all endeavors is assured. Everything is available to you—success, happiness, harmony. All is right with the world. Whatever you do now will prosper—a career change, a move to another place, a new relationship, recognition, rewards, acclaim. This is the end of an old cycle and the beginning of a new one. You have mastered the complexities of your own inner nature and feel supported by your inner resources. This is a time of supreme self-confidence and victory. You have put your trust where it belongs—in a Higher Power—and you will reap the rewards. At this time, many possibilities and opportunities are available to you, and you are completely free to choose what pleases you.

Reversed

You are being presented with a multiplicity of choices and aren't sure which one to make. You may be experiencing new facets of your own self or investigating different levels of reality. Or you may be rejecting new ideas being offered out of fear or a limited understanding. Now is the time to face the fact that the universe is a more complex place than you have been willing to admit.

Chapter 13

The Minor Arcana—
The Suit of Wands

In medieval Tarot decks, the suit of Wands represented the working class—those individuals who were attached to the noble houses as serfs. They had little choice but to follow the trade of their fathers, and they were usually apprenticed out at an early age to learn some difficult and unpleasant task. Today the Wands have come to represent whatever work you do and how you express your talents, as well as your ability to overcome odds and achieve success.

Interpreting the Wands

In a larger sense, the Wands are linked with creativity, drive, energy, enthusiasm, willpower, and outer world activities. They describe attitudes, abilities, and situations that offer the potential for success, perhaps through utilizing your talents and imagination, even though you may have to overcome obstacles in the process. Artists and craftspeople, for instance, may find that Wands appear in their readings frequently. Financial achievement may or may not be a factor; self-expression and fulfilling your potential are more important.

How the Wands are pictured varies considerably from deck to deck. Generally speaking, Wands are positive cards. The colors tend to be bright (yellow stands for optimism, red for action) and the designs or scenarios depicted are usually cheerful. Wands may be symbolized as branches sprouting leaves or flowers, wooden staffs, crude clubs, poles, scepterlike rods, or flaming torches. Sometimes these images are mixed within the same deck. As representative of the fire element and masculine force, Wands are obvious phallic symbols.

King of Wands

The King of Wands is usually shown as a dignified man, seated on a throne, robed and crowned. Sometimes he wears armor; other times he appears as a prosperous merchant king. A positive and powerful figure, he is clearly in command of the situation, confident and at ease. He holds a full-length staff or rod, generally upright but sometimes leaning against his shoulder. In some decks, this King faces sideways, and whether he is looking toward or away from other cards in a spread will have a bearing on his relationship to the reading.

KING of WANDS

Upright

Upright, the King represents a man of status and wealth, an influential and independent person who is inclined to help those he cares about. He may be a boss or a mentor, a senior business partner, or an advisor. You can rely on his honesty, intelligence, loyalty, and fair-mindedness, and you are sure to get good advice from him. If the King does not represent an actual person in your life, he can refer to a situation, which is exactly as it appears to be with no hint of deception. This card can indicate that good fortune is coming your way, perhaps in the form of unexpected help or advice, good news, a promotion, or an inheritance.

Reversed

The King of Wands reversed indicates delays in a business or creative project you are starting, however, nothing really problematic is standing in your way. If the King represents a person to you, the man he stands for will be available but won't go out of his way to help you. He won't block your efforts. He may even approve of what you are trying to accomplish on your own and lend moral support. But don't expect overt or tangible assistance.

Queen of Wands

The Queen of Wands is pictured as a statuesque woman of regal bearing. She holds a tall staff in one hand, a symbol of her authority. Often she sits on a throne, robed and crowned, but some decks show her as a well-dressed matron figure.

Upright

Socially prominent, this Queen represents a woman who is in a position of authority and shines in her endeavors. She is a "lioness"—warm, generous, and loving. She is honorable, creative, intelligent, friendly, and mature. Her advice is well worth taking, and she will be a loyal confidante or provide valuable assistance. A natural leader, she may be the head of a business, social, or philanthropic organization, or a political figure. If this Queen does not represent an actual person, she indicates that now is a good time for you to move forward in any business or creative venture you are planning. If the Queen represents you, she is an indication that you have the qualities within yourself that you need to succeed.

Reversed

If the Queen of Wands is reversed, she can represent a powerful woman who demands control over your affairs in return for her advice, support, and/or financial assistance. She wants to control social situations for her own advantage. If the Queen does not represent an actual person, the reversed card can be a warning to be careful in any business deals with women. She also advises you to avoid giving offense to the socially powerful, and to be aware of deception, greed, and jealousy.

Knight of Wands

The Knight of Wands is usually depicted as a young man on a rearing horse, in a mode of forward action. He is brandishing the wand like a weapon, but it seems more for show than to render a blow. He usually wears a suit of armor that is colorful and ornate. His position indicates that he is riding toward some encounter, more likely a joust than a fight.

KNIGHT of WANDS.

Upright

Knights are messengers and travelers, and the Knight of Wands is bringing good news concerning work or social activities. His glad tidings may relate to almost any anticipated happy event—a journey or vacation, a change of residence or job, an engagement or marriage. If this card represents a specific person, it will refer to a young man who is a relative or friend with the same qualities as the King and Queen, who are his parents in the royal family. It also indicates that the person bearing the message can be trusted and is faithful.

Reversed

Even when reversed, the Wands aren't particularly negative, but the reversed Knight can indicate a delay in a message or paperwork you have been expecting. A trip may be canceled because of bad weather or an engagement or wedding postponed, or even broken off. The reversed Knight can represent separation from people, places, or situations.

Page of Wands

The Page of Wands shows a youth, generally facing sideways and holding a tall staff before him with both hands, perhaps leaning on it. His attitude is expectant but casual. He is wearing garb similar to that of the rest of the royal court, but because he is a youth he may wear short pants. Some contemporary decks depict the Page as a girl or an androgynous figure.

PAGE of WANDS.

Upright

The Page of Wands represents a message of importance to your current project or situation, usually affecting work although it may be of a social nature. The information is positive. If the card represents a person in your life, it could be a younger relative or friend, an apprentice, student, or assistant. This Page is an enthusiastic adventurer and may be interested in international travel, foreign cultures and people, the arts, or philosophic projects.

Reversed

When reversed, the Page of Wands represents a delay, which could cause trouble. Something you were expecting might not arrive on time or a mix-up may occur. Or the Page may bring a message of unwelcome news that causes some disruption in your life or requires you to travel to put things right. If this Page represents a person, he is someone not to be trusted, or who conveys false or misleading information. Be on guard.

Ace of Wands

The Ace of Wands in the Waite and some other decks shows a hand emerging from a cloud, firmly grasping a heavy yet elegantly shaped stick that is vaguely phallic in design. Out of the wand, or club, new shoots are growing. The disembodied hand holds the Wand so that it points upward. Some decks picture only a wand, often one that is large and elaborate, like a ruler's scepter or a magician's ceremonial tool.

Upright

This Ace indicates the beginning of an enterprise, usually involving business, the arts, or finance. It shows that you have planted the seeds for a new birth—possibly a creative or money-making idea. You are now free from restraints that have hampered you in the past, enabling you to express yourself successfully, take on a new role, or forge a new identity through your work.

Reversed

The Ace of Wands reversed indicates that the process of creating a new identity or the start of a new endeavor has not yet manifested. It's still in the planning stages. You may be experiencing delays, or you might have to rethink your plans and make adjustments. You have a sense of your potential to do something new but could be hesitating because of lack of resources or confidence.

Two of Wands

The Two of Wands is an ambiguous card. It shows that a second, perhaps unexpected, factor is entering into the situation at hand, something for which your plans have not allowed. There is an element of surprise. Sometimes this card indicates a choice must be made, which could be related to your work or a creative endeavor.

Upright

You are saying "Yes" to a new enterprise with the expectation that you will achieve ownership, wealth, and good fortune. You've started something and are awaiting results. You may, however, have to deal with some unforeseen problems or encounter unexpected obstacles and opposition, such as a bank loan not coming through, a partner defecting, or a loss of support you were counting on. Sometimes this card can indicate a need to alter your course.

Reversed

This position suggests you may be in for a surprise, perhaps a nasty one. Nonetheless, you are affirming your new self-concept whether you have told others about it or not. Whether the surprise element portends good or bad will be indicated by the surrounding cards in the reading. If the Two of Wands appears with a Court card, for example, it may mean the person the Court card represents will disappoint you or make an unexpected appearance, which will change the picture.

Three of Wands

The Three of Wands represents someone who is ready and willing to hang on to what he has achieved. You can remain calm and in control of the situation, for there is no need for impulsiveness. This is a time for taking things firmly in hand and to act in a mature and responsible manner based on your experience and common sense.

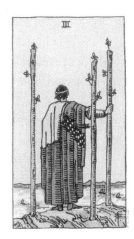

Upright

You have consolidated your situation, business, or enterprise and now can expect financial and/or personal gain. By clearly defining the role you want to play, you are presenting a positive picture to the world. This confident attitude may draw helpful people toward you or attract beneficial circumstances. You've established a solid foundation for your business or occupation and can expect cooperation from others. At this point, you are clear about who you are and what you intend to achieve. Others will respond positively to you.

Reversed

You are doing most of the work on an internal level, clarifying your needs and formulating your sense of direction. You have resolved most of the problems connected to the situation or enterprise and negotiated the tricky bits. Now you can expect things to go smoothly when you do go public with your ideas.

Four of Wands

This is an extremely positive card, indicating that your efforts to establish a project, business, or other endeavor are successful. Your position is secure and comfortable. Now you can relax and enjoy life. It's a time of respite and rejoicing.

Upright

You are enjoying pleasure and prosperity, reaping the rewards you have earned. Your finances are in good shape, and you are in harmony with your environment and the people in it. You've shown the world who you truly are and what you can achieve. It's a time for celebration and good times.

Reversed

As this is a very positive card, the reversed position means only that you are celebrating your good fortune in a quiet way. You may be expanding your property holdings or creative output without fanfare. Financial gains may be more modest than if the card were upright, but you are satisfied with your accomplishments and the sense of having done a job well. Your public image, your relationships with others, and your sense of self are favorable.

Five of Wands

The Five of Wands is about competition in economic, social, or career areas. It signifies the mad scramble for money and power, success and recognition, with concomitant excesses of greed and corruption. This card represents struggle in the marketplace. It can also indicate that you are involved in ego battles with other people in your workplace or the social arena. Often the image on the card shows five men fighting among themselves, using their staves as weapons.

Upright

New factors moving into the situation are demanding that you change, adapt, and grow. Life's not as simple as it was. New competition has moved into the neighborhood—or the industry—and you have to put forth a lot more effort to keep what you have gained in terms of money, status, and material goods. Depending on the rest of the reading and how you handle the challenges facing you, you could either suffer hardship and loss or go on to greater success and prosperity.

Reversed

When the Five of Wands is reversed, you must challenge yourself to change and adapt to different and difficult circumstances. The new competition may be cutthroat, even dishonest or underhanded. There could be litigation to resolve disputes, and your public image may suffer. Don't get involved in questionable or risky practices at this time and be careful whom you trust.

Six of Wands

The Six of Wands represents triumphing over adversity. A card of victory, it indicates good news and success. You've met the challenges to your position, work, or reputation and come through with flying colors.

Upright

Victory is at hand. You have overcome or conquered the opposition. Past self-doubt has been resolved, and you are in the process of winning some significant battles. You can expect to succeed and have your desires gratified. Gifts may be received, awards and recognition won.

Reversed

The hopes and wishes you have for your success are being delayed, often by factors over which you have no control. You feel frustrated and angry, ready to do battle to get things set right. You're being challenged by circumstances to take a stance about who you are and what you intend to accomplish. You may have experienced some kind of betrayal that has caused you to re-evaluate your self-image.

Seven of Wands

The Seven of Wands is about courage and determination. It indicates you are willing to fight for what you believe in and will stand your ground. Previously, you might have fallen into complacency but now you are ready to face challenges.

Upright

Profit and gain come only after you have firmly held off your competition or enemies. You may be outnumbered, but your determination will win the day. You are discovering inner resources you hardly suspected you had and using them to overcome obstacles. Thus, you have the advantage and will eventually achieve success by sheer force of will and personality.

Reversed

This position signifies a time of confusion. You don't know whether to hold on or back off, but now is the time for firmness and decision. Even if you're not sure which way to go, it's one of those situations where any decision is better than none at all.

Eight of Wands

This is a card of movement, action, and excitement. Things happen rapidly, and success is assured. Follow through on what you've already put in motion and start planning new goals.

Upright

You have shot your arrows into the air, and they are speeding toward the target. Now is a time for action, for initiating the next phase of your enterprise. This may involve air travel or other movement. It's an exciting and hopeful period when you are likely to be extremely busy. Positive things are rapidly

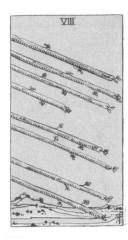

unfolding. Establish the roles you want to play and let go of those that no longer suit you.

Reversed

Movement may be unwanted, stressful, or unpleasant, such as being transferred across the country when you'd rather stay put. Go with the flow, wherever it leads. Allow yourself to be open to new experiences, but be prepared—be aware of what you're getting into. Relationships—marriage, business partnerships, family—may suffer. You may be required to reprioritize your schedule to accommodate other people's needs.

Nine of Wands

The Nine of Wands represents defending your legitimate territory. Through effort and determination, you have protected what's yours, shown courage under fire, and stood your ground. This is a card of recovery. Now you are in a strong position, and success is at hand.

Upright

Nines represent completion, and the Nine of Wands in a reading indicates that the job is done. You have had the discipline and the ability to plan well and wisely. Your relationships are developing positively, and you are moving forward with a sense of purpose and direction. If there is still opposition, your skills, strength, and courage will prevail over all opponents.

Reversed

You may be fighting a losing battle. If so, it's time to cut your losses and get out. Whatever it is, it is over, and if it hasn't worked out for you then go on to something else. Learn the lessons of failure—failure is but success's opposite and the wheel always turns. Get on with your life.

Ten of Wands

The Ten of Wands shows you taking up new responsibilities appropriate to the new cycle that's beginning now. These may seem burdensome, but you have the strength and character to shoulder them. You feel you can do anything at this time, even an extremely difficult task.

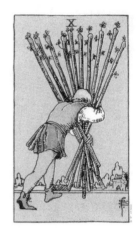

Upright

Your labor may have gone for naught, or you may be carrying burdens that really don't belong to you. You feel weary, as if the whole world is on your shoulders. It's up to you to decide whether to continue carrying the heavy responsibilities you have undertaken or if other people are shirking their part and should help out. Sometimes, one member of a family or organization gets all the dirty work for the simple reason that they are willing to do it. Make sure others are doing their fair share. Ask for help if you need it; don't let pride stand in your way.

Reversed

The burden is lifted—sometimes unexpectedly—and there is a feeling of freedom from undue responsibilities. Either you have taken the appropriate action or are about to do so. In any case, your load has been shifted, reproportioned, or removed entirely. You are learning to delegate and take on less. Pressure and stress are reduced, and you are able to enjoy life more. Sometimes, however, depending on negative influences in the spread, you may be suffering the consequences of overload—either with ill health or burnout. You may need a recovery period.

Chapter 14

The Minor Arcana—
The Suit of Pentacles

In medieval times, the suit of Pentacles, or Coins, referred to the merchant class. These cards represented tradesmen involved in buying and selling goods, building up commerce and trade routes, sending ships around the world, and getting rich in the process. Today, Pentacles are related to money, security, material goods, and the physical world in general.

14

Interpreting the Pentacles

Pentacles are often depicted as discs of gold, sometimes with a star (pentagram) or a five-sided design (pentagon) in the center. Interestingly, the pentacle is a powerful symbol in magick, used for protection against harmful influences, so there is also a suggestion that money and material resources can provide protection.

The suit of Pentacles (or Coins) has come to represent people who deal in the economy, whether captains of industry, professionals, accountants, entrepreneurs, shopkeepers, or those engaged in doing business in general. It includes bankers, lawyers, businessmen and women, stock traders—in other words, most of today's middle- and upper-middle classes. Pentacles can also symbolize those who desire to upgrade themselves financially, who understand money and how it works, and who respect the power it confers. In a reading, Pentacles usually point to an increase in the finances of the querent, and can show success in business, a raise, or relief from financial difficulties.

Therefore, in general the appearance of Pentacles is a positive note on a temporal basis. As Pentacles represent the element earth, they also indicated groundedness in the material and physical world. They can suggest concern about financial security, career, or whatever work you do as your livelihood. In some instances, Pentacles describe other types of material resources, physical capabilities, or health conditions.

King of Pentacles

The King of Pentacles is usually shown as a royal figure regally dressed and seated on a throne. In some decks, the throne is decorated with animal figures such as a lion, a bull, an eagle, or a griffin (signifying the four fixed signs of the zodiac). He may or may not be crowned, but he appears comfortable with the power money confers. Generally the King holds a single coin upright in one hand and a scepter in the other, and he is sometimes represented as a prosperous merchant.

KING of PENTACLES.

Upright

This King represents a mature man who is not only wealthy but also courageous. He is a solid citizen, reputable, dependable, and kind to others. He symbolizes worldly power in a positive sense and is experienced in handling money matters. His stability is a major factor, making him someone who can provide reliable counsel on matters of money, property, and security. He may also be a man who is cultured and refined, perhaps someone who serves as a patron.

If the King represents an actual person, he is likely to be well-disposed toward the querent—possibly he is a corporate head where the person works, or a banker from whom the querent is soliciting a loan. If the King is not an actual person, then his appearance indicates that the querent is engaged in some worldly enterprise that will meet with success.

Reversed

Some people consider this King reversed to be an extremely negative symbol, representing danger or an unwise business move. Others view the card as a warning to be aware of the small print in any contracts being negotiated. The King can also indicate unfair competition or shady business practices.

Queen of Pentacles

The Queen of Pentacles is a benevolent figure with a regal and kindly bearing, sometimes shown holding the Pentacle or coin in her lap and gazing fondly down at it. She may also be pictured standing, leaning against an ornate throne or chair. Like the King, her throne is often decorated with animal figures. She is someone who understands and respects money as a tool but does not worship it.

QUEEN of PENTACLES

Upright

This Queen represents a generous woman who is also an excellent manager in practical and financial areas. She may be a sensual woman who is at home in her body and enjoys her creature comforts. As an adviser, she favors the querent or will at least be fair. She is pragmatic and realistic and wants to see that the money she distributes produces tangible results. If the card doesn't represent a person, it shows a harvest after much labor, security, the acquisition of wisdom through experience, and prudent use of wealth.

Reversed

In the reversed position, this Queen may represent someone who will try to block your efforts. She could be merely indifferent, or actively hostile. If she is a relative or an older friend, mentor, or boss, she might be a superficial person who only pretends to want to help you. Or the price of her help might be too high; she wants to control everything. She may lack confidence and try to compensate for her own shortcomings by a display of her wealth, or she may be hiding a lack of money. If this card does not represent a person, it describes a situation where caution is due and advises you to be careful whom you trust.

Knight of Pentacles

This Knight brings news concerning money, usually good news. He is typically depicted on horseback, facing sideways, wearing armor, and holding the Pentacle before him as if offering it to someone. Unlike the Knight of Wands who is on a charging horse, the Knight of Pentacles's horse is at parade rest, calm and stable. He is poised on the edge of adventure or travel.

Upright

If this Knight represents a person, it's someone with the spirit of adventure, but who is practical and materially minded. He is good at performing any task set for him, but not likely to be a self-starter. If the card does not signify a person, it suggests a situation involving arrivals and/or departures. You may quit a job for a more lucrative one elsewhere, move to another locale for financial or work-related reasons, or experience other changes in your life relative to money, possessions, or security.

Reversed

The Knight reversed brings an unwelcome message about money, often a loss of some kind, a disappointment, or frustration due to an unforeseen delay. Existing plans may have to be aborted; delays could cause failure. If the card represents a person, he may be a young man who is unemployed or uninterested in employment. If it's not a person, this Knight shows a situation where waste, inertia, and problems with money exist.

Page of Pentacles

PAGE of PENTACLES

The Page of Pentacles is often shown as a youth standing in a countryside. He is holding the Pentacle before him, as if admiring it. His attitude suggests that he desires money or wants to achieve the means to gain it, perhaps through education. Sometimes called the card of the student or scholar, the Page of Pentacles shows one who is so intent on his lessons that he misses everything else going on around him. In some contemporary decks, the Page is pictured as a girl or androgynous figure.

Upright

The Page of Pentacles indicates good news regarding the acquisition of money or material goods. His appearance suggests someone who is intelligent, refined, sensitive to the arts, and appreciative of the good life. Ambitious and determined, he is goal-oriented. If he does not represent a person, this card indicates your own worldly ambitions and/or a message concerning them.

Reversed

This Page in the reversed position reflects someone who is lazy, unmotivated, or uninterested in furthering himself through education or work. If the card does not represent a person, it may indicate bad news concerning money matters. It can also refer to some sort of disappointment such as failing an exam, not getting into the college of your choice, or not being hired for a job. More effort and focus are needed.

Ace of Pentacles

The Ace of Pentacles often depicts a large Pentacle as the central image on the card. In the Waite deck, a hand is coming out of a cloud holding the Pentacle in its palm. Other decks illustrate the coin in a decorative manner, sometimes as a shield. The Ace of Pentacles is the card of new success, new money, new enterprise, resources, ambition, opportunity, and material attainment. In some cases, it can also represent physical or health-related benefits.

Upright

This Ace is extremely positive, predicting success for some new enterprise you are starting. You are planting the seeds for a new venture involving the acquisition of money or financial security. The Ace is a strong indication of prosperity coming to you. Be open to receive the benefits it promises.

Reversed

This Ace in the reversed position indicates that your new venture is still in the idea stage. You are laying the groundwork to achieve a greater level of security and prosperity. Your material gain will come, but it is being delayed, and you must be patient and persistent. Don't get discouraged.

Two of Pentacles

The Two of Pentacles suggests either money coming from two sources or having to juggle finances to make ends meet. In some cases, it shows a financial or business partnership. It is a positive card indicating good fortune and enjoyment. You may be experiencing financial difficulty, but it won't last. Better times lie ahead.

Upright

A message about money could be on its way to you, probably in written form. You are still in the stage of deciding which of two different options to choose. Perhaps you are concerned about financial issues and may be holding down more than one job, or moonlighting to make extra money. It's time to make a choice and stick with it even if you aren't sure of the outcome.

Reversed

You may be experiencing financial difficulties while pretending that all is well. You are juggling not only sources of income but options for change. This isn't the right time to make a change. Hang in there until the right moment presents itself. You need to overcome doubt and have faith in yourself.

Three of Pentacles

The Three of Pentacles is the card of the crafts-man, someone who has already developed skill in a profession or trade. It's time to turn these skills to profit, and success is assured. The Three of Pentacles usually shows you are planning and conferring about a future action, such as cooperating in a business venture.

Upright

You are acquiring marketable skills, preparing yourself for action in the world. You might be a recent graduate or have gone back to school to upgrade your skills or change your career. You are enterprising and may be interested in some particular area of commerce, or a specific trade or business. You can anticipate a rise in prestige and earnings. This card can also indicate a payback period when you demonstrate your abilities and begin to reap the rewards of your efforts. Or you could receive money that's owed to you.

Reversed

You aren't making the effort to acquire the new skills you need in today's changing marketplace. You may be stuck in a job you really don't like but lack the confidence or ambition to strike out and change things for the better. You need to get going—thought without action is invalid.

Four of Pentacles

The Four of Pentacles indicates a security-conscious person who is holding tight to money and material possessions. You may fear that loss is in the offing and are trying to prepare yourself by closely guarding what you have. Or you may simply be overly cautious and conservative in financial areas.

Upright

You are hanging on to something—either your possessions or a situation—in a stubborn and inflexible manner. Fear of change may be involved, or you may merely be comfortable where you are. Your fixed attitude, however, may be limiting you and blocking new opportunities for success and happiness.

Reversed

You may be trying to make something happen prematurely, or you are holding on too tightly to current circumstances. Perhaps you are quarreling with someone over money, such as in a divorce proceeding. You need to loosen up and have more trust in the universe to provide.

Five of Pentacles

Of all the Pentacles, this is the only one with a basic negative connotation. It suggests financial losses, business problems, or material lack. It can also indicate that spiritual bankruptcy is at the root of this unfavorable condition. In some instances, this card can show that your priorities are spiritual, not financial or worldly.

Upright

This Five is a warning that money may soon be very tight, that losses may ensue from ill-advised investments, or that support you had counted on won't be forthcoming, such as a grant, legacy or job. In some cases, it advises you to ask for help—from other people or the universe.

Reversed

You are being advised to get your house in order financially. Cut your losses any way you can to avoid further deterioration of your finances; if you are in debt, which you probably are, focus on getting it cleared out. Be extremely careful of any future investments. Don't take risks at this time.

Six of Pentacles

This Six shows that past financial problems have been resolved. You can afford a charitable act because your income is steady and your security is stable. You are in a balanced position concerning income and outflow. You are using your prosperity to help others. Because Sixes represent give and take, this card can also indicate a business partnership or shared financial responsibility.

Upright

Good things are coming to you and going out from you, in material terms. You are experiencing abundance, prosperity, and personal gratification. You may be in a position to support a good cause, perhaps by contributing financially to people who are struggling upward. This card can also represent philanthropic projects or providing work for other people.

Reversed

You need to recoup after a period of loss and confusion. You want to help others, but you don't have the means, and that makes you unhappy. You may be required to find a pattern that will create a sense of security for you so that you can find peace of mind.

Seven of Pentacles

The Seven of Pentacles is about receiving the benefits that are due to you, realizing the legitimate gain that you have earned by your own hard work. Like a farmer harvesting crops that he has nurtured through bad weather, you are reaping what you've sown. The harvest may still be a ways off, however, so keep tending your fields.

Upright

You've put in the time and effort and paid your dues. Now you will gain in your business or other enterprise. Not only that, but you feel great satisfaction from a job well done. Growth and good fortune are yours, well earned.

Reversed

You are experiencing disappointment or failure in some enterprise. Financial difficulties, usually the result of an unwise investment or a loan unpaid, may be causing you concern. It's a time to adjust your own attitudes toward how you use your money and look into how you yourself are responsible.

Eight of Pentacles

The Eight is a card of craftsmanship and conscientious work. It suggests developing and applying your skills in a productive manner. You know what you want and how to go about achieving it. Be sincere and persevere, and your efforts will succeed. A business or project will prosper as a result of refining your craft or improving your processes. A new venture augurs success because you are training yourself intensively with a clear goal in mind.

Upright

You are integrating old skills into a new form, or you are adding new skills. You've tried various means of making your living, and you are now finalizing how you want to use your personal resources to fulfill your needs and expand. Your sureness of purpose guarantees success. Your craftsmanship will be rewarded by increased income, opportunity, and respect.

Reversed

When this card is reversed, there is an indication that you have not mastered the necessary skills to achieve your goals. You may desire to begin some new enterprise, but a lack of ambition, ability, or clarity prevents your success. More effort or education may be necessary.

Nine of Pentacles

The Nine of Pentacles suggests independence from financial concerns and worries. You receive abundance from proper management in business or financial affairs. This card says you've arrived, accomplished your goals, and now feel secure.

Upright

You have integrated the factors of your life into a secure base. Now you are enjoying money, resources, and physical energy as a smooth combined flow. There is plenty all around you— material well-being, order, safety, and success.

Reversed

Your security is shaky, and you may be dependent on someone else— perhaps a spouse or relative—for your financial well-being. Circumstances may have caused you to lose your independence. Figure out how to regain what you've lost.

Ten of Pentacles

The Ten of Pentacles is a happy card, indicating a solid and secure life, both in business and with your family. Your work and planning have paid off, and you are enjoying the fruits of your labor.

Upright

You are emphasizing home and family at this point, now that you have a secure income to support them. You may be planning to build a new home, or buy a second vacation home. Family matters are at the forefront, and you have the leisure to concentrate on personal affairs. In some cases, this card can represent marrying into money or receiving an inheritance.

Reversed

You may be so established at this point that you are stagnating. Maybe you have retired comfortably and are just sitting around watching TV. You need to activate some growth in your life to avoid boredom. Take up a hobby, start a new business, do charity work, or teach others your skills.

Chapter 15

The Minor Arcana—
The Suit of Swords

In early Tarot decks, Swords represented the knighthood, or noble houses, which ruled absolutely by the power of the sword. Yet, this class was also aware of its obligations to protect the people they governed—the obligation of the noble class to better those under their control. Today the Swords show states of mind and mental activity, communication, psychological matters, and spiritual issues.

Interpreting thea Swords

The Swords represent events, conditions, situations, or attitudes that may be difficult or challenging. However, as a result, they also represent the growth and development of the conscious mind. When Swords appear in a reading, you may be experiencing stress or problems, but these are making you think.

An old Chinese proverb says, "Life is pain. Pain makes you think. Thinking makes you wise. And wisdom makes life endurable." It is this point of view that the Swords represent.

The suffering associated with the Swords can also be the result of over-analyzing situations. In our modern society, where left-brain logic is favored over right-brain intuition and feeling, Swords can represent the alienation that comes from cutting yourself off from your inner self.

The Swords are often depicted as unsheathed double-bladed sabers, sometimes as daggers or the magician's tool known as an athame. Although usually shown as battle swords, they have a quality of power and authority wielded for some purpose other than physical fighting. Some writers interpret the Swords as totally negative, others see a spiritual side to the Swords as well as the obstacles, pain, and difficulties sometimes associated with them. This is because we often come to a spiritual path through or after intense suffering of some kind, be it physical, mental, psychological, or emotional.

King of Swords

The King of Swords is a somewhat stern figure who is in absolute command, but who can be trusted to be fair in his judgment and decisions. He is usually pictured enthroned, armored, helmeted, and crowned, a combination of symbols that suggests not only power and authority, but a willingness to use it forcefully if necessary. In one deck, he holds a set of balanced scales suggesting both

KING of SWORDS.

justice and the sign of Libra. Some Tarot experts attest that his sign is Gemini. Regardless of which zodiacal sign he refers to, the suit of Swords corresponds to the element of Air. Therefore, his appearance often has to do with your mental processes.

Upright

This King represents a man of great strength and authority. If he stands for a person, it is someone who is involved with mental work, such as a researcher, a lawyer, teacher, someone in the communications field, or a military officer. As such, he is a good counselor with acute mental dexterity. He has a gift for thinking clearly and rapidly, and he is able to express his thoughts with considerable eloquence. If this King is not a person, he represents a situation in which mental and communication skills are called for. When he appears, you may be on the verge of a spiritual breakthrough and are ready to communicate it.

Reversed

When reversed, this King shows the negative qualities of the Air signs—fickleness, using words as rapiers to wound, gossiping, superficiality, playing one person against the other, or rigidity of opinions. If he does not signify a person, he can represent a situation in which the people around you are antagonistic to your ideas or your spiritual quest. You may have to keep these matters to yourself and not advertise them to those who are unsympathetic.

Queen of Swords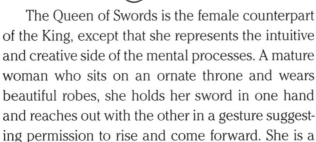

The Queen of Swords is the female counterpart of the King, except that she represents the intuitive and creative side of the mental processes. A mature woman who sits on an ornate throne and wears beautiful robes, she holds her sword in one hand and reaches out with the other in a gesture suggesting permission to rise and come forward. She is a formidable figure with power and authority, either in the mental world or in the spiritual realm.

QUEEN of SWORDS.

Upright

When the Queen of Swords appears in a reading, she may represent a single or independent woman with authority and power. Often she is someone with keen intellectual or communicative abilities—a writer, professor, lawyer, minister, business woman, or scholar. In some instances, this card may indicate someone who has endured emotional loss and separation, perhaps as a result of a divorce or death. If she describes a person, she is strong-willed and has the ability to cope with her loss and go on with her life. If she does not represent a person, this Queen can indicate that the querent is going through a difficult experience, which will open new vistas if she uses it for positive growth. This is especially true if an Ace appears in the reading, too.

Reversed

When this Queen is reversed, the person she represents is not dealing well with whatever loss is involved. There may be sadness, withdrawal, or mourning beyond reasonable limits. If the card does not stand for a person, it can represent a situation in which the querent is bogged down emotionally, wallowing in pain, letting her heart rule her head. Other cards in the spread will indicate the way out of the dilemma.

Knight of Swords

The Knight of Swords is often shown leaning forward on a fully charging horse, his sword held upright and forward as if he is ready to encounter the enemy. He is definitely on the attack and by his expression he expects to win the battle. He can represent a person who is overly aggressive or argumentative, who lives in attack mode. Or he can mean that you are aggressively pursuing a lifestyle that will allow you to live out your own philosophical ideals.

KNIGHT of SWORDS .

Upright

As a messenger, the Knight of Swords may bring bad news that relates to you personally or to someone close to you. Some kind of conflict is at hand, usually of a mental nature. There could be violent differences of opinion around you, with angry messages being sent and received. Or if this Knight is not a person, you may be so focused on your intellectual pursuits that you are neglecting other facets of your life. You may be expressing your ideas too forcefully and are antagonizing the opposition. Diplomacy may be called for in a situation.

Reversed

When reversed, this Knight loses his aggressiveness and becomes passive about a situation that requires action. He suggests you are delaying doing what is necessary, perhaps neglecting paperwork or communication. There could be serious repercussions from withholding information. If this card is not a person, it can indicate that you are mentally closed off from a situation that desperately needs attention and is thereby creating bad feeling and opposition.

Page of Swords

PAGE of SWORDS.

The Page of Swords is about risk on a mental or spiritual level. It might mean you are taking up some new line of thought or study. Many decks depict a youth standing, looking over his shoulder away from the sword he holds. He seems a bit unsure of his ability to wield the weapon although he tries to appear as if he can easily defeat any enemy. He usually wears a short garment, leather or padded cloth, instead of armor. Some contemporary decks show the Page as a girl or androgynous figure.

Upright

As a messenger, this Page brings news of problems and difficulties, perhaps relating to a younger person you know. An offspring may have failed college exams or be in trouble with the law. An element of experimentation is indicated here—either you or someone else is taking a risk or behaving in a risky manner that might cause problems. The Page is motivated by unconventional activity, which can cause strife. Overconfidence or the ignorance of youth might also get this person into trouble.

Reversed

The reversed Page is having trouble getting it together. Although this young person is attractive and charming—eager, confident, clever, active—he isn't strictly on the up and up. This Page could represent someone who is sponging off others, maybe parents or friends. Or it could indicate someone who is anxious or capable of spiteful action. Insecurity lies at the root of this person's actions.

Ace of Swords

ACE of SWORDS.

Like all of the Aces, the Ace of Swords indicates a new beginning. Most decks depict an upright sword, sometimes crowned at the tip. In the Waite deck, a disembodied hand coming out of clouds holds the Sword. The Sword and crown are decorated with living vegetation—vines, flowers, leaves, fruit. This Ace indicates a triumph over difficulties through the use of mental means or spiritual growth. It is emblematic of a major breakthrough.

Upright

A brand new lifestyle is coming into being for you. You have achieved this opportunity by dint of will and using your mental faculties at a high level. Prosperity, recognition, new development—especially spiritual growth—are sure to follow in the wake of your new direction in life. This Ace signals a birth—of an idea, an enterprise, or a child. You now are in a position of power with the possibility of manifesting your philosophy in a new way.

Reversed

As this is an extremely positive card, the reversed position only indicates delays or glitches. What you planned for on the mental plane may not come into manifestation on the physical plane as quickly as you had hoped, and this may be causing frustration and tension.

Two of Swords

The Waite deck shows a blindfolded woman holding two swords crossed over her breasts with a crescent Moon above and the ocean behind her. The card represents a situation in which it appears impossible to move forward. Because you can't figure out with logic or intellect how to proceed, you must rely on blind faith that the universe will handle things.

Upright

This card indicates stasis. You may be maintaining the situation in a state of balance by ignoring the underlying tension that exists. This is an uncomfortable position to be in, but you aren't ready to do anything about it yet. You need to speak up and communicate about the circumstances involved. For instance, it can represent a couple who really do not get along but are putting up a perfect façade to the outside world. Eventually, however, change must take place for the continued tension is unbearable. Choice is available. Remove the blindfold and look honestly at the situation.

Reversed

When the Two of Swords appears reversed, it exacerbates the above situation, except that the person actually feels helpless to make the necessary changes. If a husband and wife are at odds, one party may be unwilling to admit to the truth of the situation, making discourse impossible. This may result in deceit or disloyalty, lying or duplicity.

Three of Swords

The Three of Swords is a card of severance, signifying separation and sorrow, perhaps the end of a love relationship. However, there is the sense that the separation or breakup was needed. A relationship or alliance had outworn its usefulness, and, although there is sorrow or regret, the end result is positive. This card can also mean you feel isolated and cut off from something you love—a way of life, your home and family, a philosophy, pursuit, or job.

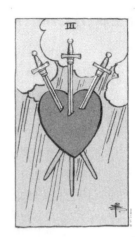

Upright

You are feeling the pain of separation right now, quite possibly in the area of love. Sometimes this card can signify a love triangle. A third party has entered into the formerly stable situation and caused the breakup, but it was ready to happen anyway. It's time to let go. Whatever has died must be allowed to disintegrate within your psychic structure. Don't try to hold on to the past.

Reversed

You are taking this separation too much to heart and not thinking clearly about the truth of the situation. You may be blaming someone else instead of acknowledging that you were a party to the breakup. You may be suffering depression over the situation, unable or unwilling to pull yourself together and get on with your life. Try to keep a clear head and don't get bogged down with what might have been.

Four of Swords

The Four of Swords is a card of respite after the sorrow or misfortune of the Three. It represents rest and recuperation, of working on your problems quietly and with faith. You feel the need for introspection and solitude, a necessary period of aloneness and contemplation to understand what happened and why.

Upright

You have been in pain, but now you are in the first stage of recovery, whether from emotional upheaval or physical illness. You are resting and taking the time out to think things through and plan your next moves more wisely. This is the calm after the storm, and you may want to retreat from other people and the world. During this time, think, plan, and re-evaluate what you had been doing before the crisis. It's time to get your inner house in order.

Reversed

You are not allowing yourself the rest and respite you need, and if you continue this way you may make yourself ill. Everyone needs a period of calm and quiet in the wake of any kind of major disruption. Refusing to make time to recuperate, both mentally and emotionally, will only worsen the situation. Take heed and take time out.

Five of Swords

The Five of Swords suggests the double-edged nature of the sword. One edge signifies defeat, misfortune, betrayal, and loss; the other suggests learning to accept the boundaries we all must face and live with. Fives are about adjusting, and this Five indicates you are adjusting to some kind of change brought on by distress or loss. It's an uncomfortable process but a necessary one.

Upright

Change is part of life, and the more you resist it, the more difficult you make things for yourself. Whatever needs to be changed—your lifestyle, your philosophy, your inner beliefs about yourself—now is the time to get to work and bring those changes into your daily life.

Reversed

Your losses have hit you hard, and you are in a state of great unhappiness. You feel hurt and betrayed, angry and discouraged. This is a time of agony, but only you can get yourself out of it. You may feel confused about why the crisis occurred, but deep down you are already aware of the reasons. You just don't want to face them.

Six of Swords

The Six of Swords indicates that you are moving away from past troubles, putting them behind you. It marks the beginning of a new phase after a time of upheaval. You have stabilized yourself and are enjoying a new peace of mind. This is the calm after the storm—a period of smooth sailing with relatively few problems ahead.

Upright

This is a time of integration—or reintegration. Harmony and ease prevail. New people you can trust come into your life. After some intense suffering, you now feel optimistic and balanced. This card can also indicate a move or a journey over water. The destination may be unknown, or the effects of the move may be uncertain, but luck is on your side, and any change you make will go smoothly.

Reversed

As this is a positive card, the reversed position simply means delays, or that the harmony you are experiencing is internal rather than being expressed externally. You may have come to a new way of thinking about your life, or you may be affirming your old beliefs and attitudes, finding a path that's comfortable for you.

Seven of Swords

When the Seven of Swords shows up, it urges caution in all dealings. Surreptitious action or indirect communications may be occurring. Nothing is quite what it seems to be, and you have to use your wit to achieve your aims. Be wary of overconfidence. You may appear to be on top now, but imprudence could still do you in.

Upright

You have got the upper hand over a tricky situation, but you still need to exercise caution in handling your affairs. Discretion and discrimination

are required, as are diplomacy and evasive tactics. You may not like this oblique approach, but you'll be more likely to achieve success this way.

Reversed

When the Seven of Swords appears reversed, it emphasizes all of the above but includes the possibility of deception. Maintain caution and vigilance in all things during this period. Stay open-minded and flexible so that you can respond to changes speedily. You may be experimenting with different plans of action, getting various points of view.

Eight of Swords

The tension of the Eight of Swords is related to that of the Two, except that the Two indicates denial while the Eight suggests the queris is conscious of the choices available. Despite this, you feel trapped—either unable or unwilling to make a choice, therefore stuck in a painful state. You are your own worst enemy.

Upright

Most writers view this as an extremely negative card. In the Waite deck, a bound and blindfolded woman is surrounded by eight swords stuck into the sand around her, like a barrier. The card describes a situation that causes great unhappiness, but you are not without resources to change matters. The bad situation is temporary and, if the card falls in the "future" position, the problem can even be avoided.

Reversed

This card reversed is a warning that what is already wrong can get worse, or that a difficult situation is approaching. Make sure all your affairs are in the best possible order. If you've been putting off paying your taxes, or getting insurance, or settling some legal matter, take care of it promptly. Your well-being depends on using your head and preparing for emergencies and unexpected calamities.

Nine of Swords

The Nine of Swords shows extreme anxiety, nightmares, tension, unhappiness, and regrets over past mistakes or misfortunes. When it appears, the querent is in an unhappy and tense state of mind whether or not the facts bear out the fear. Thus the suffering associated with this card may be mostly in your mind.

Upright

The Nine of Swords indicates that the querent is troubled by bad dreams or horrible fantasies. You may not even know where these are coming from, but deep-rooted or repressed issues are trying to surface so you can recognize and resolve them. Extreme mental torture may result as you are forced to change your attitudes and beliefs by crisis circumstances. This is not all bad, however, no matter how painful it seems. Remember that Nine is the number of completion. Thus, this card indicates that the changes you are being required to make forecast a better future.

Reversed

When the Nine of Swords is reversed, it shows intense mental anguish. It's time to examine belief systems that no longer apply to your life and that are standing in the way of your progress. You are suffering because you refuse to face the cause of your problems. Honesty is called for to gain the insight you need to resolve the situation.

Ten of Swords

Although the Ten of Swords is another difficult card, its appearance marks the beginning of the end of a period of trials and tribulations. It also signifies the beginning of an entirely new cycle. For the new cycle to come in, you have to clear away the debris of the old cycle now ending, and often this process is painful. Extreme stress and exhaustion may accompany the appearance of this card. You need to stop worrying.

Upright

When the Ten of Swords appears upright, it suggests that you need to make a clean break from the past and all its attendant pain and suffering. Whether this means a divorce, quitting a job, changing careers, moving across the country, or changing a traditional belief system, make the break and make it cleanly, leaving no loose ends. It's time to do away with previous illusions that have clouded your vision.

Reversed

When the Ten of Swords appears reversed, it is an indication that you are holding back and are reluctant to take the necessary steps to move into a new cycle. You are delaying actions or deceiving yourself about a situation. You may be making excuses for yourself or someone else to maintain the status quo, but you are only prolonging your agony. Make a choice, even if it's the wrong one.

Chapter 16

The Minor Arcana—
The Suit of Cups

The Cups in medieval times represented the clergy, whose influence in the society was second only to the nobility. In fact, it was common practice for the second or third son of a noble house to enter the Church. Although the clergy often fell short of its obligations, the local priests were frequently good people who used available resources to help their flocks. For this reason, the suit of Cups has come to represent love, happiness, companionship, compassion, and benign influences.

Interpreting the Cups

In a broader interpretation, the Cups describe emotions, love, romance, social relationships, congenial situations, culture, comfort, intuition, and the unconscious. The love shown by these cards is not just romantic love, but friendship and love of one's fellow humans as well. Kindness, compassion, and geniality are depicted in the imagery of this suit. Thus, the Cups are almost always considered positive, and if there are negative factors in the reading, a Cup card will mitigate the bad omen, help to make a situation better, or point the way to a solution.

The symbol for the Cups is a happy one. In most decks they are pictured as large, beautiful, often ornate vessels or chalices. Sometimes they appear double-ended as if they could be filled from either side.

King of Cups

KING of CUPS.

The King of Cups has a loving demeanor. He is a mature man, usually pictured seated on a throne, often with water in the background. In the Waite deck, his crown is more like an elaborate hat than a bejeweled regal headpiece, suggesting that he stands with rather than above his subjects. Rarely is he shown wearing armor—usually plain robes— so there is nothing of the militant about him. This King's expression is benign, his attitude relaxed and nonthreatening.

Upright

This King indicates a man who is kindly disposed—a benevolent father figure, who may represent your own father or someone who fills that role for you. He can also signify an older man with whom the querent either has or wants a love relationship. Whether as a friend, advisor, or lover, he is utterly trustworthy and dependent, and he can be relied upon to come through for you when you need him. Most interpretations consider this King to be a man of culture, knowledgeable about and interested in the arts, possibly himself a creative type. If the King does not represent an actual person, he indicates a situation that is favorable, especially if it is an artistic pursuit.

Reversed

Your involvement with some kind of love situation is ending, but the process should not cause much pain. You have reached a phase in your life when it's time to move away from dependency on an older person—perhaps your father or a mentor or teacher—and strike out on your own. Whether the circumstances are related to a person or to your own inner psychic process, the result is the same. It is also possible that this King reversed represents someone who is trying to get rid of you for some reason, romantic or otherwise. You need to let go and, if necessary, mourn the passing of something that was good once but is now over.

Queen of Cups

The Queen of Cups is a beautiful and benevolent figure. The Cup she holds is an ornate chalice, and she gazes at it as if she could see visions of the future inside. She wears robes that appear to be filmy and flowing, and her crown is elaborate but graceful. Usually she is pictured with water flowing at her feet, for this suit corresponds to the Water element. An affectionate and loving woman, whether wife, mother, friend, or lover, she is wise in the ways of the human heart. Her attitude is one of receptivity and approachability.

QUEEN of CUPS.

Upright

The Queen of Cups can represent any kindly woman in your life. If the querent is a man, she may signify his wife or the woman he loves. She is creative, perhaps an artist, with visionary tendencies. Her psychic ability is highly developed and tends to be accurate. However, she tempers her intuitive nature with mature judgment. If she represents the querent herself, the above qualities apply to that person although they may still be in the nascent stage and might need to be developed. If this Queen does not represent a person, the situation she describes may concern a creative endeavor, relationship, or circumstances with a positive emotional tone.

Reversed

This Queen reversed can indicate a love relationship gone sour, or someone who is having trouble expressing emotion. If the card represents a person, it can be a dishonest advisor. Be careful whom you trust with your secrets and your emotional life. If the card represents the querent, it can mean that you are playing with possible dangerous psychic matters you don't understand.

Knight of Cups

Portrayed as a handsome young man, usually sitting upright on a white horse in parade or dressage position, he holds the Cup straight out in front of him. His helmet may be winged, a symbol of the messenger. In this case, the message he brings is of love or good tidings. Usually depicted in an outdoor setting, sometimes with water under the horse's hooves, this Knight is armored only lightly. He's a lover, not a fighter.

KNIGHT of CUPS.

Upright

The Knight of Cups is bringing you a message about love, or he may represent your true love—the knight on the white horse! His appearance indicates you are deeply involved in an emotional situation, to the point where little else matters. You may be awaiting this message—such as a declaration of love or a proposal of marriage—with such anticipation that everything else seems insignificant. All other relationships pale when compared with this one. If the Knight does not represent a lover, he is certainly a friend, honest, intelligent, and willing to aid you.

Reversed

The message you hope for has been delayed or may never arrive. The relationship you yearn for may be based on deceit or superficiality on the other person's side. You may be obsessing about someone who really doesn't care that much about you and who will never make a commitment, even if he has led you to believe he is sincere. This person is fickle, likes to flirt, but belongs to the "love 'em and leave 'em" school of romance.

Page of Cups

The Page of Cups usually shows a young man in decorative short garb wearing an elaborate hat. His attitude is relaxed and open, and he seems well pleased with himself. In the Waite deck, he holds the Cup out in one hand—a fish, symbol of the Water element, peeks out of it. It's as though he magically produced the fish like a rabbit out of a hat, and he seems to expect approval. Some decks depict the Page as a girl or androgynous figure.

PAGE of CUPS.

Upright

This Page signifies a young person, male or female—possibly a son, daughter, or a younger sibling—who is bringing you a message about love. It might mean an engagement or a wedding—some situation that holds an inherent emotional risk. The circumstances may be exciting yet scary at the same time, as with a sudden elopement. Often the Page suggests naiveté or vulnerability, especially in matters of the heart. If the card represents the queris, it says you have already decided to take an emotional risk and aren't interested in being dissuaded. You are willing to give it your all and feel things will work out.

Reversed

The Page reversed shows a fishy situation, something you should look at carefully. If the card represents a person, there may be deceit involved—flattery for gain, an unwanted pregnancy, or secrecy in matters of the heart. Someone may be trying to seduce you, and you are blinded to the falseness of his or her intentions. Or you may be playing the role of the seducer, toying with someone's emotions. If so, take care. You might get hurt yourself.

Ace of Cups

The Ace of Cups shows a single large chalice, usually with water flowing fountainlike out of it. In the Waite deck, a hand emerging from a cloud grasps the Cup as if offering it to the querent. This Ace suggests a fountain of love or the Holy Grail. Other symbols such as doves, flowers, or water motifs may decorate this card. The Ace represents a gift, in this case a gift of love, of a personal or divine nature.

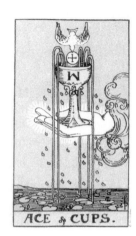

ACE ♣ CUPS.

Upright

The Ace of Cups indicates a new beginning—a new love or a one-on-one relationship of any kind. Previously unfelt emotions come into play now, perhaps as a result of seeing a relationship in a new way. This Ace can also herald a birth—of a child or an idea. This is a fertile time for emotional or creative growth, as this Ace symbolizes the consummation of something hoped for.

Reversed

When reversed, this Ace indicates delays or disappointments in love. Sometimes a new beginning doesn't develop as hoped. Difficulties in getting a new relationship or creative effort off the ground could be indicated, or something you are trying to set in motion meets unforeseen and frustrating obstacles. Perhaps this is not the right time to start something new.

Two of Cups

The Two of Cups describes a coupling of some sort—a marriage, a partnership, a union. Harmony is in the air. You may be in the honeymoon stage of a relationship or endeavor when all seems right and you think nothing can go wrong. This card can also represent a new stage of happiness and harmony in an existing relationship.

Upright

You are moving in tandem with another person now, and all is going smoothly. Whether it is a romantic relationship or a friendship, there is plenty of accord, mutual admiration, and good will toward each other. Ordinarily, this card refers to a love match between the sexes, but it can also indicate a partnership of another sort.

Reversed

Fortunately, this card has such a vibration of harmony that its reversed position isn't much different from the upright one. It can suggest delays or that the relationship may have to be kept a secret for some reason.

Three of Cups

The appearance of the Three of Cups signifies that something has been brought to completion. There is victory and success. The act of falling in love signified by the Two of Cups may have resulted in a baby, or a creative venture has produced a salable product. It's time for a celebration!

Upright

You are experiencing success and plenty, and a time of merriment and celebration is at hand. Your feelings, which may have been murky, are clearer now, and you understand your emotional patterns in a positive and growth-producing way. You're on your way now to great things.

Reversed

The Three of Cups reversed remains a positive influence, except that the gratification you are getting may be more sensual than deeply emotional. You will still have success, but your achievements may be in small things.

Four of Cups

The Four of Cups represents a state of apathy and withdrawal. However, this may be a necessary rest from the hectic excitement represented by the

Three. It's a time to get away by yourself and just drift and dream for a while before getting back into your daily grind.

Upright

You are in a state of withdrawing your emotions from a situation or a person. After intense emotional involvement, you may need some space in which to be yourself. There's a feeling of let-down after build-up, as in the postpartum blues or when you have to face the daily grind of ordinary life, dealing with all the nitty-gritties of making a marriage work.

Reversed

You may be experiencing displeasure, disappointment, or dissatisfaction with a relationship or the way a creative project is turning out. You want to tune out to get away from your negative feelings. That's okay; it is a necessary respite to regain perspective and balance.

Five of Cups

The Five of Cups signifies that you are brooding over past wrongs, losses, disappointments, or hurts. It symbolizes a state of mind that is dwelling on a painful past and refusing to look forward to a positive future.

Upright

Your unhappiness is a result of your attitude, which you can change. This is a card of choice. You can continue to brood over what went wrong, or you can turn around and contemplate what can go right in the future. You don't have to be miserable unless you enjoy misery.

Reversed

You are in a state of indecision. There's some issue about which you are refusing to make up your mind, and you are refusing to face facts. Just because there have been past losses doesn't mean there can't be future gains. If you continue in this negative state of mind, you will only make things worse.

Six of Cups

The Six of Cups signifies nostalgia and happy memories of time gone by. This card refers to a sentimental remembrance of things past. These pleasant and comforting memories can be used to better your future, to build on. Knowing that you have been happy in the past will enhance your ability to be happy in the future.

Upright

You are experiencing some feelings that are connected to your past that will shed light on your future. You are feeling calm and collected about past events, putting them into perspective, and beginning to understand how they can engender fruition in the present—a future renewal.

Reversed

A happy card, the Six of Cups reversed suggests changes in the immediate environment that will make you feel more secure. These may involve meeting new friends or making new associations. You are developing new emotional tools that will aid you in the future—an important event is coming soon.

Seven of Cups

The Seven of Cups signifies a time of great creative potential along with the energy to make use of it. Many options are available: the difficulty is in choosing the right one. This card is about fantasy and imagination.

Upright

You are looking at a number of possibilities now—too many to make an easy choice. With so many choices, you are living out different roles in your imagination but having a hard time deciding which to manifest in reality.

Reversed

You are in a state of total confusion because there's too much going on. You need a calm space where you can sort through the multiple choices confronting you. Let your feelings be your guide.

Eight of Cups

The Eight of Cups indicates a situation where the only solution is to turn your back on it and go in another direction. What's there either isn't working as expected or isn't all that important any more. The eight neatly stacked Cups represent effort that was made in vain and now needs to be abandoned.

Upright

You are wishing things might have been different, but, knowing they aren't, you realize that you have to let go. It's time to cut your losses and get out of the situation that has failed despite your best efforts. Unfortunately, this usually refers to a relationship that has reached such a state of deterioration that the only solution is to walk away from it.

Reversed

You are walking away without facing the facts behind the problem you want to escape, taking the coward's way out. Things haven't worked out as you planned and hoped, and you want to cut and run without giving the situation a second chance. If you don't, you may regret it later.

Nine of Cups

This is the best pip card in the entire Tarot deck. Called the wish card, it indicates great joy and happiness, all your dreams coming true, and getting what you wish for. It's like winning the lottery and meeting Mr. or Ms. Right all on the same day.

Upright

Even the most negative interpreters have nothing bad to say about this card. It means success, triumph, everything you want and hope for. When the Nine of Cups appears, ask yourself, "What is it I really want?" The card's answer is that you will get it!

Reversed

As above, it's hard to say anything negative about this card, even in the reverse position. The worst thing that can be said here is that if you refuse to believe in your own good fortune and take a negative attitude you can mess things up for yourself.

Ten of Cups

The Ten of Cups indicates a situation of lasting contentment, real love, domestic bliss, and complete satisfaction in all your endeavors. It symbolizes people living harmoniously together, sharing their love and their lives unconditionally. This Ten is so favorable that it can offset any negative cards in a reading.

Upright

This card is an indication of everything that most people wish for—love and harmony, happy family life, true love and compatible companionship. It's a time of completion, of reaping the rewards of what you have sown. It does not necessarily mean wealth, but it symbolizes an abundant life in the true sense.

Reversed

Delays and obstacles are standing in the way of achieving the happiness you long for. Circumstances beyond your control may be the cause, and at the moment there's nothing you can do but keep a positive attitude and hold tight while waiting for them to change, which they will.

Chapter 17

Where to Go from Here

No matter how long you study and work with the Tarot, you'll never know everything there is to know. The more you use it, the more it will reveal itself to you. Although most people turn to this elegant oracle for divination purposes, it has many other uses. In fact, the Tarot's potential may never be tapped fully, and its possibilities may be limited only by your imagination. Let the cards speak to you; open your heart and mind to their guidance. Then implement their wisdom in the ways your intuition suggests.

Using the Tarot for Personal Growth

Many people believe the most valuable role for the Tarot is as a tool for personal growth. Some decks, such as the Jungian Tarot and One World Tarot, are designed specifically to augment spiritual and psychological development. Of course, any deck—and any reading—can reveal important psychological issues that the querent needs to address, and they often do. Many spreads are designed to take into account the emotional, spiritual, and psychological dynamics that are affecting the subject of the reading, but you can intentionally choose to work with the Tarot to understand and heal particular problems in your life.

Meditation and Contemplation

As you have learned over the course of this book, meditating with Tarot cards is a simple and relaxing way to connect with your intuition through your Tarot deck. The simplest way to do this is to select a single card that represents an issue you are dealing with and remove it from the deck.

Continue meditating on a chosen card day after day, until you have resolved the concern or developed the qualities you seek. You might also wish to display the card in a place where you will see it often throughout the day. Each time you look at it, you'll be reminded of your intention.

If you feel vulnerable or uncertain in a romantic relationship, for instance, you might choose the Page of Cups to contemplate. If you are embroiled in ego battles with coworkers, pick the Five of Cups. Or choose a card that symbolizes a characteristic you wish to develop in yourself. Strength, for example, can help you build inner power, patience, and perseverance. The Queen of Cups can encourage receptivity, acceptance, and flexibility in relationships.

Relax, calm, and center yourself, then gaze at the image on the card, without trying to analyze it too closely. Allow the symbols pictured there to speak directly to your subconscious. They will trigger inner awarenesses and gently work on the conditions that are influencing the situation. As the card's meaning imprints itself on your mind, you will notice the traits you desire becoming more available to you, and/or you'll experience an increased ability to handle the situation that is challenging you.

Diagnosing Difficulties

Tarot cards can also help you to diagnose difficulties—physical as well as psychological. Let's say, for example, that you are experiencing lower back pain. You could ask the Tarot, "What factors are involved in this condition?" Then randomly draw one or more cards from the deck. In this instance, you might pick the Three of Swords, which suggests that your back pain is linked with the emotional pain in a disappointing love relationship. If you drew the Ten of Wands, you might determine that carrying a heavy load—either physically or personally—caused the problem.

Allow your inner knowing to communicate with you. Don't necessarily stick to standard interpretations; whatever pops into your mind could be meaningful. Maybe you picked The Star in response to a query about a sore throat that's been bothering you. This card usually represents hope—and indeed, it probably indicates that your sore throat isn't serious and you will soon be fine. But if The Star card in your deck depicts a woman kneeling in water, it could be telling you that your malady is connected with getting wet and chilled.

You can also use the cards as aids to healing. The Nine of Wands, for example, is considered a card of recovery. Gaze at it when you are ill and breathe in its vibrations to facilitate well-being. Or lay it on an injury to send positive energy to the wound. Some people like to position seven beneficial cards on their bodies at the seven chakra points. Although this method is not a science and is certainly not a substitute for qualified medical care, the cards can often shed light on situations and may offer guidance for healing problems.

The Tarot as a Teaching Tool

In recent years, many Tarot designers have incorporated subjects of special interest—both esoteric and mundane—into their decks. These intriguing decks not only offer users the traditional benefits, but they also provide an attractive and interesting way to learn about a new topic or field of study. For instance, the Australian Animal Tarot deck introduces querents to the wildlife of the continent. The Goddess Tarot serves as an encyclopedia of goddesses from many countries and cultures. The Tarot of Gemstones and Crystals deck teaches users about the mineral kingdom and the properties of various gemstones. The Royal Thai Tarot brings the customs, art, and history of the Thai people to Western users. From angels to Zen, whatever your interest you can probably find a Tarot deck that will teach you about it.

The Tarot and Magick

The link between the Tarot and magick is obvious. The symbols of the four suits—Wands, Swords, Cups, and Pentacles—are the four principal tools used by magicians in spell-working and rituals. The Magician card shows a magus deftly handling these four implements, and other magickal symbols and references can be found throughout the Tarot.

Using Tarot Cards in Spells

As any magician will tell you, magick is mostly in the mind. Therefore, the vivid imagery on Tarot cards provides a rich source of visual material for magicians to work with. If, for example, you wanted to attract a lover, you could choose the Two of Cups or The Lovers and focus energy on the images. Connect emotionally with the meaning of the card, then project your thoughts and feelings outward to attract a romantic partner. If your goal is to attract prosperity, select the Nine of Pentacles.

Here are some other simple ways to work magick with Tarot cards:

- Display the card on your altar to demonstrate your magickal intention.

- Carry the card in your pocket during the day to attract your heart's desire.
- Place the card under your pillow at night, so it can influence your dreams.
- Lay the card face up on a windowsill where the moonlight will shine on it and set a clear quartz crystal on the card. The crystal directs the imagery of the card toward your objective. If you know where your objective is located, point the crystal in that direction.
- Prop up the card on your altar or other flat surface, then burn incense in front of the card. The rising smoke carries your intention, represented by the card, into the cosmos.
- Put the card in a flowerpot, then fill the pot with soil. Plant seeds to indicate that you are sowing the seeds of your intention. Water and care for the seeds, and as they grow, so will your love, money, success, etc.
- Bury the card beneath a tree, preferably one that is compatible with your intention. (Refer to a book of Celtic tree magick for more information.)
- Place the card in the center of a labyrinth, then walk the labyrinth while concentrating on your objective.
- Frame a card and hang it on the wall.
- Build a ritual fire and burn the card in the fire to release its energy into the cosmos.

Tarot Talismans

For centuries, people have worn magickal talismans to attract love, wealth, health, and good luck. Tarot images make ideal talismans when worn or carried on your person. The Peter Stone jewelry company has translated artist Amy Zerner's Tarot designs into beautiful silver pendants that are perfect as magickal talismans.

You can make your own Tarot talisman by choosing a card that represents your intention. Fold the card three times and slip it into a cloth pouch. Add other ingredients that correspond to your intention—gemstones and crystals, herbs and flowers, etc. Wear the pouch around your neck, affixed to a belt, or carry it in your pocket to attract what you desire.

If you have artistic talent, you might draw or embroider the card on a scarf, handkerchief, or other garment and wear it as a talisman. Or you could paint a henna tattoo of the card on your body.

> Without realizing it, man possesses immense powers. He is "engendered from the fount of wonder and the fount of desire and intelligence." And his most vital faculty is his imagination—imagination in the sense that Paracelsus used the word, the faculty for reaching beyond himself, beyond his everyday life . . . the doors are open.
>
> **—Colin Wilson, *The Occult***

Imprinting Water with Tarot Imagery

Japanese scientist Dr. Masaru Emoto theorizes that words and pictures affect water crystal patterns. Simply exposing spring water to an image, such as those on Tarot cards, will imprint the water with the vibration inherent in the image. If you then drink the imprinted water, you incorporate that vibration into your physical makeup.

To imprint water with a particular energy that will help you achieve your objective, select a Tarot card that represents your intention. Fill a plain (no designs) glass or bottle (with the labels removed) with spring water. Tape the Tarot card on the glass or bottle, so that the image faces in toward the water. Or if you prefer, lay the card face up on a flat surface—a table, altar, mantel, or windowsill—and set the glass or bottle of water on the card. Allow it to sit for a few hours, then put the card back in your Tarot deck. Drink a little of the water each day to create within yourself the condition you desire.

The Tarot and Feng Shui

Feng shui (pronounced *fung shway*), the ancient Chinese art of placement, has gained great popularity in the West during the past decade. This school of thought, which is part spiritual, part practical, considers your home to be a mirror of you. The different rooms or areas of your home correspond to the various parts of your life—career, love, family, friends, self-image, money, creativity, health, and future. According to feng shui's tenets, you can enhance certain facets of your life or create circumstances you desire by making changes in the sectors of your home that relate to those parts of your life.

Just as there are many views in Christianity or Judaism or Buddhism, there are many different schools of thought in feng shui. One of the most popular in the West uses a tool called the bagua to determine which portions of your home are associated with which areas of your life. A simpler method symbolically relates the various rooms in your home with the various parts of your life, based on the activities that take place there. For instance, the living room is where household members and friends or guests come together to socialize, therefore this room is linked with your social life.

By using Tarot cards in conjunction with feng shui, you can bring something you desire into your life. Choose a card that represents your intention. Then locate the sector in your home that relates to the area in your life that you wish to affect. For instance, if your objective is to attract prosperity, select the Nine of Pentacles from your Tarot deck, then determine which is the "wealth gua" in your home. (Refer to a book on feng shui to find out which parts of your home correspond to wealth, love, health, etc.) Place the card you've chosen in the respective sector of your home. Performing this act demonstrates your willingness and desire to make changes in your life, and that's an important part of magick as well as feng shui. Soon, you'll begin to see your intentions manifest.

Creating Your Own Tarot Deck

Creating your own deck is the ultimate Tarot experience. Famous artists, such as Salvador Dali, as well as many unknown talents have designed original packs of cards. Artist's Inner Vision Tarot, an intriguing deck published by NoMonet Full Court Press, is the collaborative effort of more than two dozen collage artists. Although thousands of decks have been designed and produced over the centuries, there are as many possible interpretations of the Tarot as there are artists.

Whether or not you believe you have artistic ability, you can embark on this journey of self-expression and discovery. Choose whatever medium appeals to you—watercolors, acrylic, oils, pen and ink, colored pencils, pastels, woodcut, collage, fabric, crayons, computer imaging, or another medium. Give yourself permission to experiment. What matters is that the images depict your own interpretations of the cards in your own way.

Creating your personal Tarot deck requires you to design and render seventy-eight individual pictures, unless you opt to do only the twenty-two Major Arcana cards. Therefore, you should be willing to commit to a project that may take months or even years to complete.

ALERT!

When creating your own personal Tarot deck, you may choose to start with cards that depict conditions you wish to attract into your life. For example, you could focus first on only creating positive cards.

One way to approach the design process is to work on cards that represent issues that are currently in the forefront of your life. For instance, if you are resting and recuperating after an illness or injury, you might relate to the Four of Swords and decide to depict it. As you create the card, you'll come to a deeper understanding of the situation you are experiencing, and your understanding will naturally be transferred to the card's imagery.

However you decide to go about creating your own Tarot deck, you will find the experience illuminating. The interaction between your intuition and imagination will take you to places within yourself that you've probably never visited before. Invite your Muse to participate and guide you. Don't judge or censor yourself. Be daring—there are no rules here. Allow for serendipity to enter into the process and above all enjoy yourself!

Appendix A

Glossary of Tarot Terms

Arcana
Secret knowledge.

Court Cards
The four "people" cards in each suit of the Minor Arcana, the court cards consist of a king, queen, knight (or prince), and page (or princess).

Divination
The act of predicting the future, often with the aid of a device such as the Tarot, runes, etc.

Element
One of the four fundamental energies in the universe—Earth, Air, Fire, and Water. Each element corresponds to one suit of the Tarot.

Feng shui
The ancient Chinese art of placement, pronounced *fung shway*.

Kabbalah
An ancient Hebrew mystical tradition to which the Tarot has many links. Also spelled Cabala, Qabala, and other variations.

Karma
A concept of cause and effect, as taught in some Eastern religions.

Major Arcana
One of the two books of the Tarot, consisting of twenty-two cards beginning with The Fool and ending with The World.

Minor Arcana
One of the two books of the Tarot, usually consisting of forty numbered cards and sixteen court cards divided into four suits—Wands, Pentacles, Cups, and Swords.

Occult
Hidden or secret.

Pip cards
The numbered cards in the Tarot deck.

Querent
Someone who asks a question or seeks information. In a Tarot reading, the querent is the person consulting the cards.

Reading
A consultation using Tarot cards to gain insight or information.

Significator
A card chosen to represent the person for whom the reading is being done.

Spread
A pattern used in a Tarot reading to reveal insight or to answer a question.

Appendix B

Resources

Publishers of Tarot Cards and Books

U.S. Games Systems, Inc.
179 Ludlow Street
Stamford, CT 06902
203-353-8431 or 800-544-2637

✍www.usgamesinc.com

Llewellyn Worldwide
P.O. Box 64383
St. Paul, MN 55164
800-THE-MOON

✍www.llewellyn.com

Bear & Company
P.O. Box 388
Rochester, VT 05767
800-246-8648

✍www.innertraditions.com

Destiny Books
P.O. Box 388
Rochester, VT 05767
800-246-8648

✍www.innertraditions.com

New Page Books
P.O. Box 687
Franklin Lakes, NJ 07417
800-227-3371

✍www.newpagebooks.com

Red Wheel/Weiser
P.O. Box 612
York Beach, ME 03910
800-423-7087

✍www.redwheelweiser.com

Sterling Publishing Co., Inc.
387 Park Ave. South
New York, NY 10016
212-532-7160

✍www.sterlingpublishing.com

Tarot Jewelry

Peter Stone
P.O. Box 1008
Selbyville, DE 19975
800-397-8787

✍www.peterstone.com

Wellstone
P.O. Box 952
Grass Valley, CA 95945
800-544-8773

✍www.wellstonejewelry.com

Tarot Organizations

American Tarot Association
P.O. Box 102
Stoneham, CO 80754

✍www.ata-tarot.com

International Tarot Society
P.O. Box 1475
Morton Grove, IL 60053

✍www.tarotsociety.org

Online Tarot Card Distributor

The Tarot Graden
✍www.tarotgarden.com

Index

A
Ability levels, 109–10
Ace (One), 9, 47
  of Cups, 268
  of Pentacles, 242
  of Swords, 254
  of Wands, 229–30
Affirmations, 81–82
Air, 43–44, 53
Air purification, 28–29
Akashic Records, xii
Anima mundi, xii
Aquarius, 61, 74, 75
Archetypes, 3.
  See also Symbolism
Aries, 64–65
Astrology, 59–78
Attitude, toward readings,
  108–10
Awareness levels, 132

B
Black, 54
Blessing the cards, 26
Blue, 53, 54
Book of Toth, xi
Brown, 54

C
Cancer, 60, 63, 66–67
Capricorn, 78
Catholic Church, xi–xii
Celtic Cross spread, 148–50
Chariot, 66–67, 98, 103, 127,
  190–93
Collective unconscious, 55, 78
Color symbolism, 53–54
Conscious mind, 16
Contemplation, 276–77
Court Cards, 4, 7–11, 113–14.
  See also Minor Arcana;
  specific cards
Crowley Thoth deck, 17, 19
Cultural themes, 21–22
Cups, 44–45, 84, 263–74

D
Daily insights, 80–81
Death, 71–72, 100, 128, 204–6
Devil, 4, 73–74, 100, 128, 208–
  10
Diagnostic tool, Tarot as, 277
Difficulties, diagnosing, 277
Divination, 14–15

E
Earth, 45–46, 53

Earth purification, 27–28
Eight, 51
  of Cups, 272
  of Pentacles, 246–47
  of Swords, 259–60
  of Wands, 234–35
Either/Or method, 142
Elements, 42–46, 53
Emperor, 64–65, 97–98, 126,
  183–85
Empress, xii, 3–4, 64, 97, 126,
  181–83
Encyclopedias of Tarot, 19
Enlightenment, 80–82
Everyday life, 4–6

F
Fate, 3–4, 111–12
Feng shui, 280–81
Feng Shui spread, 161–63
Fire, 43, 53
Fire purification, 26–27
Five, 49
  of Cups, 270–71
  of Pentacles, 244–45
  of Swords, 257
  of Wands, 232–33
Five-card spread, 146–47

THE EVERYTHING SERIES!

BUSINESS & PERSONAL FINANCE

Everything® Accounting Book
Everything® Budgeting Book
Everything® Business Planning Book
Everything® Coaching and Mentoring Book
Everything® Fundraising Book
Everything® Get Out of Debt Book
Everything® Grant Writing Book
Everything® Home-Based Business Book, 2nd Ed.
Everything® Homebuying Book, 2nd Ed.
Everything® Homeselling Book, 2nd Ed.
Everything® Investing Book, 2nd Ed.
Everything® Landlording Book
Everything® Leadership Book
Everything® Managing People Book, 2nd Ed.
Everything® Negotiating Book
Everything® Online Auctions Book
Everything® Online Business Book
Everything® Personal Finance Book
Everything® Personal Finance in Your 20s and 30s Book
Everything® Project Management Book
Everything® Real Estate Investing Book
Everything® Robert's Rules Book, $7.95
Everything® Selling Book
Everything® Start Your Own Business Book, 2nd Ed.
Everything® Wills & Estate Planning Book

COOKING

Everything® Barbecue Cookbook
Everything® Bartender's Book, $9.95
Everything® Chinese Cookbook
Everything® Classic Recipes Book
Everything® Cocktail Parties and Drinks Book
Everything® College Cookbook
Everything® Cooking for Baby and Toddler Book
Everything® Cooking for Two Cookbook
Everything® Diabetes Cookbook
Everything® Easy Gourmet Cookbook
Everything® Fondue Cookbook
Everything® Fondue Party Book
Everything® Gluten-Free Cookbook
Everything® Glycemic Index Cookbook
Everything® Grilling Cookbook

Everything® Healthy Meals in Minutes Cookbook
Everything® Holiday Cookbook
Everything® Indian Cookbook
Everything® Italian Cookbook
Everything® Low-Carb Cookbook
Everything® Low-Fat High-Flavor Cookbook
Everything® Low-Salt Cookbook
Everything® Meals for a Month Cookbook
Everything® Mediterranean Cookbook
Everything® Mexican Cookbook
Everything® One-Pot Cookbook
Everything® Quick and Easy 30-Minute, 5-Ingredient Cookbook
Everything® Quick Meals Cookbook
Everything® Slow Cooker Cookbook
Everything® Slow Cooking for a Crowd Cookbook
Everything® Soup Cookbook
Everything® Tex-Mex Cookbook
Everything® Thai Cookbook
Everything® Vegetarian Cookbook
Everything® Wild Game Cookbook
Everything® Wine Book, 2nd Ed.

GAMES

Everything® 15-Minute Sudoku Book, $9.95
Everything® 30-Minute Sudoku Book, $9.95
Everything® Blackjack Strategy Book
Everything® Brain Strain Book, $9.95
Everything® Bridge Book
Everything® Card Games Book
Everything® Card Tricks Book, $9.95
Everything® Casino Gambling Book, 2nd Ed.
Everything® Chess Basics Book
Everything® Craps Strategy Book
Everything® Crossword and Puzzle Book
Everything® Crossword Challenge Book
Everything® Cryptograms Book, $9.95
Everything® Easy Crosswords Book
Everything® Easy Kakuro Book, $9.95
Everything® Games Book, 2nd Ed.
Everything® Giant Sudoku Book, $9.95
Everything® Kakuro Challenge Book, $9.95
Everything® Large-Print Crossword Challenge Book
Everything® Large-Print Crosswords Book
Everything® Lateral Thinking Puzzles Book, $9.95
Everything® Mazes Book

Everything® Pencil Puzzles Book, $9.95
Everything® Poker Strategy Book
Everything® Pool & Billiards Book
Everything® Test Your IQ Book, $9.95
Everything® Texas Hold 'Em Book, $9.95
Everything® Travel Crosswords Book, $9.95
Everything® Word Games Challenge Book
Everything® Word Search Book

HEALTH

Everything® Alzheimer's Book
Everything® Diabetes Book
Everything® Health Guide to Adult Bipolar Disorder
Everything® Health Guide to Controlling Anxiety
Everything® Health Guide to Fibromyalgia
Everything® Health Guide to Thyroid Disease
Everything® Hypnosis Book
Everything® Low Cholesterol Book
Everything® Massage Book
Everything® Menopause Book
Everything® Nutrition Book
Everything® Reflexology Book
Everything® Stress Management Book

HISTORY

Everything® American Government Book
Everything® American History Book
Everything® Civil War Book
Everything® Freemasons Book
Everything® Irish History & Heritage Book
Everything® Middle East Book

HOBBIES

Everything® Candlemaking Book
Everything® Cartooning Book
Everything® Coin Collecting Book
Everything® Drawing Book
Everything® Family Tree Book, 2nd Ed.
Everything® Knitting Book
Everything® Knots Book
Everything® Photography Book
Everything® Quilting Book
Everything® Scrapbooking Book
Everything® Sewing Book
Everything® Woodworking Book

Bolded titles are new additions to the series.
All Everything® books are priced at $12.95 or $14.95, unless otherwise stated. Prices subject to change without notice.